Secret Sharers in Italian Comedy

From Machiavelli to Goldoni

Jackson I. Cope

Secret Sharers in Italian Comedy

From Machiavelli to Goldoni

Duke University Press Durham and London

1996

© 1996 Duke University Press

All rights reserved

Printed in the United States of America on acid-free paper ∞

Designed by Cherie H. Westmoreland

Typeset in Monotype Fournier by Tseng Information Systems, Inc.

Library of Congress Cataloging-in-Publication Data appear

on the last printed page of this book.

For DeAnn

È il buono amore desiderio di bellezze tale,

quale tu vedi, e d'animo parimente, e di corpo

And love desired such beauty as here, was

found in mind and body bound

Contents

Acknowledgments

*A*decade ago a fellowship awarded by the John Simon Guggen-
heim Foundation permitted me to spend a year in Venice.
While I did not begin writing this book then, it was the time at
which its seed was planted and I am honored to again offer my
public gratitude to that great and generous institution. Parts of the
chapter on Carlo Goldoni have appeared in different form in *Theatre
Survey* (1990) and in *Annali d'italianistica* (1993), and I thank the
editors of these volumes for their kind permission to reprint some of
that material here.

All translations are my own, unless otherwise indicated. However, the reader shares my good fortune in that they have been
smoothed and given the idiomatic precision that only an accomplished translator like Professor Anthony Oldcorn of Brown University could have supplied. This word of thanks is an inadequate return
for the friendship with which he meticulously did so throughout the
text.

Professor Walter E. Stephens of Dartmouth College carried on
an anonymous review of the work as a reader for Duke University
Press over many months. His acute and tireless critiques stimulated
me to discover new implications in the materials at so many points
that he sometimes seemed co-author.

Barbara Norton's editorial care in shepherding a complicated text
from my irregular original into print was exemplary. Her effort, and
Peter Guzzardi's shared enthusiasm for Italy, made Duke University

Press an ideal home for this book. It was Stanley Fish who first put me in their hands, and his involvement is another marker along the route of a long friendship.

The dedication is to the scholar and companion who inspired me to begin the work and who encouraged me to continue to make it ripe for reading.

Introduction

Plautus, New Comedy, and the Anti-Plautine

*T*he details of the story that evolves here are Italian, but they should not be misconstrued as a mini-history of Italian comedy, engaging, as they do, with only a limited grouping of plays written across more than three centuries. The formal paradigm I describe and illustrate may, though, draw the awareness of other critics to features that fit other plays into a common pattern with this sampling, because no play is an island, separate from the critical pressures upon it from some literary past, from prescriptions and expectations clustering around the notion of genre. What "genre" means has become so mooted and redefined in theoretical studies of the past two decades that we still know only a single truth about it: it exists. It exists as a context that seems to revolve as a flange of terminus and beginning to literary creation. We may treat it as an insubstantial ghost, but ghosts are notorious as ancestors, lares and penates protecting the sacredness of ancient hearths; most notably, in Western comedy, that of Plautine Rome.

In response to this fact, dramatic history became self-perpetuating when Northrop Frye turned it into a description of comedic form in his classic 1948 essay "The Argument of Comedy."[1] In one way, he was helping fill in the blanks of structural analogues between the line of Plautine-Menandrian "New Comedy" and a Shakespearean comedy which, for all its "green world" in Frye's distinctions, turns out to be remarkably Plautine in form, a sort of anglicized new-New Comedy.

What becomes remarkable in retrospect is upon how few models the theoretical history of comedic form was raised and honed. Duckworth, in the first exhaustive history of Roman comedy, had only two dozen plays to work with and even so had to divide them into Alexandrine divergences of focus when he came to summarize their plots as "innocent mistakes," "mistaken identity and deception," "guileful deception," and so forth.[2] But even this constitutes riches if we recall that the arguably "pure" Shakespearean comedies constitute half a dozen out of nearly forty plays.

Nonetheless, these plays were the basis upon which a seminal theory was erected. And what exactly (or, rather, inexactly) was the "Argument of [New] Comedy"? An urban society controlled by the established ethic and greed (for power, money, sex) of a generation seeking self-perpetuation (immortality in its way, as opposed to evolution) runs counter to the libido of a second generation. The seeds are sown here for both change and repetition. The conflict of interest makes for confusion and an anxiety that reveals the "unnatural" at every turn in this history of generations, both personal and public or social. In Plautine plotting, the youngsters most often hide and deploy plans in adjacent houses of the city. Abetted by the almost asocial mischief of servant or parasite, they ultimately embrace their elders, but promise establishment of a new ethos even as they appear penitent. Blocking, plotting, and counterplotting merge in a renewed harmony.

Shakespeare, influenced by the powers of folk material, translated the Plautine city plotting into the countryside in mid-play. It was in this "green world" that one took a breather and planned for a new attack and subsequent battening upon the old town and its perennial restrictions. Chambers, Barber, and Weimann have told us most, in their various ways, about Shakespeare's divided milieu, the milieu of country immigrants in London who contributed so largely to his audience and articulation.[3] Frye's distinction between Plautine and Shakespearean New Comedy was not only a historical intuition of the soundest sort but a reflection of emerging sophistication about particulars in folk archaeology as they developed into the dramatic country-city fusions most notably examined in Barber's essay *Shakespeare's Festive Comedy* and in Paolo Toschi's *The Origins of the Italian Theatre*.[4] The movement of comedy seemed bound to its origins in natural regeneration, the comedic genre mirroring the movement of nature toward a harmony of resignation and renewal. It is worth reminding ourselves that Toschi's capstone of a career as Italy's great modern folk analyst came in tandem with Frye's *Anatomy of Criticism* and with Barber's essay on Shakespeare's festive structures derived from folk rituals: all appeared between 1955 and 1959. Toschi, in common with most students who leap the divide between indubitable popular progenitors and their dramatic offspring, saw every aspect of the commedia dell'arte as being in debt to folk formulae, and all subsequent Italian drama in debt to the commedia. The result, both surprising and inevitable, is that the city comedy of Plautus has been impressed into a regenerative folk tradition which insists that we recognize the shared contours of a plot line we call "New Comedy." Recent reevaluation offers explanation for this apparent paradox in clarifying the "festive" status of Plautus's urban comedy itself.

Erich Segal related Plautus's inversions of materialistic Roman values and social strata to the historical circumstances of his plays having formed part of the *ludi* financed by the senatorial elite as a sort of dangerous occasional "carnival" for the populace.[5] One consequence has been a close examination of Plautus's achievement as a radical and conscious new dramaturgy quite antipodal to that of its Greek sources in Menandrian comedy. Into the conservative woof of the Menandrian plot Plautus interpolated elements of the improvisational tradition associated with the shadowy indigenous farce of southern Italy's "Atellan" players, thus leading David Wiles to a conclusion that might as readily be applied to plot as to masks: "Plautus, like the Atellan actors, and like the actors of the *commedia dell'arte*, was content with a very limited repertory of stock masks. The masks of Plautus, like those of Atellan comedy and of the *commedia dell'arte*, had as their principal function to legitimate taboo behaviour."[6]

As we have come to recognize the cross-fertilization of a learned, written tradition with a popular, improvisational mode in Plautus, we have also realized that—*pace* Toschi—the commedia dell'arte historically was a reflex, not an origin or epitome, of the written drama of the Italian Cinquecento. The commedia troupes at every stage of their development mingled the dramaturgy of "improvised" playing from the *scenarii* with private and courtly performances of fully written plays that were elaborately produced; indeed, a number of the *scenarii* received a second and more prestigious literary life when they were expanded into full-length plays published by several of the more ambitious members of the commedia troupes.[7] And, in common with so much of the *commedia erudita* corpus, the written commedia dell'arte progeny were basically Plautine in plot. Further, improvisational playing from type masks, and the bold strokes made necessary for the understanding of mixed dialects by a linguistically mixed audience, militated toward the predictable closure of the Plautine pattern in commedia dell'arte productions. On the other hand, improvisation brought to the drama an especially acute sense of openness, a continual awareness that expectation might never quite be fulfilled—that the framework of plot was fragile, and the action might burst through, creating a sudden bridge into society. Both Segal and Slater gave new attention to the effects of Plautus's own crossing of such a bridge into the audience through his asides and allusions to notorious aspects of contemporary Roman mores. In the case of Plautus, these incursions were significant in content but not strategically placed so as to disturb the harmony of the New Comedy restoration plot. And this description remains accurate in discussing the illusion-breaking devices frequent enough in most commedie erudite of the Renaissance and beyond.

One also finds in Italian comedy, however, another plot paradigm, variations on a structure that is most conveniently thought of as a subgenre of Plautine New Comedy. Perhaps with more precision it might be labeled an anti-Plautine or anti-New Comedy form—tags that will recur in the pages that follow. This paradigm can be considered a subgenre because in most of its manifestations the principal elements of the New Comedy formula are present: the lover or lovers blocked by interested elders; escape or hiding within or without the city enclosing an ordered society; and an eventual harmonious reconciliation. But this describes, in these plays, a misleading surface; it constitutes the course of events as perceived by most of the dramatic characters but not by the audience. The audience itself and one or more of the observed players share the knowledge of a secret kept from the play's society at large: that there has been no denouement. In this respect, the paradigm explored in the readings that follow exploits secrecy as form, as a formal mode of dealing with a radical discrepancy between simultaneous stories unfolding in a single action doubly understood: one is the harmonious closure of New Comedy, the other an unfinished contingent plot. It is in this sense that we can speak of these plays as anti-Plautine. The play action and the witness of it are separated by all the physical and dramaturgical conventions of theater, yet the audience is placed in such a position of enforced collusion in secrecy that it becomes a formal ingredient. What we, the viewers, agree to silence is our awareness that events at the "end" are not closed back in a great circle that creates a renewed social harmony but open onto vistas of disruption and deception that belie the ludic ritualized release and restoration that have been the historic seedbed and pattern of New Comedy. The effect is a play more cynical than carnivalesque. But this, like all skeletal paradigms, is an abstract summary that can take on significance only as it is fleshed out in particular readings.

The early exemplars appear at the very beginnings of vernacular drama, and we will find developed instances in Ruzante, in the anonymous *Venexiana*, even in a yet earlier Latin academic comedy. If they are relatively few when set within the proliferation of Italian comedies throughout the sixteenth and seventeenth centuries, one finds the pattern nonetheless persisting into the eighteenth century. But the enduring and best-known model was Machiavelli's *La mandragola*. To recall the structure of this popular play in anticipation of its more detailed analysis later may serve to clarify the rough map given above sufficiently to set the reader on the way with a compass in hand.

La mandragola includes all the habitual Plautine elements. There are an older husband, a young wife, a would-be seducer aided by a clever parasite. The seducer, Callimaco Guadagni, is a Florentine long resident in Paris, where he hears an extravagant account of Lucrezia, wife to the doltish lawyer Nicia. Returning to Florence obsessed by the thought of Lucrezia, Callimaco discovers that she is as chaste as her name implies but that she is unable to bear Nicia an heir, much to his distress. The parasite Ligurio, Lucrezia's mother Sostrata, and Lucrezia's confessor Fra Timoteo all contribute pressures which, added to Nicia's own foolish gullibility, trick Lucrezia into bed with Callimaco. He has been disguised as an expendable beggar who will impregnate Lucrezia and immediately thereafter die, owing to the alleged magic powers of the titular mandrake root. Accepting the venality of society, Lucrezia, freed of any sense of guilt, accedes to her unsought but delightful situation. The ending is harmonious because there is no ending; secret pleasure between the lovers is cast into an indefinite future. For the husband, his wife's new promise of fertility and an heir bring the regenerative ending of New Comedy. For the lovers, their coconspirators on stage, and an audience drawn into silent collusion, another play promises to play on.

It is not surprising that playwrights impatient with a familiar generic pattern would produce a remarkable variation of response in altering it. But one will recognize as a substructure of each variation a matrix close to that into which I have distilled Machiavelli's action. The recognition can, here at the outset, be expedited by turning to a play that arouses antigeneric expectations by posting repeated signs of secret collusions of the sort that leave *La mandragola* with an open ending, only to turn back timidly at the last moment to incorporate a patent New Comedy close. It is the first of three unpublished plays written by Lorenzo di Filippo Strozzi, a patron to whom Machiavelli would dedicate his *Art of War*. Indeed, so closely was the play associated with Machiavelli that this untitled "commedia in versi" was first published in an eighteenth-century edition of Machiavelli's collected works. The error continued to be entertained until the end of the nineteenth century. This is understandable given the milieu in which this early play evolved. The prologue insists upon comedic decorum in much the same terms as those used in Machiavelli's *Discorso o dialogo intorno alla nostra lingua* [Discourse or Dialogue about Our Language]: that is, old men must not marry nubile young women, peasants must not speak like courtiers nor courtiers in the language of peasants, and so on. In the more detailed discussion of the *Discorso* in a later chapter, it will become evident that Machiavelli's tractate was written at some time during the decade that terminates in 1524. Strozzi's sixteenth-century biographer stated that this comedy, the first of his plays, was presented at the Medici palazzo as a part of wedding festivities in 1518,[8] that is, at the time Machiavelli was also writing *La mandragola*. The modern editor of the "commedia in versi" believes that "certamente il Machiavelli offrì la sua attenzione di cliente allo Strozzi, e che forse collaborò all'ideazione di qualche scena" [certainly Machiavelli offered his attention as a client to Strozzi, and perhaps collaborated in the invention of some scenes] (15). This is quite credible, because the play deviates from the Machiavellian double ending only after displaying a good deal of the Florentine cynicism prevalent in *La mandragola*. The plot concerns the crossed loves of Camillo and Catillo. The former is betrothed to Pamfila but has delayed their nuptials because he is obsessively attracted to Virginia, wife of Catillo. This latter marriage, however, has remained unconsummated throughout its three-year duration because Catillo, a hunchback[9] who is himself obsessed with jealousy, is rendered psychologically impotent by Virginia's disgust. There is even a recurrence of the allegorical name play in *La mandragola:* Machiavelli's chaste Lucrezia is manipulated into infidelity by her mother Sostrata ("la sua madre è stata buona compagna" [her mother used to be an easy companion] 1.1), a name shared with the mother of Strozzi's virgin bride, implying that each is the substratum, the underlying influence upon the daughters' behavior. In any event, the parasite Saturio and the part-time pandaress Apollonia also work to seduce Virginia. But at the moment of Virginia's manipulated fall into Camillo's arms, Pamfila's uncle arrives as a deus ex machina to

Introduction

regularize matters with an unmotivated series of adjustments that legally nullify both previous unions and reverse the matings (he pontificates, "Sempre ogni cosa / che vien, creder si vuol che sia a buon fine" [one should believe always that everything that happens is destined to a good end] 4.7.229–30). Camillo does get his Virginia, as Callimaco gets his Lucrezia. But Strozzi's *innamorato* wins out in spite of his plotting, not because of it; and while Machiavelli's Nicia is left with a merely chimerical dream of paternity, Catillo's sexual potency is actually restored in the legitimate bed of Pamfila: "l'uno dell'altro le donne scambierete / e così tutti contenti sarete" [you will swap the women one for the other / and thus you will all be contented] (5.4.192–93). This new harmony, then, results from the New Comedy formula of regenerative weddings—two, in this case. But it is shadowed by all the treacheries and manipulations of secret adultery that will achieve brazen success in *La mandragola*. And the final note echoes the Machiavellian sense that mutability is the only certainty to which we can pretend; this is stated by Pamfila's uncle:

> Pamfila, adunque, voglio che sia moglie
> di te, Catillo; e Virginia sia sposa
> qui di Camillo; e però vi conforto
> a far le noze, or che siete contenti,
> perché instabile è il tempo, e son volubili
> gli umani ingegni

Catillo, then, I want Pamfila to be your wife, And Virginia here to be the bride of Camillo; therefore I urge you to get on with the nuptials, now that you are all content, because time is unstable, and human inclinations inconstant. (5.5.210–15)

Pamfila's uncle has arrived without preparation. He seems cognizant of intimate affairs in a locale, physical and psychic, that he has not shared as returned resident, messenger, spy, or any of the usual role rationalizations of comic construction. Catillo queries him, in Strozzi's implicit gesture toward disguising improbability, and re-

Secret Sharers in Italian Comedy

ceives the negligible response that lovers talk, and news gets around (5.3). Cremete condones Camillo's mistreatment of his niece because he seems to know that Camillo's first love has been Virginia, and "el primo amor è quel che puote / più che altro amor ne' petti giovenili" [first love is that which can do more than any other in young breasts] (5.4.137–38). The two marriages (or one; the status of betrothal between Camillo and Pamfila is never entirely clear) are conveniently suspended for years in order to bring about the whitewashed, socially acceptable rematings of the conclusion. All of this, of course, precludes any sense of character development among the principals (the local color and quotidian details are reserved for the aged pandaress Apollonia), so that Virginia can never undergo the psychological transition that justifies Lucrezia's surrender in *La mandragola*. But further, the absurdity of the suspended marital situations underlines the truism that all of the disguised returns, the sudden reconciliations between generational rivals, between frustrated fathers and feckless sons, the discoveries of kidnapped infants through prop necklaces and cameos, all the unexpected harmonies of New Comedy that on Renaissance stages so often elicit expressions of *meraviglia* or, in Shakespeare's version, "wonder," are, at bottom, absurd. And it is a major function of the secrecy plots encountered in the chapters that follow to reveal that absurdity and its irrelevance to the actual social behavior that comedy traditionally claimed to mirror and to modify. It is in this demystifying sense, as well as a more formal one, that we can label these plays antigeneric.

Cinquecento theorists from Francesco Robortello in 1548 to Giovanni Talentoni in 1597, with countless fellow critics between, had repeated that "la maraviglia è affetto" [the marvelous is a passion] inspired in comedies by the unexpected, the sudden peripeteia (Talentoni), especially when the poet must restrict his events to the twelve hours allotted by the Aristotelian demand for unity of time as it had been refined in the Renaissance: "[gli spettatori] riguardando spessissime volte . . . che in così breue giro di tempo ogni trauaglio de' priuati si riuolga in somma letitia" [the spectators seeing many times . . . that in so brief a period of time every trouble of private citizens may be changed into the greatest happiness] (Giason Denores). Francesco Robortello, in the first extended commentary on Aristotle's *Poetics*, had put his finger directly upon the crucial problem encountered by the authors of New Comedy without really solving it. Comedy is an imitation of private life that, in an entertaining display of folly (*dulce*), leads men to virtue (*utile*). But, in Weinberg's succinct summary of Robortello's long argument, "is not the marvelous the exact contradictory of the credible, and would not the pleasure arising from it exclude the possibility of utility?"[10] Such certainly is the case with Strozzi's representation of his couples. Few of his audience could contemplate the utilization of a three-year hiatus in nuptial fulfillment even when offered the prospect of future happiness greater far. But most could appreciate the wisdom of the avuncular urging "vi conforto / a far le noze, or che siete contenti, / perché instabile è il tempo, e son volubili / gli umani ingegni." This was Strozzi's adaptation of Machiavelli's often-repeated advice that one must accept the mutable nature of human nature and the situations it creates, that one must go about one's affairs "secondando i tempi," that is, following the changing weather of the times. It is the lesson that will seem most useful to the spectators of *La mandragola* and the subsequent plays that reject the optimistic propaganda of New Comedy, a genre in which the harmonies that allegedly bridge natural and social renewal are attainable only through absurd conversions and discoveries that are "marvelous" because they stand *outside* the natural course of human experience. To sum up: Machiavelli, exploring the whims and resignations, the treacherous grasping and the venal fickleness of "gli umani ingegni," offers a touchstone in *La mandragola* for a comic form that imitates life as it is experienced without the wonderful interventions and strange discoveries that were nature's props in classical New Comedy. The rituals unearthed by Toschi, Frye, and the other heirs of Cambridge anthropology celebrated seasonal regenerations which are, indeed, nature's miracles; the sere and fallen leaf is replaced by the new sprig, the winter field springs to green life. But, as was observed earlier, Plautine comedy transported this form into the modern city, as so many

Cinquecento prologues boast. The fact goes far toward explaining the linguistic provincialism audible in many of the plays examined in this study. This is manifested most consciously as an extensive use of dialect in *La venexiana* and in the plays of Maggi and of Goldoni. Perhaps even more striking is the insistence upon local Florentine locutions and proverbialisms to the extent that we will find them foregrounded in the Tuscan of Cecchi, Grazzini, and Fagiuoli. These playwrights were creating a new realism that gave substance to a new ideal of imitation. If their drama was to speak in the provincial languages of modern men, it would also incorporate the daily experiences of men in their social provinces as they search for happiness. And here the ritual bridge between man and the natural order broke down; fertility had less to do with the magical power of the mandrake root than with Callimaco's plotting. Seldom expedited by miracles from the gods or nature, happiness seemed a jerrybuilt shelter that one stuck together against the winds of mutability. This modern drama was open-ended because it reflected a constant contingency in society that precluded the finality necessary to a *lieto fine*, a happy ending—indeed, an "ending" of any sort.

The new comedic form thus implicitly abrogates the familiar demand from contemporary generic critics that vice should never triumph in comedy, because the genre's utilitarian mission is corrective of social aberrance. Giulio Del Bene, speaking before the Florentine Academy of the Alterati in 1574, is typical when he says of the actions in comedy, "se fussero disoneste, non mouerieno a riso, ma si bene a sdegno et a riprensione, et à uergogna auuenga che delle cose disoneste per lo piu gli huomini si uergognino come cose mal fatte e da persone uitiose" [if they were dishonest, they would not move to laughter, but rather to disdain and accusation and shame, because for the most part men are ashamed of dishonest things as badly done and by vicious persons].[11] On this assumption, the critic asks rhetorically, "crederremo noi che potendo eleggersi lartifice di essa un suggetto honesto et di honeste ationi egli sia per scerne in cosi gran multitudine come son quelli della comedia piutosto [uno] disonesto, et uituperoso che [uno] honesto et gentile sendo in suo

Introduction

arbitrio di pigliare luno et laltro?" [shall we believe that the artist, being able to select an honest subject and one which concerns honest actions, will choose among so great a multitude of subjects as are those of comedy rather one which is dishonest and dishonorable than one which is honest and gentle, having the freedom to take the one and the other?] And one's response is that yes, some dramatists did make what to conservative critics could only seem a perverse choice. In their own moment of the perennial revolt of the artist against generic prescriptions, the dramatists we will watch at work chose to display morally compromised actions; chose, moreover, not to teach or purge their audience but to compromise that audience itself as well as the onstage characters. But even if compromised, the characters of these plays and the intrigues in which they engage are neither vicious nor pure. Theirs is a world wherein happiness is patched together from the contingencies of whim, or accident, or serendipity, but never by way of marvelous intervention. And maintaining this happiness appears contingent upon, to repeat the now familiar phrase, "secondando i tempi" in silence and secrecy. In another proverbial phrase we will return to later, this comedic world is "manco male" — not bad as things go.

Viewed from this perspective, Machiavelli's *Mandragola* assumes yet another historical significance. It was not until the mid-sixteenth century that the debate on the role of the marvelous in the several literary genres became central to Italian criticism. Thirty years ago Baxter Hathaway, a more incisive critic lost in the overshadowing bulk of Bernard Weinberg's compendium, sought "to define Renaissance literary criticism as a battle between a desire for realism — the depiction of everyday life as we experience it in the here and now, empirical and based on causality and human characters whose motivations are true to the life we know — and, on the other side, the age-old demand for the marvelous . . . escaping from this world of brass into a golden one of fantasy that is closer to our heart's desire."[12] Roughly a quarter century before Robortello pioneered the snowballing series of commentaries and expansions based in Aristotle's *Poetics*, Machiavelli's practice, clearly foregrounded by its intertextual relationship with Strozzi's more traditional comedy, had heralded the rising conflict of perspectives between the "golden" world absurdly engineered into being by the wondrous machinations of New Comedy and the truly new "empirical" comedy "based on causality and human characters," characters reflecting the mores and language, the opportunity and the instability, of Machiavelli's Florence.

Geography and Genres

I have said that this is not a history of Italian comedy. It is, however, a map of distribution of a comedic form where I have found it in northern Italy.[13] To keep this distinction clear, I have organized the sections that follow geographically, rather than chronologically. I have avoided chronology (and on occasion reversed it) to minimize our inherent tendency to seek that progression which leads from an origin in *A* to a full realization at *Z*. And I have arranged the plays as they fall into categories defined by three great centers of dramatic activity: Florence and Siena in Tuscany, Milan, and Venice, with the sweep of subsidiary cities between the latter two which I have roughly labeled the Veneto. The anti-Plautine open form seems to have arisen and developed almost simultaneously in these places.

One is entitled at the outset, though, to inquire about activities in their neighbor Ferrara, that other major Renaissance cultural center often recognized as the birthplace of modern drama. Why did this new open form not appear among the striking experiments here?[14] The question becomes especially urgent when one recalls that Ferrara's ambivalent cultural and political ties with Venice were represented in the theater by the interaction between Ariosto and Ruzante. Ruzante's *Moscheta* was produced at the court of Ercole d'Este for the carnival season of 1528, and the actor-playwright continued to frequent Ferrara professionally through several years (his editor comments that "si potrebbe forse parlare di un periodo 'ferrarese', compreso tra il 1528 e il 1532") [one could perhaps speak of a "Ferrarese" period, extending between 1528 and 1532].[15] Ariosto

Introduction

had produced *La Lena* and *Il negromante* in the same season and in the same court theater that saw the production of Ruzante's *La moscheta*,[16] and the Ferrarese poet may have overseen the mise-en-scène for the latter. Certainly he did serve in such a function on some occasions, since in 1532 Ruzante wrote to Duke Ercole soliciting more rehearsal time to prepare an imminent court performance, adding that "messer Lodovico Ariosto serà buono per fare acconciar la scena" [Messer Lodovico Ariosto will be fine to oversee preparation of the staging].[17] *La Lena* and *Il negromante* were Ariosto's first attempts at an original realism after the Plautine pastiche of *La cassaria* and the adaptation of the *Menaechmi* in *I suppositi*. Both failed, though, to break through the generic pattern too firmly established for a dramatist who had apprenticed in translating Latin comedy. Coincidental or not, it was in these years that Ruzante was bringing to completion his pair of Plautine experiments, *La vaccària* and *La piovana*—the latter deriving not only from the *Rudens* but also from *La cassaria*. Ruzante, though, was imposing his own experimental forms upon the Plautine pattern that had imposed itself upon Ariosto's efforts at originality.[18] Originality is, however, the claim Ariosto makes repeatedly in his prologues—so successfully that one can reasonably argue that the *idea* of a modern genius for dramatic independence and innovation was bred in Ferrara's Plautine theater.

This theater was a hybrid offspring. The calculated politicization of tournaments, palios, and such public spectacles was engineered by Borso and Ercole d'Este; the result is preserved in the zodiacal frescoes of Schifanoia that "stage" the ideal city in juxtaposition with representations of the literal Ferrara and the spectacles and spectators within its walls.[19] And it is just this reflexive scenic realism that stands for originality as it expands into the staging of local customs, types, and dialect incursions within the enveloping Plautine form in Ferrara. The Veneto and Florence, less burdened by an idea of originality, became better matrices for its development. But perhaps one may momentarily project what might not have eventuated in its neighbors had Ferrara not invented the notion of the new.

Secret Sharers in Italian Comedy

Machiavelli, like Ariosto, was both translator and adapter of Plautus, but one who more effectively wrested comic form away from his dramatic progenitor; we have begun with and will return more than once to *La mandragola* as a touchstone for the anti-Plautine structures considered together in this study. Machiavelli's personal reactions to Venice were negative[20] and any impact he may have had upon Ruzante unknown and problematic. Nonetheless, it bears recalling that *La mandragola* was performed at Venice during carnival in 1522 "per Cherea luchese e compagni . . . con intermedii di Zuan Pollo e altri bufoni" [by Cherea from Lucca and his companions . . . with intermezzos by Zuan Pollo and other comics], and that the second edition of Machiavelli's play was published in Venice in the same year.[21] It was again seen in Venice in 1526 in tandem with the *Menaechmi,* which, in contrast, was reported to be "una cosa morta" [a dead thing]. Thus, *La mandragola* predated in Venice the contributions to the comic subgenre of secrecy made by Venice's own early dramatic experimenters, Ruzante and the author of *La venexiana.* And this fact demands that one step backward to observe that Lorenzo Strozzi had been in Ferrara in 1502 to participate in the theatrical festivities surrounding the marriage of Lucrezia Borgia with Duke Alfonso d'Este; he accompanied his music instructor, Baccio di Michelangelo degli Organi, a composer intimately involved with the program of celebratory events. Here the young Florentine patrician who would become Machiavelli's patron and coplaywright encountered, among the host of attendant luminaries, Ariosto and Ruzante.[22] This can serve to remind us of Ariosto's own probable attendance at the Florentine production in 1513 of *I due felici rivali* [The Two Happy Rivals] of Jacopo Nardi, a fellow Medicean dramatist with Strozzi.[23] A new road map of the routes of communication is still approximate, conjectural paths connecting such details as these about the activities of theatrical figures conjoined from distant points. Later we will encounter another important instance in Alessandro Piccolomini's dramatic ties with Padua and with the spread of Sienese rustic plays, in spite of their high degree of local color and dialect, to Rome and Venice. It is becoming clear that when the history of Italian Renaissance drama is rewritten, it will be a revised story of a phenomenon long disguised by those generations of dramatic archivists who tirelessly recovered for us texts that were cubicled into dramatic provinces seemingly as peculiarly homogenous as the political organizations and dialects which are important parts of their context.[24] One aspect of my study is its modest contribution to our realization that the dispersion of larger forms insistently points to a pan-peninsular development that characterizes the early years of a uniquely Italian drama.

The plays grouped here differ as much in their individual strategies as they resemble one another. But when juxtaposed, as in a series of familial snapshots taken across a long period of years, that resemblance emerges as their common final form, inwardly defining if not outwardly definitive.

Il Padano to Il Veneto

Ugolino Pisani's *Philogenia:* Goliardic Prototype

*R*ape, anonymous to victim and assailant alike in the darkness of night or drunkenness, was a plot device common to Plautus (*Aulularia*) and Terence (*Hecyra*) and one inherited from their Greek predecessors. Its function, though, was to delay, even while preparing, the happy epiphanies of social concord. The act, then, was a commonplace instrument of the drama, directing its outcome toward a *concordia discors* that we have come to think of in those terms of blocking, renewal, and regeneration gathered under the rubric of New Comedy. In Italian Renaissance society, rape was an act of nature scarcely more stigmatized than it is in these Roman comedies and their Italian adaptations. We can observe, for instance, the gridwork of class, age, and violence that has been arranged for the reporting of crime and punishment in fifteenth-century Venice. Rape as such, unless it constituted an extraordinary violation of social status, did not often result in punishment. When it did, that was owing not to the rape but to the beatings and bloodshed that were often its accompaniment.[1]

Rape could be a small social accident, perhaps a recurrent inevitability, to be turned to a fortunate fault by the drama when placed at the center of structural plot movements toward comic harmony. It is when the act becomes thought that modern drama emerges as a form of human secrecy, complicity. Rape becomes dramatic when it also becomes seduction, because rape is infinitely repetitive, seduction infinitely variable.

The variability is not focused only in the psyche, although that too counts for much, but to a more decisive degree in the mode of narration. A Boccaccian *beffa* is an extended joke, a comic form in which the point of secrecy is the revelation of a secret to the audience. In dramatic enactment, the informed participants are as contingent in their possibilities as the audience. These two groups are inducted together into a secret that has a social potential too far-reaching to permit the mere pleasures of tale-carrying, the cackle at fictional cuckolds without dimension. The *novella* of seduction must, by definition, tell all the news; the drama of seduction is a conspiracy of silence with its audience, the society that sanctions and shapes it. The novella form has the mythic closure of the fairy tale: "once upon a time there was an old man and he had a young wife . . ." The dramatic form, a creation or realization of the Renaissance, remains as open as the denouement which never arrives.

In the seventh tale of the second *giornata* of Boccaccio's *Decameron* we are presented with one of the most widely and variously interpreted stories in the collection. Alatiel, the Sultan of Babylon's daughter, is the most beautiful woman in the universe. She is affianced to the young king of El Gharb in recognition of his aid in the Sultan's wars. Properly accompanied, richly accoutred, she sets sail to join her prospective husband. So begins Boccaccio's tale. Shipwreck ensues. Rescued, she is joined physically to the first of her eight lovers in his bed; yet, separated by languages, neither speaks — no one can when, as in this case, the seduction is simply the act of sex alone.[2] But it is apparent that Alatiel is no more or less a victim than is this first lover, Pericone, who must suffer death as the price of his love — like so many of the successors who follow him through a course of events that are merely fortune's accidents. Finally, Alatiel, often satisfied, is returned to her father and invents for him a tale of a long sojourn in an imaginary convent. The ecstatic Sultan resupplies the virgin bride's delayed dowry, and she again sets off to wed the king of El Gharb. This tale offers a web of intrigue in which we vicariously enjoy the lady's pleasures masked as the turns of fortune, and the good fortune, at that, of encountering such varied lovers as she has known. It is in a comic history from another time that we learn of the lie that leads her father unwittingly to dispatch his much-used virgin princess to the patient pre-cuckolded king. We join forces with the narrator in a tale of seductions carried through without language because they are without characterization. The princess is . . . a princess, the king a king, the unfortunate lovers interchangeable pawns. Men and women are creatures of the lustful lie; fathers and husbands beware. Yet, as in New Comedy, Boccaccio's tale ends in a social renewal, a celebration at a new court of an old cover-up so prevalent in the *novelle* that the word for such jokes, *beffa,* seems always on the verge of spilling over to become generic.[3] We are not, however, in the presence of that joyful malice of *I tre becchi* or *La Calandria.* Cesare Segre makes a significant observation about a key distinction that reorients the affective bearings of such superficially analogous narratives: "La novella si rivela dunque come una delle molte del *Decameron* basate su un inganno (categoria più ampia della beffa, dato che include la difesa sleale del proprio interesse, ma esclude l'animosità verso il promesso sposo)" [The novella reveals itself then as one of the many in the *Decameron* based on a deception (a broader category than the beffa, given that it includes the unfair defense of one's own self-interest, but excludes animosity toward the fiancé)].[4] Segre's observation distinguishing self-interest with or without malice toward some other offers a convenient point from which to begin this analysis of secrecy in Renaissance comedy. The convenience arises from the circumstance that Boccaccio's tale of the ever-virgin bride offers an analogue to the plot of the rebellious young humanist Ugolino Pisani's *Philogenia;* it is an analogue, though, that reveals the gap between reading and observing the performance of similar matter molded by dissimilar genres.

Pisani's Latin play was written sometime in the 1430s in the active center of goliardic theatricals at the University of Pavia.[5] Not Renaissance, not medieval, certainly not "humanistic," *Philogenia* has both affinities and individuality within the corpus of Quattrocento goliardic drama. While a number of these plays are directly drawn from the novelle of the *Decameron, Philogenia* is not. How-

Padano to Veneto

ever, it has several features in common with three other plays—all of undeterminable authorship—attributed variously to the first four decades of the century: *Poliscena*, *Dolos*, and *Poliodorus*. These all are 'original,' while yet giving a sense of familiarity with their novellalike structure around a central beffa that results in seduction and "la ricerca finale di una soluzione o compromesso che finisca per soddisfare tutti in maniera più o meno completa" [the final search for a solution or compromise that may result in satisfying everyone in a more or less complete manner].[6] Except for the derivative *Poliodorus*, however, only Pisani's play demands an ultimate collusion in silence which is shared by the auditor. The relevance of Boccaccio's tale of Alatiel is that of an analogue, not a source; *Philogenia* is novellesque without being derived from the *novelle*. Also analogous in some respects to other near-contemporary Latin student plays, it extends the implications of a final scene that conceals as much as it discovers. It is this aspect of dramatic independence that may justify the speculation that *Philogenia* is the first thorough experiment in a new comedic form.

The plot of *Philogenia* is as simple in outline as its implications are complex. Epiphebus is desperately in love with the nubile virgin Philogenia. She is seduced into eloping from her parents' home, but Epiphebus must displace her from his own house to avoid discovery, a displacement during which she is shifted from the care of one to another of his friends, each of whom abuses her. Finally, in order to have Philogenia more readily at his own disposal and to throw off all pursuit, Epiphebus arranges her marriage to a cloddish young peasant, Gobius, with the aid of two prostitutes who pose as her relatives and vouch to the country man for her modest upbringing. The tale of Alatiel is brought from the court into the country-city class conflicts that will emerge as a standard feature in Ruzante's pre-commedia dell'arte canon.

The early scenes (there are no explicit divisions) focus upon cynicism about women pretending to flee love in spite of their desire, a foreshadowing that is soon confirmed both in Philogenia's soliloquy and in the action as Epiphebus rhetorically woos her and wins her elopement. This extended 'philosophic' foreplay upon the passions occupies nearly a quarter of the text. But once repression of instinct is overcome, the action runs slapdash through the middle and tosses Philogenia from bed to bed. The final half of the play is fully occupied with another seduction, more complicated than the first: the seduction of Gobius into marriage with the supposed virgin and of Philogenia into marriage with the peasant.

The principal deceptions of the wooing are the gross stuff of perennial sexual satire. Epiphebus—whose love will quickly lose its first heat—is warned about the folly inherent in animal passion by his coeval counselor Nicomius, who promotes reason as being that self-conserving attribute that man shares with the gods. And in his own manner, Epiphebus uses his reason to promote his passion; he argues that the lover, like the archer, must be persistent: "Balistarii namque solent ab arcu plerumque sagittas centum emittere priusquam signum attigerint et forte fortuna exulabit una que statim in metam statuetur" [Archers usually must send forth from the bow at least a hundred errant arrows before hitting the bullseye; but usually one finally almost by chance will hit the center] (178). And persistent he is; drawing Philogenia onto her balcony, he feigns death, invoking this same image of the bow: "O diva Venus, tuque Cupido qui me arcu et face tua feram hanc inesorabilem non modo amare sed insanire compullisti, succurrite pariter, obsecro" [O, divine Venus, and you, Cupid, who with your bow and your power have driven me to love with the madness of a savage beast, I implore you in like manner to hasten to my aid] (194). Nicomius's wildly passionate animal has been hunted down by the savage heart of the huntress, the nubile virgin; as so often in the poetry of the succeeding century, Diana is transformed into Venus. Philogenia, as adept as Epiphebus at acting through her passion, pretends to a suicidal Liebestod by threatening to fling herself from the balcony "postquam sic datum est fatis" [since one sees it is the law of fate] (194). This calculated

Padano to Veneto

rhetoric of action promised in *mauvaise foi*, combined as it is with the rhetorical calculations of Epiphebus, both confirms and undermines Philogenia's own consistent expression of her passivity in the hands of the gods. It is confirmed insofar as Epiphebus will seduce her into a situation of permanent degradation, using her in the beffa that is the old heritage of the play's plot.

Within the personally secret, generically public lies of lovers, however, are buried more cues to the secrecy that makes life comic rather than tragic in form. Philogenia *is* a nubile virgin. But one who is aware of her stunted status, aware of her right to seek nature's redress from parental suppression: "Quoad enim viro maturam virginem servare hedes opportet? Ad annos usque sedecim dici audio; ego vero vigesimum iam nacta sum meam in rem malam" [How long is it proper that a virgin ripe for a man should be kept in custody at home? Until she is sixteen, I have heard; yet I am already twenty and still in this bad state] (180). Either Philogenia has passed on a lie about her age to Epiphebus, or he has perpetuated it as a further sordid detail of the beffa engendered upon the hapless farmer and cuckold Gobius, for Epiphebus explains to Gobius's brother (and marriage broker) Zabinus, "virgo ista annos sedecim vix nata est" [the girl is scarcely sixteen] (239).

It is not only the betrayed girls and the betraying rakes of society who prefer to live their lies in secrecy. Epiphebus has cynically learned the way of the older generation, of the parental world become so much more self-protective than in the old Plautine (or New Comedy) cast of blocking *senes,* as we learn when he assures Philogenia:

Parentes autem tui cum te abesse domo comperint, clam omnibus id facient. . . . Parentes enim eiusmodi fere omnes sunt: interminatus filiis ne quid sceleris, flagitii, inhonestive commitant et eos observant quantum in ipsis est. . . . Sed . . . si quando forte superata parentum omni cura et vigillantia, filii, ut humanum est, quicquam flagitii impudentieve admiserunt, illud continuo sua prudentia occultari volunt neque causam sui dedecoris in publicum afferre student.

Your parents, when they know that you have run away from home, will keep it secret from everyone. . . . Almost all parents are like this: so that their children do not fall into wicked, flagitious, dishonest ways they warn and watch them as well as they are able. . . . But . . . if evading every care and vigilance of their parents, children, as is human nature, should do something shameless, the first care of the parents is prudently to hide things so that the cause of their dishonor does not get about in public talk. (190)

I say that Epiphebus has "learned" this insight into the universality cutting across the generational boundaries supposedly dividing the dramatis personae of classical comedy because Philogenia's father verifies the younger man's sense of a new and harder society unknown to Plautus or Terence in his immediate reaction to his daughter's defection: "primum cautio nobis sit, ne qua exeat. Si quis roget ubi sit, quid faciat, egram simulemus" [the first care for us must be that nothing gets out. If someone should ask where she is, what she's doing, we will pretend she's sick] (200). If Philogenia is fulfilling her animal needs, so may (no, *must*) the parents in their own appropriate mode: "Nobis reliquum hoc pauculum vite nostre degamus perpetua in leticia" [That little of life that remains to us, we must pass happily] (204).

Philogenia appears to be an abused and abandoned child of a social order in which there remains everything but the explicitness of that slavery found in the classical models. She is a maiden reared in the demanding mores of Italy, tossed about not only by the whimsical gods but by the calculations of parents and lovers—an overprotected and undervalued girl kept too close to home too long. Secret plots, however, have a way of reshuffling the drama's principals. Philogenia's secrets are her own, but her ownership is endorsed by the church. She is liberated into happy disaster to be Epiphebus's pleasure and Gobius's promiscuous country wife by the machinations of the prostitutes Servia and Irtia when they join forces with the priest Prodigius, devotee of the high gods Jove and Venus, authorized by some "primario pontifice" (260) to take confession from Philogenia. This ambiguous Prodigius, the "miracle worker," stands somewhere between Christian and pagan in his rites and in his concepts of sin. But let us begin at the beginning again, with Philogenia's abuse and her collusion in the dilemma it produces before returning to the later collusion through which the priest will extricate her conscience.

Epiphebus is not alone as a prime mover of Philogenia toward apparent disaster. He himself is always acted upon: if his friend Nicomius warns him against women, his friend Emphonius offers to hide the fleeing Philogenia in his own house. But once finding herself there, Philogenia finds a voice more forward than that of Emphonius himself. As he settles her in and sets out to recover Epiphebus and bring him to his hidden love, Philogenia speaks excitedly to her new host, but not only about her errant lover: "Obsecro, quam primum vos domum recipite; nimis enim crutior in solicitudine" [I pray you, come back home as soon as possible, because I'll be tortured by worry] (216). Before Prodigius appears to work his confessional cleansing, then, we have all parties silenced against their potential for instrumenting a peripety: Philogenia, Epiphebus, Emphonius, Philogenia's parents. Plot has become a tangled web without promise of a comedic outcome. But Prodigius, as the public representative of morals, and Gobius, as the uncharacteristically youthful cuckold, stand in the wings to play out old roles in defining a new context in which cynicism replaces symmetry.

Philogenia's father simply wants that natural pleasure that is possible once he has given nature's due to generating and bringing another generation to desire. He may have cost himself some pain by retaining her a little too long at home, but once Philogenia has fled, he will play without remorse. As will they all.

Emphonius sets forth the plan for Philogenia to be married to Gobius not only as a convenience for Epiphebus but as an advertisement for the future: all sorts of women will learn the new way these rakes can guarantee marriage and more general pleasures simultaneously — or, at the least, a mutual recourse abetted by men "quibus satis abundeaque" [when satiated with them] (222). Pisani makes it clear that this is not an elitist class conception by providing a parallel cynicism in Gobius's brother and advisor Zabinus, who recognizes the commonality of sexual ennui in city and country as he promises the youth, "ad ne ante mensem ista uxore saturabere ut quocumque aspicias, uxores decem tibi videantur cernere" [before a month passes this wife will satiate you so that wherever you look you will seem to see ten wives] (242).

Turn now from the principals to their respective instruments, the prostitutes and the priest. Accustomed to wicked actions, the prostitutes nonetheless are in such debt to Epiphebus for favors over a long period that they cannot refuse him their help now in passing off Philogenia to Gobius as a pious virgin. If Epiphebus's past benevolent offices for the women remain yet another little secret nested into the set of concealing Chinese boxes, they ingenuously view the plan to marry Philogenia under false colors as participation in "piam et sancta rem" [a pious and holy affair] (246). In this context they feel called by some odd combination of conscience and superstition to have the bride shriven of past sins—purified, that is, from just the "venial" sexual sins that they have in common with her. But to be certain that all goes smoothly, one of the prostitutes hurries ahead to the church to acquaint the priest with Philogenia's situation and with the marriage plan.

The confession is a prolonged catechism of irrelevant sins (avarice, gluttony, etc.) into the midst of which is thrust the relevant question: "Veneri autem quantun indulsisti?" [But how much have you resisted Venus?] (258). Philogenia breaks down in spiritual panic: "Mi pater, plurimi mei copiam turpiter habuere" [Father, many have abused me filthily] (258). This echoes Epiphebus's description of the situation he admittedly has created: "Ubi ego vidi virginem hanc pernoctare opportere modo aput hunc, modo aput illum et pluribus usui turpiter esse" [I see the girl must pass the night first with this one then with that, and many have used her shamefully] (246). The solution, of course, is the marriage to Gobius, which will not only save Philogenia's reputation but will raise her conduct to the dubious level of his society's mores, as prescribed by Epiphebus: "Tu enim imitari disces quod mulieres bene ac provide factitarunt sumperque tucius amatore suo potite sunt, cum nuptui tradite sunt" [In fact, you must do as good and prudent women do who, married, nevertheless receive their lovers to betray with them their nuptial vows] (224). But even as he leaves for the country to treat with Gobius, Epiphebus snickers some double entendres about her waiting meanwhile with Emphonius: "concinite quicuid . . . oblecta te interim quantum potes et bene vale" [sing something together . . . divert yourselves in the meantime in good spirits] (226–28). When Epiphebus has departed, Philogenia confides to Emphonius that she realizes Epiphebus is beginning to disencumber himself of a waning passion. Emphonius gives her false reassurances (it was he, after all, who explained to Epiphebus that the cuckolding marriage would serve as an advertisement to bring them other women), and the scene ends as he takes up Epiphebus's musical sex metaphor: "Sed parendum est quidem Ephiphebo [*sic*], qui abiens ut concinemus imperavit" [But we must obey Epiphebus who in going out ordered us to sing together] (230). Now we should remember that first night at Emphonius's house, when the ambivalent Philogenia urged him to hasten back and not leave her alone, as here she responds to Emphonius's innuendo of invitation: "Hac in re bona fide utar" [I'll do my best to sound a good chord] (238). These are small clues, though, that Philogenia may be less than wholly victimized, clues almost swept aside in the whirlwind of cynical worldly passions with which she is surrounded. To read them clearly, we must return to that moment of distraught confession to the priestly miracle worker Prodigius, who is on the verge of earning his name.

When Philogenia admits that many have abused her "turpiter," Prodigius asks the pivotal question: did she submit willingly? In holy confession the answer will remain secret: "Istud quidem minime . . . [sum] nimium credula ut sumus omnes adulescentule. Quare me opportuit multorum libidini inservire" [In small measure . . . I have been too trusting like all young girls. Therefore many have been able to subject me to their desires]. The absolution is unconditional:

"Id ergo peccatum non est . . . te innocentem esse dico" [Therefore this is not a sin . . . I declare you to be innocent] (258). And with this assurance, Philogenia can open to the audience the secret of her future as well as her past: "Heya, diis igitur gratias ago, quod sumper absque noxa libidinem meam explevi" [Oh, how I thank the gods, that with such punishment I can discharge my pleasure] (258). There is collusion here, of course, far more flagrant than that one finds in *La mandragola* amongst Fra Timoteo, Sostrata, and Lucrezia.[7] Pretending to ignore Philogenia's delight, Prodigius's double entendre reinforces her future: "te hortor et impero sic facere pergas ut cepisti" [I exhort and command you to continue in the way you have begun] (260). Carrying this benediction upon venereal pleasures, Philogenia leaves the priest to rejoin the prostitutes. And with them she again encloses the secret of desire that had so briefly and opportunely been revealed. The priest, she tells the women, absolved her, "astinendum mihi tamen deinceps mandavit" [ordering that I abstain, though, from now on] (262). What will follow, of course, are Gobius's cuckolding upon Philogenia's projected trips into the city for trysts with Epiphebus and Epiphebus's adventures with other women, to be, like Philogenia, "enjoyed to satiety." A wiser and older *contadino* perhaps opens the endlessly repetitive future of everyone when he tells Gobius why he himself prefers nubile young girls to more experienced women (not knowing that even now Philogenia the bride has passed from one category into the next in which he notes the secret ennui endemic to love). Mature women, comparing a man to the husbands or lovers who first taught them the arts of love, may find him wanting and "recall it in bitter secret" (*egre clam ferunt*) (266).

Li sei contenti:
Galeotto del Carretto's Vernacular Prototype

Pisani was a brilliant young student playing upon the language and a genre he had learned and playing a formal antinovellesque trick

Padano to Veneto

upon the stuff of the novella as well. Not so "il Magnifico Cavaliere Galeotto del Carretto," a native of Monferrato who spent his youth at the Milanese court, dedicated a lost play to Beatrice d'Este, and upon her death established himself as a major political courtier at Casale, despite a brief exile. We know a good bit about his theater from his long correspondence with Isabella d'Este. In these letters, however, he fails to speak of *Li sei contenti,* a five-act prose comedy written in semi-Tuscan, presumably for the festivities surrounding the marriage of Federico Gonzaga to Maria Paleologo in 1517.[8]

The play offers a paradigmatic model for *La venexiana* (probably nearly contemporaneous), *La Betía,* and such later practices in anti-Plautine form as Fagiuoli's *Non bisogna in amor correre a furia* (to which Carretto's early piece has the closest family resemblance).

Mastallone, a wealthy householder, covets and beds Cristina, maidservant to his wife Iulia. Iulia—abetted by her other maid and confidante, Brunetta—cancels the humiliation by enjoying Mastallone's servant Graziuolo. The parasite (in a fully classical sense of the role) Stoppino, who acts as shrewd adviser to Mastallone, completes the contented sextet by obtaining Brunetta. Everything is revealed by the time the conclusion arrives—and nothing.

What in summary sounds so patently Plautine in effect turns the festive form upon its head, as the domestic discord of a proper *mariazo* is intended to do, performing an exorcisory function in the context of wedding rites. There is a deep current of unresolved ambiguity beneath the surface action, in which the secret affairs of every party to deception are revealed by counterdeceptions as transparent as the original illicit actions. Everyone will learn everyone else's secret without much difficulty, with a little aid from chance at convenient times. An example illustrates Del Carretto's casual attitude toward the mechanics of plotting. A serving boy in the household of Mastallone, a character otherwise supernumerary, just happens to overhear the maidservants gossiping about their mistress "over-sleeping" ("io era in luoco che udi' ciò che ragionavate de la nostra patrona" [I was in a place where I couldn't help hearing what you were saying about our mistress]) and as casually entrusts them

("Giura di tenermi secreto" [Swear to keep what I tell you a secret]) with the news that, finding a door locked against an errand he was performing and looking through a crack ("guardando per una fissura") he discovered the padrona Iulia romping in bed with Graziuolo (3; 100–111). With such important disclosures so easily emergent, one infers that the playwright is flaunting the folly of hoping that secret actions can remain hidden. Graziuolo has made his way into his mistress's bed with the tried and trite means of a threat to kill himself, a threat that foreshadows the extravagant beffa that will be arranged to reconcile Iulia and Mastallone. But the reconciliation will be necessary because Graziuolo, soon to be observed *in delicto flagrante* by the boy, has himself overheard Mastallone's plotting with Stoppino to placate *his* illicit *innamorata* Cristina. Again, the preposterously casual plotting is foregrounded with an authorial wink at its weakness. Having dispatched him on an errand, Stoppino gloats, "ora che Graziuolo è ito . . . noi possiamo parlare . . . senza suspetto d'essere uditi" [now that Graziuolo has gone . . . we can speak . . . without fear of being heard]. But the servant has simply turned a corner to hide and eavesdrop—and comment ironically to himself and the audience upon Stoppino's belief that he and Mastallone can be secure in their private plottings: "Forse che sì e forse che no" [Maybe yes and maybe no] (2; 98).

When all of the coincidental discoveries have brought on psychological chaos, Del Carretto introduces the elaborate enterprise by means of which Mastallone undertakes to reassure Iulia that there will be no further erotic peccadilloes: he proposes voluntary castration. This constitutes the ultimate foreclosure upon that comic form one thinks of as festive regeneration. Mastro Bertuccio (the *castratore*) arrives with his irons, and there is a small playlet within the Plautine play gone awry, a vaudevillesque *lazzo* as Stoppino directs and Iulia watches while Mastallone is stripped and strapped down for the iron. Wife and husband both relent before the damage is done, but with a new emphasis upon truth and dissimulation melding into the language of a shaky pax domestica. Mastallone is left to sum things up in the role of a sexual accountant:

Padano to Veneto

Poiché tu vuoi così e m'accenni ch'io faccia quanto mi piace, e io anche ti do licenza che tu faccia quanto ti piace. Datti pure buon tempo con Graziuolo, che io mel darò con Cristina, e sia da qui inanzi comunanza di quanto c'è, . . . e ciò che è fatto, sia fatto.

Since you want it this way, and tell me that I can do as I please, I also give you liberty to do whatever you wish. Enjoy yourself with Graziuolo, as I will give myself a good time with Cristina, and from now on let everything be in common, . . . and let that which is over and done with, be over and done with. (5; 140)

Once the socially more elevated couple have agreed upon the price for evading marital and comedic precedents as they have been generically understood, Stoppino asks his own reward: "vi prego siate contenti che ancora io talvolta possa sollazzare con la Brunetta, che tanto amo" [I pray that you be content that I also may sometimes enjoy myself with Brunetta, whom I love so much] (5; 141). This completes the structural concinnity, as that century would have said, of *Li sei contenti*. All six seem content with their gains; odds seem evened in this early practice upon Plautus in the northern cradle of Italian drama. But it is not so. All is bad will and wary compromise; the notion of "contentment" is contaminated with the ambiguity epitomized in Graziuolo's ironic "forse che sì e forse che no."

To be paid in one's own kind is neither contentment nor a promised end toward which one plots. A mid-Cinquecento writer left a distinction that might summarize the pseudo-solution of Del Carretto's play, observing that "Chi schernisce, sente contento della vergogna altrui, e chi beffa prende dello altrui errore non contento, ma solazzo"[9] [He who derides feels contentment at the shame of others, and he who plays a trick receives from the error of others not contentment, but pleasure]. Mastallone's pleasure is too tainted to leave him content with his new situation; yet it is a pleasure to be enjoyed. He locates his place between the dilemma's horns in a self-debate carried on before the audience alone. His decision to choose silence defines a subgenre as it develops in collusion, as I will often repeat in the pages that follow, with an audience that shares the secret:

Io sto in dubbio dei casi mei, s'io parlo, è male. Se taccio è peggio. Se l'attosco, mi scuopro per becco publico, se non le accurto la vita, m'allungo le corna! Insomma io non so quel che mi faccia. Se parlo, io scandalezzo me e lei, e la vergogna sarà commune. . . . Pure quando ho ben pensato, trovo esser menor male il tacere e fingere non intenderlo.

I don't know what I should do; if I speak out, it's bad. If I say nothing, it's worse. If I poison her, I reveal myself publicly for a cuckold; if I don't shorten her life, I lengthen my horns. In short, I don't know what I should do. If I speak out, I bring down scandal on myself and on her, and the shame will be common. . . . Yet, when I have thought it through, I find the lesser evil is to be silent and pretend to understand nothing. (4; 121)

La venexiana

La venexiana is a text surrounded with secrecy. First published some four hundred years after its creation, reconsidered fifty years later yet as a *drame à clef,* it defies decipherment: the author unknown, the source only possibly a half-revealed scandal from the palaces of Cinquecento Venice.[10]

One can use the occasion of this mysterious text, so full of local color as to have evoked detailed historical interpretation, to review an aspect of classical comedy I have not touched upon. Plautus, straightforward about his adaptations of Menander and the lesser Greek dramatists, nonetheless is recurrently self-conscious in his prologues when he mentions the settings of his originals. He insists upon the limited size of his own theater in comparison with Menander's Athens and Sicily, insists upon the necessity of compressing them into small rooms, creating with this maneuver a simultaneous foregrounding and disruption of place. As a consequence, in Plautus's theater the fable of love intrigues became all, as it would in Pisani's analogous concentration of erotic travels characteristic of *novelle* and exemplified by those of Alatiel. But Plautus *did* lightly sprinkle his text with identifying allusions to the inherited exotic settings. And these were settings into competition with which Renaissance *commediografi* were thrust as contemporaries of the reborn Plautus. Struggle as they would, Plautus's own self-conscious struggle with the settings of his Greek originals predetermined the Italians' insistence upon place. But the modern dramatists' revolt was to make their settings those of the writer and audience, as Plautus had not dared to do. Venice, Ferrara, Florence, Siena: these were the places whose local color was incorporated into classical forms until they burst.

The place in this instance is Venice, and the plot of *La venexiana* begins and ends, like its history, in secrecy. Iulio, a handsome young stranger (from Padova? Lombardia? or a stranger place without a name? One never knows because his autobiography deals in the self-concealing lie),[11] arrives in Venice. He is sighted by and excites a young bride of an inappropriately older man; he is sighted by and excites a lusty widow. Their respective maidservants solicit him, each successfully, and each with the help of the porter gondolier Bernardo. The first night it is the turn of Anzola the widow; the second night, that of Valeria the misdisposed bride. On the first night the younger woman has been left waiting while Iulio makes love to the widow; the second night the widow is left waiting while the wife makes love to Iulio, hoodwinking her old husband.[12] The play ends at this point. All is carried out in literal darkness. And Cupid is not only blind, *cieco,* but a master of silence into whose secrets the author allows us entry only if, as he says in an address clouded in Latin, "Tu lege, disce, sile" [read, learn, be silent] (67).[13] If this is a final admonishment, it does not differ from the assumptions of the prologue, where everything is promised as a peep behind the social and dramatic curtain: "Tutti, vi prego, prestate orechie e in alcuna parte non vi turbate, se quello, che da sè è da passar sotto silenzio, oggi di nostri mimi senza vergogna serà publicato" [Everyone, I beg, lend your ears, and do not be disturbed at all if that which in itself should be passed over in silence shall today be made public by our actors] (71). These, prologue and epilogue, are immediately engulfed into the plot proper, however. Foreword and coda become commentary.

In the first scenes we meet Valeria and Anzola in juxtaposition, each with her maidservant. And each maid is independent, irritated at pretentious mores, a confidante of her mistress. To coin an oxymoron, the nubile wife in a May-December marriage is frustrated at her maid's silence when the latter has encountered the lusty outsider Iulio without bringing him home. Speech and silence are twinned, desire and distance: "Ti fa' çiò che te digo mi; e tasi" [You do what I tell you; and keep quiet] (79). And when we turn to the widow Anzola she is introduced in bed with her maid Nena, who coyly refuses to understand her mistress's heated passion for the foreign body of Iulio.

Nena: Aveu frebe? Lasseme un puoco tocar.
Anzola: La frebe xè qua entro, nel cuor.

Nena: Have you a fever? Let me just feel you.
Anzola: The fever is here inside, in my heart.
(79)

But the widow is both more open and more secretive than the bride: she activates a fantasy of love with Nena as surrogate Iulio. Nena urges her mistress back to her own bed, but Anzola objects: "Voio star qua. E, se ti vul che dorma, gètame cussì le to braze; e mi sererò gli ochii, e te crederò el fio [I want to stay here. And if you want me to sleep, throw your arms around me like this; and I'll close my eyes and imagine that you are the young man] (83). Anzola concludes the first act with this secret lesbian embrace: "Cara Nena, fa' un puoco el sbisao per mio amore" [Dear Nena, play the macho bravo with me a little, for my love] (85).

The monitory language of silence continues to thread the play

Padano to Veneto

33

from this point through the final warning—"disce, sile"—as a metonymy for the form of the fable. The morning after her night in Anzola's arms, Nena awakens with her worrisome assignment to bring Iulio to Anzola—a difficult task if one is to "farlo secreto," and only to be accomplished by the connivance of her friend Bernardo the porter "che xè pratico, secreto e fidato de casa" [who knows what he is doing, can mind his own business, and is a person trusted by the house] (87). When she encounters this friend, Nena's first demand is that he share and simultaneously keep Anzola's secret, even as it had been Anzola's command the night before: "Ti volio dir un secreto," explains Nena, "ma tasi" [I want to tell you a secret . . . but keep it quiet] (89). And when Bernardo has agreed to spirit the young stranger into Anzola's house, Nena's final admonition is "Ma tasi, ve'!" [But remember, be quiet] (91). When Bernardo has arranged for Iulio to come to Anzola imminently, the widow pleads: "Bernardo, che ti abba secreto" [Bernardo, keep it a secret] (105), to which he responds that everything is to be considered forgotten once he is paid for love services rendered. And he is faithful to his promises. If act 1 offers the lesbian embraces of Anzola and Nena so graphically, the third-act lovemaking between Iulio and Anzola is a detailed triumph in the verbal translation of fucking. Bernardo and Nena eavesdrop upon this vivid lovers' bed-talk, but in the name of silence rather than that exploitation common to servants in the comic pattern: "No parlar pì. Aldi zò ch' i parla da basso" [Say no more. Listen to what they're saying downstairs] (117). When lust has been satiated, Iulio has the male penchant for embroidering the act with talk, but the widow shushes him like a child: "Tasi e dormi, ché voio far a mio modo" [Be quiet and go to sleep, because I want to enjoy in my own way] (119). And when Bernardo glides this stranger away in his gondola, he too quiets all queries about names or circumstance: "Quest è ol bel de la segur: ol manegh. Domà vel dirò, ch' adès non recordi vergòt" [This is the beauty of the axe: the handle. I'll tell you tomorrow, for I can't remember anything now]. And Iulio acquiesces in his good fortune's desire to remain anonymous: "Se tu non vòi, non voglio anco io" [If you don't want to (tell), I don't want to (know) either] (125).

The following day Valeria's maid seeks out Iulio, who not only missed his rendezvous with the young wife but feels a conscientious, yet wavering, loyalty to the widow, who has given him a golden chain as a token to bind their secret ("me ha dato el core e l'anima; e non ha voluto palesarsi" [she gave me her heart and soul; but didn't want to identify herself] [127]). He is invited again by Valeria and, though suspicious of a trick, elects to keep this new assignation precisely because it is a different form of secrecy from that demanded by the widow—it has the advantage of the unknown: "Lo experimentar è cosa bellissima, per aver avantaggio in cognoscer" [Experimentation is a wonderful thing, which gives us a chance of wider knowledge] (131).

The stranger, the widow, the young wife: were it not for the dramatis personae, they might have no names (as Anzola has insisted), except at a crucial juncture of recognition, where identification is inadvertent. Valeria recognizes the golden chain Iulio wears as belonging to Anzola. In disappointedly dispatching Iulio back to the widow, Valeria employs an ambivalent phrase which implies her own termination of their aborted affair and a plea for silence about their near indiscretion: "Nè voio dir altro, ca tàser, da qua indrio" [And from this moment on I don't plan to say anything, just keep quiet] (137).

Iulio accepts the coincidence that has aborted his unsought adultery with the wife and turns it to a new stroke of good fortune as he contemplates his return to the widow, now resolved to remain with her, "restar cum un peso solo. Perché doi sono troppo; non a me, ma a un gigante, se fosse ben mazor de Atlas" [to stay with one burden; because two are too many for anyone; not just for me, but for a giant, even if he were bigger than Atlas] (139). When Bernardo returns to set up a second night with the widow, he speaks only in suggestive metaphor, which Iulio accepts without interpretation: "Entendo; no più, mo taci: so" [I understand; enough said; be silent;

Padano to Veneto

I know] (143). Before Bernardo can return in his gondola to carry Iulio to Anzola, however, the young man encounters Valeria's maid, begging him to come to a love tryst with her now contrite mistress, and Iulio's so recent proverb about the impossible task of juggling two lovers is replaced by another: "andarò a Valeria, per mutar cibo" [I will go to Valeria, to change diet] (147). And he will use the widow's own secrecy as an instrument to camouflage his secret encounter with Valeria. When Bernardo arrives, Iulio insists that he will not step into the gondola until the pandering servant reveals the widow's name. As Iulio anticipates, Bernardo conveniently refuses to betray his employer, but he promises to seek her permission to make the revelation later.

Then Iulio is led to Valeria, who professes her consuming passion for him. Iulio responds in kind as they meet at her door, and she draws him inside with another proverb of hidden passions: "el se suol dir che el xè matiera parlar cusì a la scoverta, perchè i venti ha orechie e occhi" [people say it's crazy to talk out in the open like this, because the winds have ears and eyes] (151). Inside the house, Valeria draws her new lover deeper into the metaphoric space of ecstatic silence, into her bedchamber. Reminding us at the close of the play that she is married, that this is a night that may or may not be repeated, that may be a beginning or an end, she turns to her maid-confidante and orders, "sera la camera e va' su a Miser Grando, che no çiga . . . di' che ho mal e che per questa sera, non voio che nisun me rompa la testa" [close the chamber door and go up to the old "Master" so that he doesn't start screaming . . . tell him that I feel sick and don't want anyone giving me a hard time this evening] (153).

But before this last dissolve, the shrewd and secretive Bernardo promises that the love triangle will proceed indefinitely with the chain of lies that prevents the comedy's entering into the form of Plautine resolution. Recognizing that Iulio's refusal to go again to Anzola until he learns her name is a mere ploy to gain this night's freedom for an opportunity to "mutar cibo," Bernardo opines to himself: "A' l' ho mi entisa, che a' volì slongarla a domà" [I've

Secret Sharers in Italian Comedy

understood very well, that you want to put it off until tomorrow] (149). Tonight here, tomorrow there, always under the open secrecy of lies to lubricate the lubricious merry-go-round.

A great deal of futile speculation has focused upon the Latin explicit, seeking to tease out the authorship of *La venexiana*. But the two final distichs sum up the plot stuff of a young man, a wife, and a widow, "quorum mihi nomina tantum" [of whom I know only the names], as if to imply, "I could say more if I would." My conjecture is that these lines were spoken as an epilogue in some form exclusive of the injunction to read, the Latin itself another pretended shield against full disclosure. But even so, we know too much, and are warned to join the conspiracy of silence: "Tu lege, disce, sile."

Ruzante: *La Betía*

The flytings of the protodramatic mariazi are surprisingly exemplary of what we have internalized as the structural norm of New Comedy: a *concordia discors* that ends just where this folk genre began, in marriage. The folk model in which married couples — generally peasants — quarrel was developed for presentation at weddings and offered as a sort of satiric exorcism of domestic demons to both high and low cultures throughout the Italian peninsula in the Renaissance; we find important versions simultaneously at the turn of the Cinquecento in the Veneto, in Tuscany, and in Campania.[14] The mariazi took on literary form at this time in the *egloghe* and commedie by members of the Sienese Congrega dei Rozzi and their immediate predecessors, a development we will discuss in detail in the following chapter; in the *farse cavaiole* of the *mezzogiorno;* and in the Tuscan materials collected largely by Lorenzo de'Medici and his companions and preserved in Giulio Ferrario's invaluable early anthologies.[15]

There is no need to rehearse again the emergence of Beolco-Ruzante from the pre-commedia performers of the Veneto except to remind ourselves that the long, sustained versification of *La Betía* was a tour de force that bridged two comedic developments. It

Padano to Veneto

37

carried Beolco's rustic protagonist past the pseudo-folk *impasto* of *La pastoral* onto the level of full-length drama, just when Machiavelli also was revising the Plautine formulae in Florence. Beolco would insert Ruzante into such Plautine adaptations later (*L'anconitana* and *La vaccària*). But at this point in the early 1520s he was making a classic (if anticlassical) comedy from the resources of the mariazo, doing so in the context of the mariazo's origins but melding them in the interests of a dramatic mold that has been exemplified in *Philogenia*. The mariazi imaged discord as exorcism of the perils to contented marriage; that was the social function of a form. The flyting done, the dancing done, the actual wedding ceremony turned to celebration of what Plautus had dramatized: lovers made fertile in their conjugal consummation.[16] Beolco, though, took the folk form seriously enough to extend it into plot, to relegate and reverse its assumed reassurance of social and formal continuities into a more cynical shape which had been foreshadowed by Pisani. *La Betía* is a comedy of the silenced future.

One may pause momentarily to recapitulate a sociological formula that has become almost paradigmatic, having been offered as a container for diverse historical materials owing largely to the influence of Lucien Febvre and the *annales* historians. It reads similarly in almost all cases, with variants inserted for local printing demographics, varying views of what constituted literacy, and the societal structures of extra-urban cultures in France, Italy, and England. There existed in that period from the rise of Venice and Florence, from the beginnings of a French cultural consciousness, from the Elizabethan consolidation of literary language, on through the eighteenth century a double class system in Europe based not upon material production but rather upon the availability of written materials. The question has become: where could the tools of literacy permeate, and what were the probabilities that the technology of reading rendered them significant in the production of cross-cultural comprehension? The paradigmatic answer goes roughly like this: there is a literate high culture with access to the classical past, to Greco-Roman language, history, and the generic forms of that past. There is another low-cultural tradition that has access to a wholly different but no less ancient set of forms and norms and languages (which were demoted to dialects). The very accident of birth established educated recipients of the high culture as sharers in the low-cultural heritage of their environs. This was notably the case in fifteenth-century Italy and carried over into the preservationist landmarks of dialects and folk forms in such works as *La Nencia, La Tancia, La fiera,* or *Il lamento di Ceccho*—all these (like the later *comme-die ridicolose* in Rome) being imitations, adaptations of traditional forms as well as dialects by educated members of the high culture. This dipping into the folk well has been more continuously visible in Italy than elsewhere, although its theorization has centered in France. Early versions of the paradigm formulated a one-way traffic in which a high-culture writer could use his incidental birthright of a regional dialect and history as realistic filler between the interstices of generic skeletal structure. On the other hand, the prisoners of low culture, whom we have come to call the "folk," had no access to the classical tradition. Once put in this way, though, the paradigm begins to raise more sophisticated doubts than it settles. One recalls, for instance, that the *Bibliothèque bleue* was itself based upon texts originally available only through a class-divided educational system, as was the *opera dei pupi* in Sicily. More generally, the high-low axis has been replaced in the sociology of Italian literature by Camporesi's development of an agrarian-urban axis.[17] In this formulation, the ritual constructs of agrarian culture permeated modern Christian rites and habits of mind with continuing force until the Seicento Counter Reformation began to sap their energies in a new urban and court culture sponsored by both church and state. The parish priest, who had once been a sacred *buffone* bridging the contadino's pagan vestiges of thought with the modern apparatus of the church, now became the preceptor and warden of a panopticonlike social edifice.

These discussions are relevant to Beolco's formal move in *La Betía*. Rather than the privileged cannibalization of a folk culture by archaeological poets such as Lorenzo de'Medici and his associates, Beolco essayed a restructuring of form that would force classical

Padano to Veneto

39

genres not only to acknowledge but to surrender to popular materials. He instrumented, in this, a landmark stage in Italian comedy's formal triumph over Plautus.

The story line of *La Betía* is as easy as Pisani's, but Beolco's apparent New Comedy plot expands into a play so lengthy and episodic as to offer a rough precedent for Michelangelo il Giovane's *La fiera* a century later, both in extension and in the intention of creating an anthology of folk forms, types, and customs. If the mariazi constitute a subgenre of the flyting *contrasti*, *La Betía* appropriately opens with a characteristic debate about the ills of marriage and the evils of women. Its instigation is the teenage *villano* Zilio's obsession by his love for Betía, but its participants are frame characters who emerge for their contrasto only to disappear forever at its end; they are plot irrelevancies but generically indispensable. Their appearance is a first sample of the surprises, the unsettling of expectations that thread the whole of *La Betía*. The younger villano Bazarelo wanders in looking for his escaped stallion in a field where Zilio is being comforted by his more mature married friend Nale, a cynic about love (the opening and closing envelope of Bazarelo's cameo insists upon the lost horse, a reference imprecisely, and unmistakably, loaded with sexual irony). Soon the senex Barba Scati joins the group. He runs through an exasperating contrasto on love and its emblematic imagery with Bazarelo, the pompous but patient Barba Scati offering in his analysis a parodic version of Bembo's commentary in *Gli asolani*.[18] A brittle cynic and an aged bumbler become the authorities on idealistic love for the stricken youth, Zilio. Platonism is interrupted by crass pragmatism; the former is undermined by authorial parody and the latter by the absence of Bazarelo's horse, symbolic of machismo lost. The stunningly unexpected upshot of the debate explains the appropriateness of this insistent symbolic insertion into the pastoral foreground. Generically we know that the young must overcome, that the green fuse must thrust aside old shibboleths—that is the function of love contrasti, of mariazi, of New Comedy. They share a formal interest in renewal. But suddenly Barba Scati, aggravated in the extreme by Bazarelo's refusal to keep to expected form in the tradition of contrasti, himself turns pragmatist in physically beating the young cynic into abject terror—at least momentarily. Age has triumphed over youth and its animality; when Bazarelo departs, it is Zilio who rejects his arguments and reevaluates his symbol: " 'l no sa d'Amore. / E questo perché a tut'ore / el sta a le stale" [he doesn't know about love. This is because he is in the stables at all hours] (1.1126–27). The last phrase says all that can be said against natural lust: "arende a gi anemale" [along with the beasts] (233). But then, as Barba Scati resumes his discourse upon the trappings of love, we are not forgetful of the foolish abuse his advice to Zilio is doing to the argument of Bembo. Zilio and Nale sit before us like children in a familiar pastoral setting, but a setting now disturbed by the violence arising between low- and high-cultural stereotypes gone awry. The protagonists, like the audience, begin to find themselves pressed out of the bounds of expectations that Beolco's choice of theatrical forms have induced, in what Ruzante calls *il mondo roesso* (the world upside down); we are tumbled through the looking glass, shattering its frame.[19]

Act 2 opens with another long plot irrelevancy as Zilio, Nale, and Barba Scati enter, picking their teeth, belching, farting, and shitting after a meal they have immensely enjoyed at the *osteria*. If this action serves no surface function, it is an episode that vividly illustrates the carnivalesque exaltation of what Bakhtin calls the "lower bodily stratum," another turning upside down as the tail supplants the head, as personal boundaries, like social and generic boundaries, merge; intake and output collapse into a process of scatalogical interchange.[20] Bakhtin's inspirations were such episodes as Gargantua's urinary flooding of Paris, but the symbiosis between the *canti carnascialeschi* and the *sacre rappresentazioni*, the culinary artillery of carnival deployed against Lent, were equally pertinent examples of this persistent train of bodily glorification in popular culture of the Italian Renaissance. And again Beolco weaves his apparently tangential folk stuff back into the web of plot as Nale instructs Zilio in courtship, using his own wooing of a wife for model. One sings,

Padano to Veneto

one dances, one wheedles, and one finally unites the scatological and sexual by catching the enamored farm girl in the outhouse when she goes to piss. The lesson incorporates a crescendo of repetition of that favored profanity of *La Betía:* "pota del mal drean," an untranslatable running exclamation that brings together front and backside in an epigraph upon the lamination of excretory and sexual functions that is at the heart of this cultivated emergence of folk forms into a post–New Comedy.

Nale's advice upon wooing is genuinely well meant toward the bashful teenaged Zilio. Instructed, the boy sallies out to encounter Betía, only to have lust make him immediately unlearn Nale's lesson of gradualism. He confronts the surprised girl with a direct verbal assault. Betía says, "A' son con te me vi' " [I am just as you see me], and Zilio responds, "A' no te vego za'. / El besognarae che te foíssi spogià" [I haven't seen you yet. / You have to be undressed] (2.603–5). Even the nubile (a term brought into question later) girl cannot play into this crude bid and fights off Zilio's more physical attempts with a threatening rock and with tears of frustration aimed at this ineptitude that deprives both parties of the resolution of their natural desires. When she leaves, Nale returns to undergo almost equally astonished frustration at Zilio's failure. But the more experienced man rethinks the situation, restructures the plot. Into secrecy. If Zilio is a stupid youngster, Nale the married man has not failed to notice Betía's attractive availability. If he has once helped Zilio toward fulfillment in good will, he can do so again in bad faith. At the end of the second act he reroutes Zilio's siege of Betía by recommending an *alba* to mollify her mortification. Youngsters are hired to sing beneath her window in the morning. But this time the wooing is upon his own behalf. As Zilio departs, Nale explains his adulterous intention to share Zilio's orchestrated triumph. The older Barba Scati has beaten young Bazarelo, and the older Nale will use Zilio as his instrument. In love and war, the dominance of the elder protagonists overturns both popular and classical form. Closing act 2, Nale turns to the audience to warn: "Mo tasí pur, vu, / cara bela mia brigà, / no disí zà / a Zilio niente de questo; / perché a' verí presto presto, / se a' tasí, un bel papolò" [And the lot of you, my dear companions, keep quiet, / don't say anything to / Zilio about all this; / because you'll soon see / some beautiful double talking, if you keep quiet] (2.851–56). We are now cokeepers of the secret. Nale will, of course, betray us by revealing everything himself, in the usual comedic formula—but this time only to complicate the rather easy complications analogous to those in *Philogenia*. Nale arranges an alba (*mattinata*) to open act 3. This is yet another timeless genre introduced into the sinuous structure of *La Betía* and serves to draw Betía into Nale's proposal of a marriage with Zilio which can become a ménage à trois. Eagerly accepting, the girl steals as many of her mother's household goods as she can carry, and all seems to be going well until Nale explains to Zilio the accord under which Betía has been seduced from home. Nale claims to have been the first affected with love for her; he claims and wheedles, but Zilio is desperate at this betrayal. And, in her way, so is Betía: "Mo no m' aí prometú / tuti du esser un? / E che ognun / serà me bon marío?" [But didn't you promise me / both to be one? / And that each / will be a good husband to me?] (3.621–24). For Nale, compacts are the visible superficies, but secrecy is really the structural way of the world. And for an audience there is the divided loyalty to Zilio's attractive innocence and to Nale's exasperated knowledge of how that stupid innocence can be turned to everyone's simultaneous gain. But as act 3 ends, Betía's mother breaks the impasse by hauling her daughter back to the house, the senex figure in female guise drawing a line through the plot action that seems to restore it to the pseudo-contingencies of Plautine comedy, if with a modern turn.

Act 4 appears to complete this generic familiarization, with some popularizing embellishments. Falling under the generic shadow of the *sacre rappresentazioni*, Nale, having temporarily convinced Zilio that his proposal of sharing the bride had been a joke—again insisting upon the audience's silent complicity in his bad faith ("Brigà, stè pur mo a vêre, / e no ghe di' niente" [Companions, just stay and watch, / and don't say anything to him], 4.117–18)—draws up a troop of rustic soldiers armed with spades and spears to spirit

Padano to Veneto

Betía from her mother's captivity. The mother counters with her own ill-equipped troops until the innkeeper Taçio not only makes peace between the comic armies but promises a marital knot will be tied between the two young people. All seems settled. But nothing is so. The mother faints away; the daughter faints on the assumption that her mother is dead. Buckets of water revive them into a mock renewal of the death and resurrection so often practiced by Arlecchino, who will come after, and in the folk *maggi* which came before. This female pair are uncomprehending participants, though, unassimilated types replacing the male roles of the old New Comedy. Taçio, host of the adjacent inn, is tacitly empowered to perform the semi-acceptable rites of a *matrimonio all'osteria* (inn marriage). Thus he mediates to assure a wedding between Zilio and Betía. Everything seems concluded in the usual comedic festivities: a little eating, drinking, bedding. A return to form as the neighbors gather and grace once again seems to come under the rubric of fertility. But there is a fifth act.

Act 5 remains to play out the action in a dubious direction. It seems an exciting finale, a farce set into tension with the mariazo, a proto-tragicomedy exploiting traditional characters within a new matrix. This last act opens where classical comedies close: with a marriage. Taçio plays a verbose authority presiding over the matrimonio all'osteria, a recognized ceremony of union often performed in evasion of the church.[21] But the ground of comedic and marital harmony shakes as the ceremony advances. Betía's mother boasts of her daughter's skill at cooking and serving the League's troops during the recent war: "ela sola serví / a mezo el campo de Spagnuoli e Toeschi" [she alone served half a camp of Spaniards and Germans]. The Slavic mercenaries, *i stralivuoti*, emptied their purses for the privilege of lodging with mother and daughter, who "l'ha vogiú con tuti amistè" [wanted to be friends with all of them] and "la gi ha serví de note e dí" [served them night and day] (5.291–320). Taçio picks up the flyting double entendres, which may be only rough joking or may boast before the slow innocent Zilio of how Betía has served the invading troops in more than one sense:

Taçio: Toràvela mo un tron
per far piasere a un?
La serve a comun;
Pensè se la è serviziale!

. . .

Menega: O quante volte a' l'he vezú sola
a essere a le man con du!

A la fin la gi ha metú
de sota da ela.
O quante volte la meschinela
è stà tolta de miezo

per farghe el piezo,
uno d'ananzo e l'altro da drio!

Taçio: Would she ever take a tron [lira]
To make it pleasant for one?
She serves them all in common;
Imagine how serviceable she is!

. . .

Menega: O how many times have I seen her
all alone coming to grips with two!
In the end, though, she got them
both beneath her.
O how many times the poor thing
has been caught in the middle
to get the worst of it,
one in front and one behind her!
(5.325–47)

Padano to Veneto

This implied history of whoring in the big wars, if missed by Zilio, is not by the audience. But Nale's persistent hope of making a third party, a second husband to Betía, has eaten into the younger man's sanity to the point of precipitating attempted murder. Zilio attacks Nale when the latter, closely following the betrothed couple ("Caminè, madona la sposa e sposo" [Get going, madame bride and bridegroom], he mocks), boasts to the audience *sotto voce* that "a' son el moroso" [I am the lover], and that he will make a "monton" of Zilio, that is, a stupid ram, a stud fool, to cover his own play with Betía. And Nale smugly turns again to the audience with a verbal wink of embracing complicity: "Tasí pur, vu, brigà, tasí!" [And the lot of you keep quiet too, don't say a word!] (5.408–18). But it is too late; Zilio has heard the overreacher and in a fury stabs him. In the aftermath, Taçio, kneeling over the fallen form of Nale, not yet knowing that he is, in fact, superficially wounded, emphasizes the folly of broadcasting to the winds what should be secret: "El no ghe acaziva zà no / che el diesse quele parole chí. / El vê [a] che Zilio iera lí, / e che lo 'l desea pur aldire, / e sí no posse sofrire / de voler frapare" [He certainly didn't need / to say those things here. / He saw that Zilio was there, / and that he had to hear, / and yet he could not stifle / the desire to joke] (5.459–64). But Nale seems incurable in his indiscretion, taking advantage of his wound to test his wife Tamía in a slapstick version of the widow-of-Ephesus pattern so popular in the Renaissance. In this instance, though, it is not his own secrets which he exposes. Playing-acting his own ghost, he elicits Tamía's queries, at first horrified, then mountingly curious. The presumably dead man unexpectedly hears the news that his wife has never loved him and that, for a good long time, she has had as a lover Meneghelo, a bully (escapee from the Veneto's *alla bulesca* tradition).[22] Nale is no fool, even if resident among fools, at least this time. Admitting that he has exaggerated the effect of Zilio's blow so that he could test Tamía, he secretes the secret by displacing her confession into a supposed dream — which he refuses to remember. The couple are reconciled, but beyond the boundaries of dream, Zilio is finally persuaded to join in a quartet of love, satisfying Betía's original compact for two husbands, Nale's connivance at two wives, and Tamía's need for two men. And Zilio, of course, the boy wonderer, is showered with the sudden sexual riches of the *matrimonio all'osteria* that no church ceremony, no comic precedent, could have bestowed. Still half-chiding Nale, Zilio nonetheless makes a not disinterested peace with pleasure: "Vuotu che tra nu a' fazén / i quattro continti? / Se ti te continti, / a 'son zà contentò" [You want us to pool resources to play / The four contented people? / If you're happy, / I'm quite contented, too] (5.1425–28), a sentiment immediately echoed by Tamía and Betía together: "E andón a far . . . i quattro continti" [So let's go and be . . . four happy people] (5.1445–46). They have made a sexual quartet not uncommon in the novelle,[23] but here one ritual marriage expands to envelop and save another. *La Betía* appears, if perversely, yet recognizably Plautine at this penultimate moment. But not to an audience that recalls a recent unexpected consequence of Nale's ghostly testing of his wife. Not only has she revealed the existence of the secret lover Meneghelo, she has married him. Coming on the scene just as a disturbed Nale's "ghost" has exited, Meneghelo asks Tamía: "mo quando / vogión far el mariazo, / adesché quel moltonazo / de to marío è morto? / T'aressi mo un gran torto, / s'te dirè mo de no" [but when do we want to get married / now that that great ninny of a husband of yours is dead? / You would be doing me a great wrong / To say no now] (5.1043–48). Tamía, grasping his hand eagerly in troth plight, does not say no. Nale views the scene while hidden and goes through several psychic contortions, blaming himself for his foolish game, advising the spectators that widows must always take on the first comer, accustomed as they become to having a man, but concluding, against the ocular proof, that "abenché a' tegno fremamen / che mia mogiere no 'l farae mé" [nevertheless I really believe / that my wife would never do so] (5.1147–48). As the *quattro continti* leave, Meneghelo emerges, watching their departure. Both shocked and disgusted at Nale's resurrection, nevertheless he closes the play with a speech that restructures its ending as a quincunx, that most open form with which the Renaissance brought together the sexes, odd and even, and imaged the future through the mark of God. The irony is quiet and all-embracing: "[a] quel che a' vezo, / i cre' far i quatro continti, / e sí a' sarón i çinque!" [from what I see, / they think they are going to be four happy people, / And instead there'll be five of us!] (5.1463–65).

Siena: Piccolomini's *Dialogo* and

the *Rozzi Rusticali*

"*P*iù che un dialogo la direi una commedia minima, poiché l'elemento comico vi soverchia felicemente quello trattatis-tico" [Rather than a dialogue, I would call it a comedy in miniature, inasmuch as the comic element happily dominates that of the trea-tise]. This is Diego Valeri's description of Alessandro Piccolomini's *Dialogo della bella creanza delle donne* [Dialogue of Good Manners for Women] (1539), commonly known as *La Raffaella*.[1] This judg-ment has become a commonplace among critical historians of the plays of Piccolomini and those of other members of the Accademia degli Intronati, of which he was the master theatrical spirit. Siena's Congrega dei Rozzi, which had produced any number of dramatic *commedie villanesche*, was succeeded by the intellectually elite Intro-nati, who made Siena, as Ariosto had done for Ferrara, a center for modern Plautine comedy. The academicians provided, along with Piccolomini's *Alessandro* and *Amor costante*, Bargagli's *La pellegrina* and the group triumph of *L'ingannati*, both of which have been attributed in large part to Piccolomini from his contemporaries on-ward, in spite of his own disavowals.[2]

Bella Creanza and Female *Destrezza*

La Raffaella is a young man's experimental venture into the popular genre of a tractate developed in dialogue. Since Piccolomini never experimented with the form again, never developed the extended systematic discussions of *Il cortegiano* or the large body of overlapping essays that constitute Tasso's *Dialoghi*, one might have missed the significance of *La Raffaella* had its author not gone on to become a playwright.[3] And had he not almost immediately written penitent palinodes upon his early piece with an oration, *In lode delle donne* [In Praise of Women], given before the Intronati (the prologue of the Academy's *Gl'ingannati* was addressed to its guests, the "nobilissime donne") and again in the exhaustive *Institutione di tutta la vita de l'homo nato nobile in città libera* [Education for the Whole Life of a Nobleman in a Free City] (1542).[4] Appearing so closely after its publication, these retractions of the views expressed in *La Raffaella* served a double purpose as titillating invitations to read that dialogue, without yet being wholly ironic. Nor was the conduct-book title "della bella creanza" itself ironic at first glance, the dialogue in fact providing extensive sound advice on appropriate dress, the judicious use of cosmetics, and general household economy. But the manners reflecting good breeding go considerably beyond this appropriateness in dress and address to embrace decency in adultery. The skill of Piccolomini's control in *La Raffaella* emerges in his shifts of register on a linguistic spectrum from the entirely literal to the openly ironic. The shifts, adroit as are the love arrangements always at the focal center of the dialogue, are epitomized in the gradual merger of two terms threading throughout *La Raffaella*'s argument, terms connotatively antithetical: *creanza* and *destrezza*. The former carries with it implications of the education, the breeding that results in proper public comportment; the latter carries the ambiguous implications (*sveltezza, modo destro, espediente* [agility, a dexterity, expedient]) of moral prestidigitation. Only at one point do the words seem to meet in the lexicographic judgments of the Crusca: *creanza* is "costume derivante dall'educazione ricevuta . . . col quale . . . si comporta . . . nel compimento d'un qualche atto" [the habit deriving from the education one has received . . . with which . . . one comports oneself . . . in the execution of any given act], while *destrezza* is "abilità, bravura o simile, in una data arte"; "agevolezza, modo opportuno, di far checchessia" [ability, skill or such, in a given art; ease, the opportune mode of doing what thing soever]. Piccolomini's little educational tract for young women inverts the expectations stimulated by its title: *bella creanza* is redefined as the expediency of female *destrezza*.

We are left to determine why this particular dialogue took that particular form which prompted Valeri's conclusion that "più che un dialogo la direi una commedia minima" or led Daniele Seragnoli to find in it "una struttura da vera e propria scena di commedia" [a structure of a genuine comedic scene]. Exploring this question will draw *La Raffaella* into the family of dramas gathering together here, prepare one to expect to meet other relatives in Cinquecento Tuscany, and lead us to expand some comments made earlier concerning Boccaccio, the novella, and (Pisani's) dramatic structure.

La Raffaella, like *Gl'ingannati*, is addressed to the female cohorts of the Intronati, "a quelle donne che leggeranno" [to those women who will read it]. And here in the preface the irony of its title begins, Piccolomini ("conoscitor delle bellezze e virtù vostre" [connoisseur of your beauties and virtues])[5] already denying any intention "parlar in biasmo di voi donne" [to speak in dispraise of you women]. He praises his readers with a straight-faced account of how his dialogue will reinforce their natural virtues; straight, that is, until he boasts that he will teach them how "con gran destrezza si elegga uno amante unico in questo mondo, e insieme con esso goda segretissimamente il fin dell'amor suo" [with great skill one may select a single lover in this world, and together with him may enjoy the consummation of your love in the fullest secrecy] (3). If some will be surprised at gentlewomen even thinking of lovers, the author will reeducate them in "come questa cosa dell'onore s'ha da intendere" [how this matter of honor must be understood] (4). And honor becomes prudence, secrecy in love:

voi sarete piene di tanto prudenza, ed accortezza e temperanza, che voi sappiate mantenervi e godervi l'amante vostro . . . così nascosamente, che nè

Siena

l'aria, nè il cielo ne possa suspicare mai; in questo caso dico e vi giuro, che non potete far cosa di maggior contento, e più degna di una gentildonna.

You will be filled with such prudence, and cunning and temperance, that you may know how to keep and enjoy your lover . . . so surreptitiously, that neither the air, nor the sky could ever be suspicious of it; in this case I say and I swear to you, that you could not do a thing of greater contentment, and more worthy of a gentlewoman. (4)

This last ironic phrase is more than a promise; it is an admonition: "il menar gli anni gioveni senza conoscer amore, si può dire che sia il medesimo che star morte sempre" [to live one's youthful years without knowing love, one might say is the same as being continually dead] (5).

Thus introduced, Piccolomini's hornbook of adultery is couched as an instructional conversation between young Margarita, recently married, and "Madonna" Raffaella, an older visitor. Margarita's isolation and hunger for social contact is emphasized at the beginning as she chides the older woman for the infrequency of her visits. Raffaella demurs with the excuse that an old and poor woman (she underlines her poverty at every opportunity) can only annoy and bore a young person; she is nothing but a leftover life, "una che é d'avanzo in questo mondo" [one who is superfluous in this world]. She has noticed, of course, that Margarita is always busy, but busy at the embroidery and sewing that suggest her lonely isolation. Margarita herself reminds Raffaella "quanto mia madre avea fede alle vostre parole e a'vostri consigli, e quanto consolazione ne pigliava: e il medesimo fo io" [how much my mother put faith in your words and your advice, and how much consolation she drew from it: and I do the same] (8). Already one has received hints at a past that effectively places both women: the younger married one someplace upward on the social scale, the elder an authority with persuasive power established at an early stage of their association. Raffaella is quick to grasp the implications of Margarita's ennui with marriage and to begin to turn the girl's confidence in a mutually beneficial direction. Raffaella's lesson to Margarita and young Piccolomini's ironic instruction of his "gentildonne" in the arts of "bella creanza" are underway.

Raffaella insists upon two topics: her own weight of sin,[6] and how visiting Margarita painfully reminds her of that sin and of her dereliction of semimaternal duty in not warning the young wife to avoid it in her own life. Playing on Margarita's growing curiosity, Raffaella pretends to have been unable even to carry out her accustomed religious rituals in the past few days, as the need has grown in her to illuminate the girl. Her sin, that sin which Margarita must avoid, is having been deaf to nature's carpe diem anthem until too late. She owes Margarita a lesson in pleasure, which begins with delightful admonitions "usar sempre qualche bella foggia nuova, cercar d'esser tenuta bella insieme e savia, esser amata da qualche uno . . . e simili altri piaceri onesti da donne giovani e gentili" [to always wear some beautiful new fashion, to try to be considered beautiful and good at the same time, to be loved by someone . . . and other similar honest pleasures of young and gentle women] (11). "Mi fate maravigliare" [You astonish me], cries her flustered auditor, pleasantly shocked to hear her sense of what we may call *creanza onesta* so radically violated.

And just here the dialogue turns dramatic. Raffaella laments that, were there time, she could detail Margarita's potential *vita nuova*, "che vita dovrebbe esser la tua" [what your life should be like]. Desperate to probe deeper into this previously forbidden cornucopia of potential delights, Margarita pleads: "come tempo? . . . non potiamo aver tempo più comodo: siam sole, e a voi non penso che importi molto il partirvi" [what do you mean "time"? . . . we could not have a more convenient time: we are alone, and I don't think you have any pressing reason to leave] (12–13). Raffaella's platitudes on her poverty are suddenly turned to account as bait: "non posso oggi star da te: voglio andar a riscuoter certi danari dalla tua zia"[7] [I can't stay with you today: I have to go to pick up certain monies from your aunt]. "Che v'importa riscuoterli oggi o domani?" [What does it matter to you whether you get paid today or tomorrow]?

Siena

In response, Raffaella boasts about her pride that hides her poverty from all but Margarita, to whom she admits that "non ho briciola di pane in casa" [I haven't a crumb of bread in the house] (13). Margarita rises hungrily to the bait: "In fine non pensate di partirvi: non mancherà pane nè altro, mentre che ne avrò io" [Come on now, don't think of leaving: there will be no lack of bread or of anything else, while I have any]. Raffaella teasingly takes up Margarita's own argument against urgency, pretending to accede to her curiosity only when Margarita admits that "poichè m'avete accesa a questa cosa, non vo' che passi oggi ch'io non intenda minutamente il parer vostro" [now that you have gotten me all excited about this, I don't want today to pass without my learning in great detail your opinion] (13). At this point the dramatic action retreats into the instruction that will constitute one generic dimension of the *Dialogo,* but not without a final merging of the dramatic vehicle and its thematic tenor. Raffaella fears that, if she begins, "nel mezzo de'nostri ragionamenti verrà il tuo marito . . . e romperacci ogni nostro disegno" [in the middle of our discussion your husband will show up . . . and spoil all our plans]. Margarita reassures her teacher-confidante with a cold description of the current state of her marriage: "di mio marito non ci è pericolo, chè egli ha due mesi che egli andò in Val d'Ambra a riscuoter non so che grano e denari, e non è ancora tornato . . . vi posso giurare che da due anni in qua che io venni a marito, non è stato, acozzando tutte le volte, quattro mesi intieri con esso me" [there is no need to worry about my husband, because it has been two months since he went to Val d'Ambra to collect I-don't-know-what grain and monies, and he still hasn't returned . . . I can swear to you that in the two years since I got married, putting together all the times, he hasn't spent four whole months with me] (15). Raffaella seizes this as an entry point for her seduction. The husband is complacent but careless; therefore, both a vulnerable and a justifiable candidate for cuckolding. "Tu veggia," Raffaella enthuses, "di pigliartili [piaceri] con tal ingegno, e con tal arte, che il tuo marito più presto abbia da comportarlo volentieri che da pigliar un minimo sospettuzzo dei casi tuoi" [you must take care to grasp pleasures for yourself with such ingenuity, with such art, that your husband would sooner have to tolerate them willingly than to take the least suspicion from your actions] (16–17). And now Margarita reveals herself an apt pupil—indeed, she seems to have intuitively anticipated the techniques she must "learn." At least, she can assure Raffaella that "il mio marito è la miglior pasta d'uomo che voi vedeste mai; e di quelle cose che io mi disponessi, crederei farli creder che le lucciole fossero lanterne" [my husband is the best-natured man you could ever see; and as far as my decisions go, I think I could make him believe that fireflies were lanterns] (17).

Piccolomini's reader has progressed a quarter of the way through this conduct book to find himself in the situational exposition of a potential New Comedy. The dialogue, though, is faithful to the instructional mode the title promises. Raffaella sets out first on dress, exhaustively detailing materials and ornament of appropriate richness, emphasizing consistency and yet originality in style ("non lasci mai foggia che sia buona" [don't miss out on a becoming style]). This accomplished, she turns to cosmetics with a beautician's practiced eye, then moves on to the *portatura*, the carriage of dress and self, with little hints of peepshow flirtation carried off with careful disingenuousness:

quando ancor ella avesse bella persona, e ben disposta, occorre alcuna volta ai bagni, mostrando non pensare a ciò, bagnarsi in tal ora e in tal luogo che de alcune fessure puossi esser vista . . . e di tutto questo intendo che una giovane abbia da cercar destrissima occasione . . . che altri non s'accorga ch'elle l'abbia fatto avvertitamente; ma ha da finger con rossore, . . . o con qualche altro finto segno d'onestà, d'aver avuto dispiacer che tal cosa sia avvenuta.

and even if she has a beautiful figure, and is well arranged, still, when she goes to the baths, she should bathe, as if she were doing it unconsciously, at such an hour or in such a place that she can be seen through some crack . . . and in all this I intend that a young woman should seek out a very opportune occasion . . . so that others do not realize that she

Siena

has done it intentionally; but she must pretend to blush, . . . or with some other simulated sign of honesty, to have been displeased that such a thing should have occurred. (38–39)

Onestà is taking on the duplicitous connotations earlier attached to *bella creanza*. In the ensuing instruction in household economy, a short course in home economics, one discovers that it is aimed at manipulating the husband, culminating in transporting disingenuous *onestà* from the baths to the hearth: "Venendo poi il marito, ella ha da farsegli incontro, e mostrare di rallegrarsi di vederlo; e se non lo fa di cuore, almen finga di farlo" [When the husband arrives, she must go to meet him, and show how delighted she is to see him; and if she can't do this from the heart, at least pretend to do so] (43). Indeed, one must "mostrare almeno fingendo, di avere desiderio di compiacere il marito" [show at least by pretending, one's desire to please one's husband] (44). And almost immediately Raffaella develops the potential necessity for occasional subterfuge into permanent role-playing in the pursuit of pleasure. Cataloguing a spectrum of diversions from balls and country outings to private encounters, the instructress teaches that a young wife must create a mask of hedonism that will hide from view any extraordinary amorous excitement: "ha da farne professione; e massime a mostrar al marito di esser inclinata dalla propria natura a tali cose, acciocchè . . . non suspichi per questo cosa nessuna di male" [she must be open about it; and especially show to the husband that she is inclined to such things by her own nature, so that . . . he may not suspect by this anything bad] (44). The secrecy of life is codified in Raffaella's summary rule: "nascosissimamente copra la varietà dei pensier suoi" [with the greatest secrecy cover the variety of one's thoughts] (45).

Even the quotidian details, though, are turned to dramatic purpose. Raffaella, recommending a skin softener, provides a moment of farce as she rehearses an endless recipe for its manufacture. Margarita's bewilderment at the impossible instructions enables Raffaella to coopt her as a customer for her own cottage industry: "non te ne curare, perchè te ne farò io sempre che ne vorrai, e t'insegnerò ad usarla" [don't worry your head about it, I'll always make you as much as you want, and I'll teach you how to use it] (28). The unsuspected pandaress is evolving as a unique character, one knowledgeable about town, living by her wits and her friends, a gossip without a good word for any woman out of her sight. Both her parasitic opportunism and her backbiting are epitomized in a single comic vignette when she recounts a personal experience to illustrate a general point of hygiene: "la lordezza della persona genera spesso cattivo odore in una donna, che è cosa vituperosissima: e poche sere sono ch'io lo provai dormendo a sorte con la moglie di messer Ulivieri" [dirt on the body often generates a bad odor in a woman, which is a very blameworthy thing: and a few evenings ago I had proof of it, sleeping by chance with the wife of Messer Ulivieri] (31). Who is this noisome lady? Who is Margarita's aunt, and what are her money dealings with Raffaella? "Bianchetta, che è il più balzana ch'io vedessi mai" [Bianchetta, who is the most harebrained woman that I've ever seen] (20), is a sister of whom Margarita complains that she wears too much perfume (34); Fioretta and Roffina, who use the same toiletries (27); Loretta and Mascarina, who wear skin-toned rouge (29); twenty-two-year-old Bambagiuola, who already is without a "dente che buon sia" [good tooth in her head] (29); Andrea, who apes the manner of that Cassilia (36), about whose hair "fu fatto un sonetto da uno degl'Intronati" [a sonnet was written by one of the Intronati] (33)—Siena is crowdedly peopled with all the women who are Margarita's rivals in fashion and in the game of love. There is an entire cast of characters who are missing from the "stage" but not from the action implicit as bourgeois life in *La Raffaella*. So the dialogue of good manners is simultaneously a drama of social satire played out both through and around the protagonists. If the beginning pages have been dramatic exposition, the middle has been instruction in *la bella creanza*. The last part will be the dramatic development resulting from the uses and abuses of a modern *ars amatoria*.

With the younger woman prepared, Raffaella broaches the subject that is the final end toward which this tutorial in deception provides the means, the choice of men: "resta da dire . . . l'avvertanzia

Siena

ch'ella ha da tenere verso gli innamorati suoi" [it remains to speak of . . . the caution that she has to have toward her lovers] (52).

Everything else, from ballrooms to beauty, "senza amore, son proprio come una bella casa la vernata, senza il fuoco" [without love, is just like a beautiful house in the winter, without a fire] (52–53). But the chosen lover must not be too young nor too old. The young will be too flighty, too proud, too boastful of conquest; the old will be too jealous, too physically disgusting, too impotent. And both will share the worst of faults, a lack of natural secrecy, "e farà pigliare sospetto di molto" [and will make many people suspicious] (54). *Segreto, secreti, segretamente, secretissimi*—these are words that run chorally throughout Raffaella's catalogue of choices to be avoided. Not only are the callow and the aging dangerous from this point of view, but also foreigners, married men, and especially the popular kiss-and-tell dandies. Such a playboy's "segreto venga palese in pochi dí" [secret becomes public gossip in a few days], since "fanno mille pazzíe da fare accorgere le mura di tutti i loro fatti" [they do a thousand mad things to make even the walls become aware of their affairs] (56).

By this process of elimination we are to suppose that it is logic that leads to a description of the worthy lover. He will be "fra l'ventisette e ventotto, nel qual tempo il discorso è maturo, e si ha già la pratica delle cose dell'amore" [between twenty-seven and twenty-eight, at which time one's discourse is mature, and one already has practical experience in things of love] (60); he will be of noble birth, handsome, modest, and above all "segretissimo"—"sappi fingere, e ricoprire i suoi pensieri, . . . e costante e infiammato" [he will know how to feign, and to cover up his thoughts, . . . he will be both constant and inflamed]—in love of his mistress (62). She, in turn, is obligated "amare l'amante suo unicamente, con tutto l'animo" [to love her lover alone with all her heart] because constancy is one of a lover's two virtues; the other is "tenerlo segreto; perchè la segretezza è il nerbo d'amore"[8] [to keep him secret; because secrecy is the knot of love] (63).

As Raffaella proceeds emphatically to reinforce secrecy in the management of contacts with the lover so as to avoid "il minimo sospettuzzo, nel marito o in altri" [the slightest suspicion, in her husband or in others] (64), Margarita admits confusion: earlier Raffaella had said that husband and household were the first things that a woman must cherish; now the contrary seems implied if "l'amore dell'amante passi ogni cosa" [love of the lover should be above everything else]. Raffaella brushes aside these contradictions with the reminder that one is true to the lover, but "con li mariti basta a finger di amarli" [with husbands it is enough to pretend to love them] (66). She rushes on to describe to the girl what pleasures are to be found when lovers meet in "luoghi segreti" [secret places]: "quando sono insieme, sien lontani da ogni finzione; e debbano unirsi con tutto l'animo, col corpo . . . e con quel che più si può" [when they are together, they must be far from every pretense; and they should join themselves together with their whole minds, with their bodies . . . and with whatever else they can] (69). All of Margarita's earlier training in *la bella creanza* balks at this inversion: such secret sex wrongs the husband. Raffaella sneers that in sexual acts "torte sono quelle che si fanno col marito" [wrong are those (things) that are done with the husband]. But this will grow horns upon him, Margarita whines with a faltering will. Raffaella responds with the ageless argument for adultery as a victimless crime: "Corna sarebbero, se si sapesse; ma, sapendo tener la cosa segreta, non so conoscere che vergogna gliene segua" [They would be horns, if it were known; but, if you know how to keep the thing secret, I don't see what shame could follow to him from it] (70). The last remnant of resistance crumbles; Margarita now only laments that so few ideal lovers are to be found. And the immediate reason for the lessons implanted by Raffaella's dialogue now becomes the climactic revelation of Piccolomini's dramatic action. The pandaress unmasks to play her trump card: "ne conosco ben qualch'uno io, benchè pochi ne sieno" [I happen to know one or two myself, although there can't be very many] (76). She has come prepared to trade upon all the needs she has created in Margarita, from lotions to the lover. The deal is quickly consummated. Raffaella knows a magnificent man wild with secret

Siena

love for Margarita. The girl speaks with the joyful fantasy of a child just at the point of innocence lost: "Iddio il volesse che fosse vero!" [Would to God it were true!], she cries out for this phantom ideal. But drama and its *mezzana*, its panderess, both need an incarnation of the verbal portrait: "Non conosci messer Aspasio? egli è colui che io ti dico . . . e che vi [non] mancarà mezzano fidato . . . sarò io" [Don't you know Messer Aspasio? He is that one I'm talking about . . . and so that you will not be wanting for a trusted go-between . . . I will be that] (77–78). As Raffaella leaves to activate the liaison, Margarita pledges payment: "madonna Raffaella, udite una parola: volete pane o cacio, o prosciutto, o cosa che io abbia, domandate" [Madonna Raffaella, hear one word: if you want bread or cheese, or ham, or anything that I have, just ask for it]. The old opportunist takes the long view: "Domane te'l dirò poi quando tornarò da te; e pensati che d'ogni cosa ho bisogna" [I will tell you tomorrow, when I come back; and you can be sure that I have need of everything]. Her last farewell builds upon this with ominous irony: "ci sarà tempo a ogni cosa" [there will be time for everything] (80). *La Raffaella* ends without closure, Margarita's door having just opened to house the parasite's nameless and omnivorous future greed.

And what of the lovers' joys about to begin? Margarita has swallowed her lesson in secrecy as greedily as Raffaella her more material prizes: "Il mio marito non è in Siena; e quando ci fosse, mi dà bene il cuore di esser savia abbastanza, se già la fortuna non mi è contraria" [My husband is not in Siena; and even if he were, I am confident of being skillful enough if, indeed, fortune is not against me] (80). But *will* fortune cooperate? Margarita has heard a riptide of rumor about Aspasio that her desire washes under: "io aveva inteso che egli aveva finto con delle altre ancora, e che egli non amava se non a sua posta; il che mi par che sia specie d'ingannar donne" [I had heard that he had pretended with some others, too, and that he only loves as he pleases; which appears to me to be a sort of deceiving of women] (79). As she and we stand poised upon the verge of the first day of Margarita's *vita nuova*, we share her secret and her excited trepidation at adventure to come. There is no plotting a course for the fall of this fool of fortune.

It is this particular conjunction of openness and complicity (already uncovered in the plays from the Veneto) that is both justification and impetus for treating Piccolomini's dialogue as drama. *La Raffaella* is not a proto-novella; we do not serve as auditors for a story being told. As was suggested when distinguishing Pisani's play from its Boccaccian analogue, a novella is a history, a completed stage of some protagonist's affairs that has been told to or shared by a teller who is retelling it, as we may do in turn. Removed from the continuity of fluid events, the story becomes a narrative coin to be passed from hand to hand. As was the case in the second part of the *Quijote,* it may even pass back into the hands of its original. If there is more to come, that is another story.

In the Italian drama of complicity, the auditor cannot tell a story, only share in its contingency: first, he has made a pact of secrecy ("Tu lege, disce, sile"); second, and crucial to the dramatic form as distinguished from the novelistic narrative, the auditor does not know the outcome—the event presented is not detachable from its indefinable movement into the future. The presentational form makes certain that there can be no auditor who eventually will cut the thread of action and knot it into a history by becoming a storyteller.

Drammi rusticali and the Rozzi Dramatists

Although the academy calling itself the Intronati (the ironic name suggests those stupefied by the crack of some cataclysmic sound) left a significant theatrical heritage, neither Piccolomini himself nor the academy's other members ever produced a stageable anti-Plautine play analogous to *La Raffaella.* Piccolomini's dialogue itself, however, rather than being an eccentric anomaly, seems to grow almost inevitably from the rich comedic soil of Sienese drama in the early stage of Italian theater. Some years before the formal organization of the Intronati, Sienese authors were creating a large body of *drammi rusticali;* this dramatic form and some of its originators would anticipate the formation of the Intronati into an academy under the less elite rubric of the Congrega dei Rozzi, a title ironically—but nonetheless accurately—boasting of the members' rural roughness, their lack of literary refinement in a classical tradition. The Rozzi and the overlapping pioneers of Sienese drama, the *comici artigiani* (artisan players), wrote, performed, and published dozens of commedie and dramatic egloghe from the earliest years on throughout the entire Cinquecento. These included mythological pastorals abounding in courtly shepherds and nymphs, but the backbone of the tradition—with obvious infusions from the maggi and mariazi—is the love life of Tuscan villani (peasants). With unselfconscious abandon, the affairs of shepherds and nymphs are mixed with the rustic world of the realistic villani, and the coarsest rustic may on occasion encounter Mercury or Cupid.

Curzio Mazzi, the definitive bibliographer of this corpus that we may, for convenience, label the Rozzi rusticali, extracted a general pattern to which the plays conform with surprising consistency.[9] I will paraphrase Mazzi's epitome at some length in order that its relevance to the subgenre toward which Piccolomini's dialogue naturally gravitates will become obvious.

The rusticali focus on a single event that presents the customs of the villani along with their omnipresent psychology of "cunning and rascality." For the most part, the action's motive center is love, always presented as vulgar, even indecent, but concluding (in Mazzi's superbly chosen phrase cannibalizing the *lieto fine* [happy ending] of Renaissance tragicomedy) "con fine più o meno lieto" [with an ending more or less happy]. Most often, a young villano is enamored of a beautiful *contadina,* frequently the wife of a rustic senex, "brutto, avaro, strano" [ugly, avaricious, uncouth]. The suitor reveals his love to the woman and she rejects him, but only until the opportune time arrives. When opportunity is ripe, the woman consents to her lover's requests, but—anticipating Raffaella's counsel to Margarita—she arranges that their practice be hidden from the husband or, should the girl be unmarried, from the father, mother, uncle, or other figure of authority. However, there are various complications: the husband is preternaturally jealous, or there are a pair of younger rivals for the same contadina. Between husband and lover, or between the rival lovers, there is an escalation from dangerous questions to name-calling to scuffles and armed combats in which some saner friend takes a part. These agons are rendered ridiculous through absurd weapons and monstrous verbal challenges, succeeded by equally exaggerated cowardice that makes the actual encounter anticlimatic. The most interesting, and not unusual, turn is taken when a mutual friend prevents the physical combat and persuades the rivals to let the woman exercise her choice. She proposes some new rhetorical or musical contest (for song is a constant feature of the rusticali) and finally acts the dubious pacificator. Professing the worthy motive of not wanting to offend either, she takes both as her equally fortunate lovers ("per togliere la cagione delle liti e per non disgustare alcuno, dice di prenderli ambedue per amanti, e promette fare l'uno e l'altro contento e felice" [to take away the cause of the quarrels and not to offend anyone, she pronounces for taking them both as lovers, and promises to make both the one and the other content and happy]).

Such a matrix appears ideally designed to invite variations on the conflicts and rustic accommodations found in the open endings of *Philogenia* or *La Betía*. And the Rozzi dramatists supplied close analogues across the country landscapes of their large corpus. Legacci dello Stricca wrote two of the earliest, *Mezzucchio* and *Tognin del Cresta*, first published, respectively, in 1516 and 1518. The *Mezzucchio* has a cast of three villani, the contadina Vica, and her mother. Mezzucchio, enamored of Vica, goes off to fight his rival when his friend, Strifinaccio, tells him that the girl loves the third villano, Schiribilla. Strifinaccio stops them and persuades them to go with him to Vica for her choice. Vica, meanwhile, driven by the desire to see her lover, tricks the mother and escapes into the countryside. Here she encounters the villani and submits to hearing their

Siena

ridiculous boastings about their wealth. To settle matters pleasantly, Vica accepts them both as lovers, only to inform them at this stage that she already has a third lover — swearing them to complicity in sharing her favors and in keeping all the secrets from her mother and the uncle with whom they live. The conclusion is "un ballo tondo con il canto" [a circle dance with singing], a sort of parodic exclamation mark at the end of this formal parody of the usual *mariaʒo* conciliations and harmony: the suitors praise Vica because "vuol che tutt'e tre siam buon frategli, / E di segreto ci vuol far godere. / E di segreto" [she wants all three of us to be good brothers, / And secretly she'd have us take our pleasure / And secretly].[10]

In *Tognin del Cresta*, Tognino, an aged and avaricious villano, is desperate. His padrone demands payment of a debt he has run up, as a closing dance lyric reports, "fra taverne, fiaschi e gioco" [between taverns, bottles and gaming].[11] Tognin is given the ultimatum of payment or prison; under this threat, he trudges off to Siena to try to sell or pawn his pitifully catalogued *masseriʒia* (housegoods). Meanwhile, his fellow Lenzo, best man (*compare*) at his earlier nuptials, meets Tognin's sharp-tongued young wife Gista in the fields. She has already complained to the audience about wasting herself upon a miserable old husband, while boasting of suitors aplenty: "i' ho alme [sic] duo par di gaveggini [vagheggini] / . . . Due n'ho, tra gli altri e più be' ballerini, / che farebbon le pietre inamorare / Co' lor be' salti, giravolte e inchini" [I have at least two pair of admirers / . . . And two especially, the most beautiful dancers / who could make the stones fall in love with them / with their lovely leaps, turns, and bows] (110–14). In this youthful agility they contrast quite literally with old Tognin, who, returning from the trek to Siena, complains, "Appena sotto le gambe mi regge, / se dove io ho andar fusse di longa, / non mi ci condurrìen un par di tregge" [My legs can scarcely hold up under me. / If where I had to go was very far away, / a pair of ploughs couldn't get me there] (208–10). This is not Legacci's only structural contrast, though. No sooner has Gista made her casual claims than Lenzo demonstrates how, in his timidity, he has misjudged her to himself. He blurts out that he has been her silently ardent admirer: "i' v'ho già più d'un anno ga-veggiata" [I have loved you now for more than a year] (141). He guarantees he is "secreto," and Gista is quick to say that, could their doings be kept quiet, "N'ho di far chesto più voglia che voi" [I have more desire than you to do this] (170), to which Lenzo responds with the confident promise, "Segreto come al forno il vo' tenere"[12] [I wish to keep it as secretly as if it were shut up in the bake furnace] (177). The anticipated *beffa* of cuckolding is cut short, though, when, the lovers having laid their plans, Tognin returns and voluntarily pawns Gista into Lenzo's keeping in exchange for a loan that will keep him from prison. Lenzo and Gista smugly gloat over how the old *balordo* (dolt) has been "impaniato a mo' d'un tordo" [caught in birdlime like a thrush] (423), but Tognin reverses the trick upon the tricksters, boasting how cleverly he has gotten rid of the expense of a wife he doesn't want and has no intention of reclaiming (448–59). Time passes; Gista becomes pregnant, and a greedy, ignorant village vicar calls Tognin, Lenzo, and Gista before him for an inquiry into irregularities. Finding nothing against cohabitation between bride and best man in his legal guides—the novelle and satires of Boccaccio and Burchiello—the vicar tries to send Gista back to Tognin; Tognin refuses her, Lenzo objects, and the vicar solves the problem by authorizing shares: "perfin che te li rendi, sia comuna" [she will be held in common until he pays you back] (693). Gista is delighted to become common property: "la casa prometto a tutt'a due / tener pulita e ben rigovernare" [I promise you both to keep the house cleaned and in good order] (695–96). Tognin has one last, dangerous suggestion about the rules: "un può tenerla il dì, l'altro la notte" [one can keep her during the day, the other at night] (702). The vicar closes the door, leaving the audience along with the love trio to follow once again advice similar to that ("disce, sile") offered by the author of *La venexiana* to *his* audience: "Non si facci di questo più romore, / l'accordo è fatto" [Let's not make any more fuss about this, / the pact is made] (703–4).

Such lightly developed anticipations of the subgenre of secrecy appear again in Siena in the middle years of the Cinquecento with the anonymous *Pippa* (1547) and the *Capotondo* (1550) of Salvestro Cartaio, perhaps the most widely known of the Rozzi dramatists under the congregational pseudonym of Fumoso [the arrogant].

The *Pippa* is interesting as a simpler echo of the *Mezzucchio*, with the rival lovers ultimately sharing in friendly fashion. Where the odd party corrupts the balance of pairings in *Mezzucchio* and *La Betía*, *Pippa* as play and as eponymous maiden suffers no such complication. Brodacchietta and Sgraffigna, both villani, vie for Pippa, the daughter of the village mayor, Ton Fruconi. When they come to blows, the rivals are parted by the mayor and Pippa herself. Not Pippa alone but this time the entire quartet in conference determine that the two *innamorati* of the *campagna* will divide the pleasure of Pippa's company equally between them: "Così tutti restano contenti e cantano una canzona su quest' accordo"[13] [That way everybody is happy, and they all join in singing a *canzona* about this accord].

If the syndic status of Ton Fruconi gives a patina of social dimension to *Pippa*, it serves only as local color. In Fumoso's *Capotondo* this dimension becomes functional toward shaping the frustrated "conclusion." Aldo Borlenghi does not much exaggerate the political overlay when he finds the play

un esempio dei più staccati e freddi dell'insolenza e dell'indifferenza e insieme dell'acutezza però d'osservazione dei contadini, che hanno la peggio e s'adattano senza urti o dispiacere alle vergogne quasi nell'atto in cui ancora rodomonteggiano a vendicarle, e con consapevolezza piena della propria situazione.[14]

one of the most detached and cold examples of the insolence and indifference, but at the same time, of the acuteness of observation of the peasants, who get the worst of it and adapt themselves without clashes or disappointment to their disgraces almost in the act in which they also boast of avenging them, and with full consciousness of their own situations.

The title figure, Capotondo, is *mezzano* to the city gentleman Podrio. Their object is Meia, young wife of the old villano Coltriccione. As we enter the situation, Meia is visibly pregnant through the agency of Podrio, a fact Coltriccione laments with his more nearly coeval mother-in-law. Without naming names, the old man claims his place among the generic cuckolds of comedy:

> [Meia] ha'l corpo molt'enfiato, che vuol dire?
> Egli è almen ch'i'non l'ho cavalcata,
> ch'i' so stato chiocciccio, de' mesi otto:
> o 'n che modo costei donch'è 'mpregnata?

> Meia's body is quite swollen up; what does it mean?
> It is at least clear that I haven't mounted her,
> Since I have been a sick old wreck for eight months:
> In what way, then, has this one gotten pregnant? (1.45–48)

Biagia, the mother, scolds, threatens, and cajoles Coltriccione throughout the play, cowing him; Sberlenga, another villano who makes futile attempts upon Meia himself, joins with Coltriccione in a pusillanimous confrontation with Podrio and Capotondo from which the villani retreat; Capotondo himself plays the Arlecchino-like zanni in stealing money Podrio has sent to Meia and in taunting Sberlenga while the rustic is trying his ploys upon Meia; the whole is a familiar compound of New Comedy elements adapted to the commedia rusticale.

There is, however, a thread that runs from the "Prologo rusticale," written for the Rozzi performance, throughout the play. Ironically alerting the auditors to a beadroll of clever obscenities, the "Prologo" apologizes for Fumoso's pretended lack of deviousness:

> se ci sentite dentro qualche male,
> che dicesse un po' troppo a la scoperta,
> scusatel; ché 'l poeta è dozzinale,
> e che non sa andar sotto coverta
> perchè egli è rozzo . . .

Siena

If you should hear inside something wicked,
That is said a little too openly,
Excuse it; because the poet is a hack,
and doesn't know how to go under cover
because he is heavy-handed. (11–15)

"Coverta," though, might be used to describe the whole impression one takes away from *Capotondo*. When Capotondo sets off to Meia with Podrio's invitation for an afternoon of sex, the feckless servant promises to carry his master's greetings with the message, as he phrases it, "che vorreste far quella faccenda" [that you would like to do that business]. Podrio cries out in alarm at this crude directness: "Oh! digliel più coperto" [O! say it to her less plainly] (1.26–27). Biagia has spied Podrio entering to find Meia "in un modo segreto" [in a secret manner] (1.58–64). "Mantien segreto" [stay secret], demands Podrio (1.70); "C' è poche persone, come me, secrete" [There are few persons as secretive as I am], boasts Sberlinga (1.152); when Capotondo attempts to persuade Meia to keep secret his theft of monies meant for her, he is discovered by Podrio's demand to know "Che parlare è qua . . . a la secreta?" [What talk is this . . . in secret?] (3.88). Misadventures over, Podrio and Meia's mother agree upon terms for reconciliation and Meia's return home. The husband receives grain, oil, wine, and the assurance that Podrio has not passed on the pox to Meia. Missing the point of all the secrecy, Capotondo, hitherto shrewd, at the penultimate moment becomes himself the simpleton he thinks his *padrone* to be; when he hears arrangements being made for Meia's return, he is bewildered: "Oh gran menchion, padron, che sete state; / non degavate rendergliela adesso" [O, what a great fool you have been, master; / you shouldn't have given her back to him now] (3.192–93). The secrecy has not been in the action—that is all too clear—but in the unspoken agreements that even Capotondo misses. In the manifest representation of a young and illicitly pregnant wife being bartered back to her cuckolded husband we recognize a parody of the reconciliatory harmonics of the mariazi. This is, obviously, not uncommon in the Sienese rusticali.

But in *Capotondo* the preposterously resolved action is a screen for the covert collusion of contadini and their *padrone* in a continuing arrangement of relations that have had a little face lift. All angry passion bought off, Meia and Coltriccione go out together in the happy accord silently managed by Podrio, of whom Meia brags: "M'ha fatte lui quelle carezze a mene, / fussi stata suo' moglie" [He has given me those caresses / as if I had been his wife]. Coltriccione replies with a last line that closes the play in order that all can pretend to "andar sotto coverta" [go under cover] congenially. Of Podrio, Coltriccione can now conclude, "ch'egli m'ha viso d'uom da bene" [to me, that one has the face of a true gentleman] (3.212).

The earliest known example of these rusticali is the *Commedia d'Amore contro Avarizia e Pudicizia,* published in 1514 and written by Mariano Trinci, usually known as Manescalco; in later editions, which were numerous, the play was known from its beffa as *Il bic[c]hiere* (The Glass).[15] It is not only the earliest but also the most interesting rusticale in its foreshadowings of *La Raffaella.* The beffa is enveloped at beginning and end by scenes of Cupid taunting his bound captives, Avarizia and Pudicizia, who are incarnate in the padrone Senile and his young wife Erifile. Cupid tells the personifiers that "poco vale una segreta gloria" [a secret glory has little value] (56), as a rationale for introducing the action of the rustic affair. Erifile, lamenting the mismatch with Senile, has already learned honorable deception: "ecco lo sposo mio ch'ora esce fuore, / convien mi sforzi di fargli accoglienza, / per onestà coprendo il duol del core" [here is my husband coming out now; / it's proper that I force myself to make him welcome, / for honesty (honor) covering the pain of my heart] (94–96). Senile realizes that he is stereotypically ridiculous in being an aged lover, but is nonetheless infatuated to the degree that even his equally predictable comic avarice is unable to deflect his thoughts—until the villano who is his nameless dependent, bitter at Senile's miserly treatment, taunts him with puns on impotence. This flyting is juxtaposed with the quite different laments of young Pulidoro, also desperately infatuated with Erifile but helpless because, through jealousy, "Senil d'attorno a lei mai suol

Siena

levarsi" [Senile is in the habit of never getting far from her] (189). His ambiguously named servant Fidele assures Pulidoro that he can succeed as a pander and recruits Senile's servant Rubino into the seduction plot. Rubino, like the unhappy villano, has pledged vengeance upon Senile for his miserly cheating.

Rubino proceeds to convert Erifile to love gradually, in a mock-educational conversation to which we have seen a close analogue in the stages through which Margarita passes under the tutelage of Raffaella. Rubino laments that Erifile's parents have chained her to Senile, hints at her self-defeating obstinacy (so *pudicizia* takes on ambiguity), and suddenly announces the unexpected advent of a young lover: "Il Cielo provisto t'ha di tal'amante, / di bellezza, e virtù, tal ch'io vò dire, / che a Venere un tal uom saria bastante" [Heaven has provided you such a lover, / of such beauty and virtue, that I would say / that such a man would be sufficient for Venus] (322–24). Like Margarita, Erifile reacts with honest shock — *pudicizia* in its best sense: "Come credi ch'io voglia acconsentire? / Piacere a uom che non sia mio marito, / taci, Rubin, ch'io vo' prima morire" [How can you believe that I could wish to consent? / To please a man not my husband, / Silence, Rubin, because I would die first] (325–27). Taking up the twin arguments that Raffaella will employ, Rubino emphasizes a carpe diem theme and threat ("Aspetta che t'increspi il tempo il viso, / e sien canute le dorate chiome" [Wait until time wrinkles your face, / and your golden tresses turn white]) and simultaneously argues that private sin is no sin: "Chi credi che palesi un tal segreto?" [Who do you think would reveal such a secret]? This, as in La *Raffaella*, is a clinching argument. Feigning reluctance, Erifile eagerly reads Pulidoro's impassioned letter and at once answers it: "Rubin darali tu per me risposta, / ch'i'amo onestamente, e voglio amare, / ma far contro a l'onor non son disposta" [Rubin, you give him for me the reply / that I love honestly, and want to love, / but I am not disposed to do anything against my honor] (387–89). Honesty has already become interchangeable with secrecy, though; without a pause Erifile sends her innamorato permission to visit her that very night — disguised as a woman. He arrives, Rubino opens the door, and without a word between the lovers, they close themselves from sight. Or so it seems.

Simultaneously, the angry villano encounters Senile outdoors and torments him with jeers about his wife's infidelities. Ironically confident, Senile sets out to prove her chaste. He produces the *bicchiere* of the title, a magic glass that cures troubled fantasies: "qui dentro si vedrà le cose vere, / che in vita mia mai mi disser bugia" [here within one will see things as they are: / never in my life did they tell me a lie] (537–38). Exuding hubris, Senile flags down a passing schoolboy and instructs him to relate what he sees when he looks into the *bicchiere*. What he sees, of course, is the "fantesca" entering Senile's house, embracing Erifile, and throwing off his disguise; as he watches, the secretly exposed lovers escalate their play, fondling and biting until the boy cries in alarm: "i'non vo' più vedere, / che cominciano a far le porcarie!" [I don't want to see any more, / because they are beginning to do filthy things] (654–55). Heart crushed, Senile goes to confront the couple in his house. The action is concluded with an artful rush. Senile reveals how "Feci uno sperimento in un bicchiere" [I made an experiment in a glass], and Pulidoro calms the old man with the assurance that the magic glass is an old wives' tale, replacing the fear of cuckoldry with that of ridicule. "Semplice è quel che in queste cose crede" [one who believes in these things is a simpleton], he explains, adding that they must keep Senile's mistake secret if he doesn't want to be "favola alle gente" [a laughingstock to people] (740, 749, 755). Senile is satisfied to reject the truthful optical "illusion" and enter into a permanent state of unwitting collusion in his own cuckolding:

> né darò fede a tali illusioni.
> Tu, Pulidor, poi che campato m'hai,
> governa, e reggi ogni mia facultà,
> e del mio, come me, padron sarai.

> nor will I give faith to such illusions.
> You, Pulidor, seeing that you have saved my life,

Siena

71

govern and administer my every faculty,
and of my goods, even as myself, you will be master. (760–63)

With this last turn, Mariano Manescalco's little play of self-cuckoldry built around the beffa of the *bicchiere,* anticipates that beffa built from the mandragola myth that within three or four years will lead Messer Nicia to open his house and bed to Callimaco in Machiavelli's Florentine setting.

Boccaccio and Cinquecento Drama

As formal reflex, perhaps even homage, to this Sienese heritage, it is not surprising that Piccolomini should have written *La Raffaella;* nor should one be surprised that an intellectual member of the Intronati should have transported a country genre into the city.

That neither Piccolomini or any other Intronati member should have prepared a stageable version of an analogous anti-Plautine play subsequent to Piccolomini's experiment in *La Raffaella* is explicable on a number of counts: Piccolomini's personal aspirations and the academy's elite reputation are the most obvious. Before leaving it, though, one can use the example of *La Raffaella* to make a just peace with that Boccaccio who seemed thrust to the margins of dramatic history by my remarks in relation to Pisani's *Philogenia,* remarks returned to above.

Piccolomini consciously experimented with foregrounding one genre, the dialogue, as preparation for its being cannibalized, thoroughly swallowed up into another genre, comedy. Initially appealing to generic expectation by title and fulfilling that promise in the material form of its subject—*la bella crean{a*—*La Raffaella* places the "dialogue" in parentheses that make it a vehicle for the problematic final form it is given as protodrama. It is in light of this lamination of genres that one may agree with Nino Borsellino when, looking at the numerous adaptations, he says, "la commedia del Cinquecento sembra organizzarsi come un *Decameron* teatrale . . . *Il Decameron* è in questo senso un grande zibaldone teatrale"[16] [the comedy of the Cinquecento seems to organize itself as a theatrical *Decameron* . . . the *Decameron* in this sense is a great theatrical commonplace book]. If the novella cannot be drama because, no matter how tessellated with secrets, it is a closed story, a completed history, nonetheless, like the dialogue *La Raffaella*, it can be placed within the parentheses of dramatic form without abandoning its generic features. As Borsellino remarks of the Boccaccian beffe found in so many plays, "pur sceneggiata, essa resta *storia*, implica la complicità del pubblico con un evento derisorio che esso accetta come rappresentabile in quanto iscritto in un codice di comportamento narrativo col quale ha da tempo familiarizzato" [even when staged, it remains a *history*, it implies the complicity of the public with a derisory event which they accept as representable insofar as it is inscribed in a code of narrative comportment with which they have long been familiarized] (16). Once that dramatization was made on the scale we find in the Renaissance, however, the novelle become "new" in a happy contamination, "un processo incessante di riscrittura che coinvolge non soltanto il testo riscritto (le commedie) ma anche quello riscrivibile (il *Decameron*)" [an unceasing process of rewriting that involves not only the rewritten text (the comedies) but also that one that is rewritable (the *Decameron*)] (21). Boccaccio became a major source because his beffe so often employed situational groupings also found in classical comedy (old husband-young wife, parasite-innamorato, etc.) and developed them in extravaganzas of unmatched complexity. But the source itself, while remaining a collection of histories, borrowed another *almost* formal dimension from its borrowers: "Il *Decameron* in quanto testo destinato alla lettura, non alla rappresentazione, non può produrre analoghi schemi e rapporti teatrali, ma può suggerirli ed evocarli" [The *Decameron*, insofar as it is a text destined for reading, not for representation, cannot produce analogous theatrical schemes and relationships, but it is able to suggest and to evoke them] (40). These observations on the *Decameron*, like the placing of Piccolomini's *Dialogo*, are reminders of the power drama possessed to pull other genres into its orbit in the Cinquecento.

Siena

I have not wanted to leave the impression that any of these Sienese plays are fully realized developments of the formal pattern we have begun to trace. They were designed to exploit the complications of a beffa or, at most (as in *Capotondo*), a social conflict and collusion. They were not designed to examine character by turning its various facets to the light. And psychological exploration culminating in incertitude upon the part of characters and audience is certainly the fixed pole of an emerging subgenre of secrecy. Piccolomini's dialogue becomes dramatic precisely when it begins its rich offering of gradual characterizations through almost covert glimpses of behavior, past and present.

When that has been acknowledged, though, there remains visible at the heart of these brief plays a structure of problematic resolutions of plot stunningly similar to that which will be developed across centuries, using the same rivalries and collusions to arrive eventually at the semi-denouement of Goldoni's *villeggiatura* trilogy.

Moving attention from the plays of Siena to those of Florence, written in the same years of the Cinquecento, reveals a radical shift in conceptualization, even as the plot matrix remains stable. With Machiavelli, comedy is abandoning the campagna for the city—returning, that is, to its old Plautine habitat. And it is transferring the motive power of the beffa from the cause of actions to the cause of reactions. It is not to forget Ruzante's personality, so dominant a presence as to transcend Beolco's plays and their author alike, to suggest that Machiavelli will establish character in comedy.

Florence

*S*ometime just before 1550 Anton Francesco Doni described a double performance of Machiavelli's *La mandragola* and Giovan Maria Cecchi's *L'assiuolo* in the Palazzo Vecchio at Florence:

> Per la fede mia che in Fiorenza non fu fatto mai sí bel trovato. Due scene, una da una parte della sala e l'altra dall'altra; due prospettive mirabili, . . . due comedie piacevolissime e di nuova invenzione; la *Mandragola* e *L'assiuolo:* fatto che era il primo atto di questa, seguitava l'atto di quella, sempre accompagnandosi l'una l'altra, senza intermedii, in modo che una comedia era intermedio dell'altra. . . . Io non credo che si possi far meglio di queste due comediette; le sono una gioia. Il Machiavello e Giovan Maria mi posson comandare. Oh che belli intelletti![1]

> By my faith, there has never been done in Florence anything so clever. Two stages, one at one end of the hall, and the other at the other end; two admirable perspectives, . . . two very pleasing comedies and of original invention; the *Mandragola* and the *Assiuolo:* presented so that when the first act of one of them was over, it was followed by the first act of the other, one play always accompanying the other, without intermezzos, so that one comedy was the intermezzo of the other. . . . I don't believe anyone could write anything better than these two little comedies; they are a jewel. Machiavelli and Giovan Maria may command me. Oh, what marvellous intellects!

This constituted an extraordinary theatrical experiment. But it was an event that implicitly acknowledged the tradition that was flourishing in Florence as in Siena and the Veneto. These twinned plays have continued from their own time as critical and popular peaks of Cinquecento drama in Italian. Probably not spoken in this performance was Cecchi's *prologo*, which recalled the New Comedy tradition while disavowing it: "vogliono fare spettacolo d'una Commedia nuova nuova, fatta . . . per voi; non cavata né di Terenzio, né di Plauto, ma da un caso nuovamente accaduto in Pisa"[2] [they desire to stage a fresh new comedy . . . for you; derived neither from Terence, nor Plautus, but from an event newly happened in Pisa]. Cecchi emphasizes the particular eccentricity of his play's focus in that it does not conclude "in mogliazzi, siccome sogliono fare le più delle commedie" [in marriages (the word also refers to a type of mariazo), as most comedies usually do] (128); that is, with the generic and formal base of the rusticali so dominant in neighboring Siena. Cecchi, of course, was himself recalling Machiavelli. But *L'assiuolo*, Cecchi's adaptation of *La mandragola*, is almost as impenetrable in its linguistic detail as are the northern dialect plays. If it does not adopt the linguistic variations of Tuscan villages reflected in the Sienese rusticali and sought out by Lorenzo and other preservers of dialects soon to be imperialized by Tuscan, *L'assiuolo* is, from one perspective, a ribbon of Tuscanisms demanding such a length of annotation that modern editions bear comparison with the explanatory translations of Ruzante or *La venexiana*. This is not surprising from a Florentine who boasted that from birth he had never been out of sight of the Duomo ("dal ceppo, che non ha perduto / la cupola di vista"[3] [from his family's origins, he has not lost / the cupola from sight]), and certainly not surprising from Cecchi, the gatherer of Florentine-oriented metaphors in his *Dichiarazione di molti proverbi, detti e parole della nostra lingua*. In another sense, though, *L'assiuolo* offers so many surprises, coming in the wake of Machiavelli, that it will be most profitable to account for it, to give an account of its independence, before we turn to renew dramatic acquaintance with *La mandragola*.

Secret Sharers in Italian Comedy

Giovan Maria Cecchi's *L'assiuolo*

"al buio, messer, sí"

Titles come to our attention first. In our earlier trio of plays from the Veneto and its environs, they brought persons to the forefront: Philogenia, Betía, la Venexiana (although the last may refer only to the place). The Florentine focus is upon things, talismans, things become talismanic as participant metaphor: *la mandragola* (the mandrake), *l'assiuolo* (the owl). There is nothing initially subtle in either image, but the shift of emphasis from personal history to metaphoric generalization is worth attention. A first realization suggests that the Cinquecento dramatists may be returning to the narrative womb of Boccaccio—actions, as they discovered, easily repeated with a reassigning of names. Implicit in the *Decameron* was the infinite retelling of beffe. Akin to his predecessor Scheherezade and successors in erotica, Boccaccio discerned that naming was the best mask for anonymity, for revivifying old jokes with a few syllabic shifts. But something destabilizing happened when metaphor displaced the easy play of names, when Machiavelli displayed the mandrake root or Cecchi the owl as emblem. No one takes seriously Cecchi's claim that *L'assiuolo* was a piece of Pisan history, because it would not have mattered. Cecchi wrote of the owl, not Messer Ambrogio. And the owl was a bird of night, blinded by light, horned like the cuckold, and (so becoming the source of Messer Ambrogio's password, *chiù, chiù*) hooted. Here one may begin the process by which literal plot and metaphoric structure, the replacing of nominal titles by Florentine emphases upon things, begin to reveal a new dimension.

One can recall the few plays by Plautus titled from objects: *Aulularia, Cassaria, Rudens.* The precedent only foregrounds the new turn taken in the Florentine Renaissance. Plautus's titles point to properties, properties in each case crucial to the mechanics of the intrigue plot but never infusing the play with that metalife into which a brilliantly centralized symbol can raise the particulars of comic incident. By underlining their advances over Plautus, one does not want to be drawn into exaggeration about the skill of Machiavelli

Florence

77

and Cecchi in understanding the language of symbolic things. As a check, we have only to remember how skillfully Goldoni will manipulate a fan from prop into the symbolic center that is everywhere and whose circumference is nowhere in *Il ventaglio*.[4] Yet the tradition is emerging here in Florence as it does not in the early Venetian plays, or in those of Ariosto. To make the issue of a new symbolic dimension clear, though, one must fully integrate it with the secret form we have been exploring.

The first layer of secrecy is a familiar mechanism by which countless dramatists attempt to domesticate the improbabilities of mistaken identity to some degree of social verisimilitude. This is the device of combining a few local-color hints with a seasonal *carnevale* setting for the transvestite and other masquerades and disguises that stretch the audience's imagination more severely than that of the author. At nearly the close of his career as dramatist, Cecchi summarized these elements in the prologue to *Le maschere*, a verse extravaganza about Florentine carnival that was itself presented during the carnival season in Florence:

> . . . in questi dì del Carnovale, la
> Maggior parte degli uomini . . .
> . . . o e' vanno, o e' desiderano
> Per disfogare i capricci che vengono
> Nella testa, di andare attorno in maschera,
> . . .
> [La] Scena è Firenze, cosa molto solita
> A lui . . .

> . . . in these days of Carnival,
> most men . . .
> . . . either go about, or desire to go about
> Loosing the caprices that come
> Into their heads, of going about in masks,
> . . .

Secret Sharers in Italian Comedy

The scene is Florence, a very usual
setting for him [the author]. (1.29–31)

So it is in *L'assiuolo*. As a disguised servant observes to his master, "se noi avessimo le maschere, noi parremmo duo mattaccini" [if
we had masks, we would look like two clowns (figuratively, "crazies")], to which it is replied, "o mattaccini, o matti grandi, non
importa; a me basta non essèr conosciuto; e poi noi siamo per carnovale" [little crazies, or grown-up madmen, doesn't matter; to me
it is enough not to be recognized; and it's Carnival anyway] (169;
4.2). The carnival setting and the subsequent practice of disguise is
further advanced by the coyly overdeveloped device of having the
young wife escape her old husband's jealous scrutiny by attending
one of those carnival comedies played by the girls of the nunneries,
a practice remarked upon by such *dilettanti* as Grazzini and Cecchi
himself, of course, in this play.[5] If carnival masking and playing is a
creaking device, it is nonetheless a device that sets the intrigue in a
sort of penumbra that goes with the darkness in which much of it is
enacted.

The beffe that are the nodes of action are suggested ultimately
by the *Decameron* (3.6, 8.4, 8.7),[6] and the geometry of characters is familiar. The senex (Ambrogio) with a young wife (Oretta)
is lusting for the widow (Anfrosina). A darker note of what one
might tag "social" incest emerges when one of the two young rivals
for Oretta (Giulio and Rinuccio) is disclosed to be the widow's
son. There is the literally named stupid zanni attached to Ambrogio (Gianella), the *pinɉochera* (religious hypocrite) (Verdiana), the
servant-confidante, and the servant (Giorgetto) who concerts the
whole action in the interest of his young master (Giulio). And there
is Oretta's unattached sister (Violante). Few surprises, then, seem
probable from such tried and tired ingredients, especially from the
Plautine-oriented Cecchi. But *L'assiuolo* was drawn from and into
the other tradition, that anti-Plautine form we have been following.

The opening situation is an overlap of secrets revealed and secrets retained. As a student at the university, Giulio has taken rooms

Florence

in the convenient home of Rinuccio, a youth who soon becomes his friend. He has also fallen desperately in love with Ambrogio's young wife Oretta. But he has withheld all signs of this love because Rinuccio has unwittingly revealed himself as a rival and "m'ha conferito questo suo amore, e del continuo mi ragguaglia di tutti gli andamenti, e vuole che io gli aiuti" [has confided this love to me, and continually tells me all its developments, and wants me to help him] (131; 1.1). Already situation is beginning to unfold into form. Having revealed his own secret and Rinuccio's secret revelations alike to his servant Giorgetto, Giulio employs the universal alibi—"I' so che tu sei segreto e fedele" [I know you to be secret and faithful] (132)— saving himself from direct recognition by displacing the qualities he (perhaps subconsciously) finds lacking in himself. Cecchi's novel turn upon rivalry, and upon the novelistic turn (Palomon and Arcite) that rivalry takes when exploiting the notion of one soul in bodies twain, is the hypothesis that Giulio can embody contradictory qualities, can be lacking simultaneously in secrecy and faithfulness even while employing both. In him antonyms become oxymoronic. But it is a possibility that can be convictively developed only in an action bathed in betrayal and silencing.

Immediately upon Giulio's confession to Giorgetto, Oretta's maid Agnola comes seeking Rinuccio and is flustered at finding him with Giulio, because "io vi conterò certi segreti che importano" [I will tell you certain important secrets]. Giulio's perfunctory offer to leave them in privacy is indignantly rejected by Rinuccio, who ironically cuts short Agnola's attempt at discretion, misplacing her distrust of Giulio upon himself: "O i' crederei che la metà delle parole, che io ci ho speso attorno, bastassino a fare che voi mi fidaste molto maggiori segreti che questi" [I would have thought that one half the words that I have spent would have been enough to make you confide in me far greater secrets than these]. So endorsed, Giulio turns good faith to bad with his sinister Tuscanism: "Madonna Agnola, dite pur sicuramente; ché per me sarà il tutto sotto terra" [Madonna Agnola, speak confidently; because with me everything will be buried] (134–35; 1.2). What follows immediately is the feminine parallel to Giulio's double situation of confidant and confider. Agnola has gone to see the little nuns' comedy with Oretta; Oretta has sat beside Rinuccio's mother, who has whispered to her the secret propositions of the girl's lusting old husband—secrets revealed only in whispers—while Agnola has overheard all that she now reveals to the incestuous son and lover. And all this silence and discovery is carried on within a barrage of Florentine popular expressions, linguistic dodges, metaphors, in a subterfuge that would have challenged the hardiest Florentine sampler of the various quarters and their jargons, mannerisms, and inherited imagery. The language of this new "Italian" was clear; the meaning would have been gleaned, the phraseology triumphantly but sporadically understood by the "others" who were its alleged secret sharers. They could, of course, come inside only as could the audiences for the dialect polyglot from the Veneto's proto–commedia dell'arte performances. They could pick out and transliterate situationally available proverbialisms to which they had not been born. The evidence for Cecchi's having teased a balance between his audience's Tuscan and their inability to penetrate the mountain of Tuscanisms he philologically excavates and dramatically employs is not the roll call of annotations in modern editions but Cecchi's own anthology, a gathering no more philological than *L'assiuolo,* of "molti proverbi, detti e parole della nostra lingua" [many proverbs, sayings and mottos of our language]. A dictionary for foreigners in their own language; a play written in a local Esperanto. Which stylistic maneuver, of course, provides its reattachment to a dialect form (cf. Dionisotti, pp. 96–97 below), and echoes the open secrecy of the plot.

In interlocked versions of the bed trick, it is arranged that Ambrogio, disguised, will place himself in Rinuccio's bed for a supposed rendezvous with Anfrosina. Oretta, disguised and pre-informed, will arrive hoping to unmask her husband's treachery. But Rinuccio will lock the old man in the cold courtyard and impersonate him while making love to Oretta. Rinuccio explains all of this to Oretta's maid, adding that he isn't sure whether he will ultimately discover his identity to her mistress: "potrebbe essere che io me le scoprissi, e

Florence

potrebbe essere di no" [maybe I will declare myself, and maybe not] (149; 2.5). Then, doing homage to his indebtedness to Callimaco's creator Machiavelli, he avows, "io m'andrò accomodando al temporale" [I will proceed accommodating myself to the hour's events]. This phrase is embedded in numerous allusions to following fortune. "Io ho buona speranza, né posso credere che la fortuna non voglia dare buono esito a'miei amori, avendo loro data sí bella occasione" [I am of good hope, nor can I believe that fortune does not wish to give my loves a good outcome, having given them such fine occasion], Rinuccio says in the most extended instance (167; 4.1). The impetuosity, the buoyant mood, the youth of the speaker all recall Callimaco as model and echo the landmark metaphors of the twenty-fifth chapter of *Il principe*. The initial phrasing, though, is a direct reminder of Machiavelli's familiar version of change as constancy to time: "secondano e'tempi" [following the times] he had put it in an early letter, and perhaps its most notable expansion was that advice he offered Giovan Battista Soderini: "perché i tempi et le cose universalmente et particularmente si mutano spesso, . . . veramente chi fosse tanto savio che conoscesse i tempi et l'ordine delle cose, et accomodasse a quelle, harebbe sempre buona fortuna"[7] [because times and things universally and particularly change often, . . . truly, someone wise enough as to know the times and the order of things, and to accommodate to them, would always have good fortune].

Secrets everywhere maintained, even in the physical act of whispering ("Chi è? dite si piano / Io dico piano, perché la mi disse che io facessi che le serve non sentissino" [Who is it? You speak so softly. / I speak softly, because I was told to do so in order that the maidservants would not hear] [160; 3.3]) and metaphoric muteness ("Non dubitate, i'sarò più mutolo ch'un pesce" [Don't worry, I will be dumber than a fish] [164; 3.5]). The noncommunication of Tuscan babel blinds the audience to suggested nuances; the whispered plans blind the others. These observations return us to the centrality of the title symbol, to *l'assiuolo*.

Ambrogio begins to earn identification with the owl early in a passing realistic detail of aged nearsightedness: "È questa qua madonna Verdiana? ella mi pare; mai no; anzi sí; in fatto la vista non mi serve più" [Is this Madonna Verdiana? It appears to be her; but no; rather yes; in fact, my sight doesn't serve me well anymore] (142; 2.2). The association is sealed as he enlists his zanni to stand watch upon his expected love tryst. The sign will be a password, Ambrogio suggests, proposing one and another until Gianella unwittingly suggests the owl's hoot that emphasizes Ambrogio's obtuseness and the metaphoric night of the fable's form, in which all is secreted beyond language (it is appropriate that Ambrogio's last suggestion is a Florentine corruption of the password used by recent Spanish occupation troops):[8]

Ambrogio: Aspetta; e'dirò come si diceva nel '32 la notte per Firenze: *Chies aglià?*
Gianella: Che? gli è troppo sofistico: oh non lo terrebbe a mente un abbaco; . . . ma fate così; volendo che io venga, fate tre volte *Chiù*.
Ambrogio: O cotesto è un cenno da assiuolo![9]

Ambrogio: Wait; I will say what they said at night throughout Florence in '32: *Quien es allá?* [Who goes there?]
Gianella: What? That's too complicated: I couldn't remember it if I had an abacus to keep count; . . . but do this: when you want me to come, go *Chiù* three times.
Ambrogio: Oh, that's what owls say! (165; 3.5)

The sign agreed upon, the clever servant Giorgetto will make explicit Ambrogio's natural aptitude for the role: "sta nella corte in chiusa a contraffare l'assiuolo a più potere; che m'ha fatto quasi smascellar delle risa, sentendo così gentilmente cantare in assiuolo; e forse che e'non si studiava" [he's shut up in the courtyard imitating an owl as hard as he can; I almost split my sides laughing, hearing him singing so sweetly in owl's language; and you can imagine whether he wasn't trying] (173; 4.6). Always slower than his servant, Giulio in recounting affairs cannot understand the motive behind Ambrogio's symbolic birdsong accompanying his own cuckolding:

Florence

"mentre che noi stemmo insieme, il vecchio nella corte sempre fece assiuolo; non so io che diavolo di fantasia gli s'era tocca" [while we were together, the old man in the courtyard went on hooting like an owl; I don't know what the devil struck his fantasy] (185; 5.2). Later, his own folly as active adulterer and passive cuckold partially revealed, Ambrogio will seal the blindness theme ironically: "È il diavolo che m'ha accecato" [It is the devil who has blinded me] (192; 5.7).

Horns and blindness and bedevilment by youth: the usual accompaniments of the senex extend the *assiuolo* of the title into a walking metaphor of self for Ambrogio. As I earlier remarked, however, the Florentine (we should now admit, the Machiavellian) mode went beyond this. The owl sees, after all, but only in darkness. And darkness is the setting, nature, psychology, and form of *L'assiuolo*. The nodal expression of all these aspects arrives with Giulio's confessions to Rinuccio about his secret adultery with Oretta, the replacement of Ambrogio by himself, a similar substitution for Rinuccio, and so on. His friend, aghast at developments, exclaims, "Tutte queste cose dovettero seguire al buio" [All of this must have taken place in the dark]. Giulio responds for himself and for the play: "Al buio, messer, sí" [In the dark, yes sir] (183; 5.2).

If Ambrogio is the old caged bird growing horns in the darkness, that same darkness is the element in which the others are becoming wiser to the ways of the world. It is time for a resumé of the intrigues. And a reminder of the earlier remark that the faithless and loose-tongued Giulio is both and neither of these things.

First, there is the action that begins from Plautine commedia erudita commonplaces with a purposeful establishment of expectation. When the clever servant Giorgetto arrives in Pisa from Florence to find his master Giulio enamored of Oretta but trapped by his mores into friendship with his rival, Giorgetto is disgusted. A not unfamiliar setting, this. Nor is it unexpected that Giorgetto would maneuver to set things right in his young master's interest. Directed by Giorgetto, Rinuccio sends Ambrogio a letter supposedly from his mother, Anfrosina, a letter inviting him to her while the young friends Rinuccio and Giulio are out of the city. Rinuccio then is led to hope that he can enter Ambrogio's house and Oretta's bed. But Giulio and Giorgetto have written Oretta to induce her to discover Ambrogio in Anfrosina's bed, where Giulio awaits (and mates) her. Nothing is unfamiliar here but one addition that seems at first an awkward tagged-on mechanism for concinnity: the duped Rinuccio entering Ambrogio's house finds Oretta's sister Violante instead and enjoys as happy a coupling (*al buio*) as does his treacherous friend. These adulteries and cuckoldings could be analogues for New Comedy intrigues familiar before and after *L'assiuolo,* except that in Cecchi's adaptation the old action has been converted into the new Machiavellian form. Cecchi, though, having learned everything else from him derivatively, learned how to do what even Machiavelli did not do. He saw (strange predicate for an action developed in so many ways *al buio*) how to incorporate an analytic discussion of this drama within the fable itself. A clarifying dialogue in the dark, *L'assiuolo* reaches back and forward in dramatic history as the most self-articulate exemplar of open closure.

Giulio has betrayed and used in his own behalf the love secrets of his friend, even to the Machiavellian point of substituting for him in bed. Finally he confesses these psychic and sexual abuses. The result is to place a stamp of collusion upon friendship, a friendship in which both parties share the profits. Giulio's paradoxical innate loyalty leads him to aid Rinuccio's battle strategy for capturing Oretta, in spite of himself and his selfish machinations with Giorgetto, this allegiance to friendship being part of his "fortune": "io sono di questa maledetta natura che se un mio amico mi cerca d'un consiglio, e'bisogna, se me n'andasse la vita, ch'io gnene dia il migliore ch'io so" [I am of this cursed nature that if a friend asks me for a piece of advice, for the life of me, I must give him the best advice that I know how] (155; 3.1). Had he been speaking to someone other than the scornful Giorgetto, this might seem camouflage, since he derives the pleasure of Oretta's bed by way of tried tricks, a rather lesser Callimaco. And Oretta echoes Lucrezia's disguised but resigned anger: new lover and old husband have made her "quella che io non fu mai, né mai ebbi intenzione d'essere" [that which I never was, nor ever had the intention of being] (171; 4.4). In for a penny, in for a pound, however, and she asks only . . . privacy, that she "non perda in pubblico quello che voi in privato perder fatto mi avete" [not lose in public what you have made me lose in private] (179; 5.1). But she finds her jeopardy doubled, as both suitors converge in knowledge of her adultery with one. Heroine or victim of converging, if contradictory, situations, Oretta begins the development of a final resolution of all problems which one can denominate an anti-denouement. Nothing is to be discovered: "Messer Giulio e messer Rinuccio, così esca io della presente sciagura con quiete de'miei (il che mi pare impossibile) come io sono e sarò sempre vostra" [Messer Giulio and Messer Rinuccio, if I can only get out of this present disaster without scandal (which seems to me impossible) so I am and will always be yours] (180; 5.2).

The two friends are in the strange situation of the loyal Giulio's having two-timed Rinuccio, yet whose appeal of natural innocence, we know from his frustration with Giorgetto's scolding, is nonetheless genuine. He had every hope of betraying his friend, as he managed to do, Giulio admits, but he offers Rinuccio a complicating paradox: "chiedendomi voi come amico consiglio, volli più tosto dar contro a me, quantunque contro all'animo mio, per non mancare all'ufficio dell'amico vero, che mancare a voi, e giovar a me" [when you asked my advice as a friend, I preferred to go against my own interest, however much against inclinations, in order not to fail in the office of a true friend, rather than to let you down to my own advantage] (182; 5.2). Only Giorgetto knew how to turn innocence to mutual pleasure, to transmute faithfulness, and betrayal, to twin beatitudes of love: "Giorgetto, a chi, come voi sapete, io dico liberamente sempre tutti i miei segreti" [Giorgetto, to whom, as you know, I always speak freely all my secrets] (182; 5.2). The close of *L'assiuolo* turns this imitation of *La mandragola* into a sophisticated form discoursing upon itself in a fashion Machiavelli never imagined. It is appropriate here to recall what was said earlier about novelle versus drama. The story of Giulio, Rinuccio, and Oretta would be an ancient history of fortunate lovers in the former genre; as dramatization, it becomes perpetual future, the audience, like the principals, secret sharers who must say with Rinuccio, "io vi perdono ogni cosa" [I pardon you everything]. He so addresses Giulio when the latter admits that he has desperately loved Oretta from first sight and that, in spite of friendship and his actual aid to Rinuccio, "segretamente ho tentate diverse vie per trovarmi con lei" [secretly I have tried various ways to be alone with her] (181; 5.2).

When he finds himself there, all is in the dark, in whispers and treacherous innocence. She has believed him to be Ambrogio in search of the widow; so believing, she has first accused and rebuffed him, then succumbed — with pleasure: "E' non è 'l primo che non vuol cenare, e poi cena per sette" [She is not the first who doesn't want to dine, then eats for seven] (184; 5.2). Oretta had remonstrated, but Giulio had persisted in projecting a future and, from some ambivalent self-interest and selfish friendship, had included Rinuccio in it. As he explains to the latter:

Ma io non volendo che questa fosse l'ultima volta, siccome l'era stata la prima, e andandola trattenendo, non possendo credere che voi non tornaste, tanto le dissi e predecai, ch'io la convertii a volere a voi e a me tutto il suo bene.

But I, not wanting this to be the last time, as it was the first, while I was holding her back, not being able to believe that you would not return, spoke and begged so much, that I converted her to love you *and* me with all her heart. (185; 5.2)

And all the while this multiple pact was being negotiated, the old husband sang his symbolic chorus: "il vecchio nella corte sempre fece l'assiuolo" [the old man in the courtyard kept on hooting like an owl].

All having been arranged with Oretta, who came in chaste innocence and found an endless love feast, *il vecchio* must be silenced.

Florence

Threatened with public ridicule for his own aborted amours, Ambrogio agrees to send away his spy and doorkeeper Gianella and "giudicare d'aver la più fedel moglie che sia in Pisa, e perciò a concederle che ella vadia e stia dove le pare, senza che egli sia a farle la spia attorno" [to agree that he has the most faithful wife in Pisa, and therefore to allow her to go and stay wherever she wills, without his being around spying on her] (193; 5.8).

There is a last twist to the plot, added as seal and symbol upon relationships newborn. Rinuccio must recount how he, going to Oretta's bed without knowledge of the tricks that have drawn Oretta away, found her sister Violante for a night of love. That which conspired to place Violante in Oretta's bed was the presence of the child of Oretta and Ambrogio, offspring of the young wife and *il vecchio rimbambito*, the old man in second childhood, against all logic of the genre: "un puttino di tre anni, e perché egli è loro unico, il vecchio lo tiene nel letto suo; e dovendosi ella partire, perché e'non rimanesse solo, fece entrare la sorella di lei nel suo letto, accioché la gli avesse cura" [a little boy three years old, and because he is their only child, the old man keeps him in his bed; and when she had to leave, so that he wouldn't be left alone, had her sister get into bed to take care of him] (186; 5.2).

"Al buio, messer, sí." While Ambrogio hooted the owl song as he gained his horns, the little boy in the dark was presiding over the eternal passage of blind love, symbolic Cupid carrying out his task. But not in the way of Puck in the forest. He is already the product of unholy wedlock sealing the secrets of cynical pleasure that constitute the anti-Plautine comedy of which *L'assiuolo* is exemplar and upon which it becomes commentary. A dialogue, as we said, of clarification in the dark. Another oxymoron.

Antonfrancesco Grazzini (Il Lasca): *Il Frate*

There was a middle term between *L'assiuolo* and *La mandragola*, written by Cecchi's Florentine rival and fellow, Antonfrancesco

Grazzini, better known by his academic pseudonym of Il Lasca (the carp). Both were dramatists, both made *campanilismo* a boast in every available context, and both, aware of the changes made in the language under the aggrandizing impulse of Grand Duke Cosimo, made collections of Tuscanisms of a conservatory nature. It seems inevitable in critical retrospect that each would have turned to Machiavelli's dramatic *capolavoro* in which there is so much of Florence, in which he suggests of Messer Nicia with grave ambivalence toward the vaunted Florentine provincialism, "voi non siete uso a perdere la Cupola di veduta" [you are not used to losing sight of the cupola] (65).

Grazzini shaped a less fully developed vehicle than *L'assiuolo*. But his farce *Il frate* (The Friar), directly invoking Machiavelli, preceded Cecchi's play by nearly a decade (1540) and doubtless served as a stimulus to which Cecchi reacted in reactivating this new form that embraces the audience in a conspiratorial pact. Grazzini's prologue almost directly invites Cecchi's rivalry as it would be evinced in the later five-act structure when he announces that "le farse non son commedie e la sua [Grazzini's], sendo farsa, non viene ad esser commedia; percioché quelle in cinque sono, e queste in tre atti distinte e divisate"[10] [farces are not comedies, and his (Grazzini's), being a farce, is not a comedy; since comedies are distinguished and divided into five acts, and farces into three]. Cecchi himself would much later attempt to define and defend the *farsa* form in the prologue of *La romanesca*. But at this earlier time, Grazzini was setting his irregularities over against the supposed classical form of the younger dramatist. In his burlesques, Grazzini looks at the emerging popular troupes and declares:

> Hanno i poeti questa volta dato
> del cul, come si dice, in sul pietrone,
>
> . . .
>
> così da Zanni vinti e superati,
> possono ire a impiccarsi i letterati.
> Tutti i comici nostri Fiorentini

Florence

son per questa cagione addolorati;

e Lotto e il Cecchi al fin, piccin piccini,

con tutti gli altri dotti, son restati,

parendo questa sorba loro arcigna,

e il Lasca chiude l'occhiolino e ghigna.[11]

The poets have put their asses on the slab this time, as we say,

. . .

So, beaten and subdued as they are by the Zanni,

The men of letters can go hang themselves.

This is why all our Florentine comedy writers

are in mourning;

In the end, both Lotto and Cecchi, of small account anyway,

are tossed out along with the rest of the learned,

since their fruits now seem sour,

and Il Lasca winks and snickers.

It is to something similar to this new method that Grazzini alludes in the prologue to *Il frate,* when he comments on farce:

dunque le appartenenze tutte delle commedie non se le appartengano non già per questo: che vi si faccino vedere cose impossibili e fuori al tutto d'ogni verisimilitudine; ma sendoci qualche cosellina non così bene osservata, non dovete troppo curarvene.

so you will not find all the appurtenances of comedies, and not just for this: that things impossible and wholly beyond any verisimilitude are shown; but if there is some little detail that is not too well observed, you ought not to be too concerned about it. (93)

And he does not take great care. Indeed, a large part of the pleasure of *Il frate* is the flaunting of the improbable in its whirlwind mechanism; the thought seems capable of producing the deed with immediate effect.

Grazzini's is a simpler story than *La mandragola* before or

Secret Sharers in Italian Comedy

L'assiuolo after, more Boccaccian in this simplicity: once upon a time there were an old man, a young wife, and a venal priest.[12]

Neither Boccaccio's triangulation nor Cecchi's neat squaring of the love circle could provide for the priest in their geometry, but Grazzini, even in the prologue to *Il frate,* as in its title, emphasizes the priest and uses Machiavelli's precedent to deflect censure: "condurre in scena un frate . . . non sia così grave peccato come molti lo fanno; percioché nella *Mandragola* . . . venne in scena un fra Timoteo de' Servi che confortò santamente a ingravidar la moglie di M. Nicia" [to bring a friar onto the stage . . . may not be so grave a sin as many make it . . . seeing that in the *Mandragola* . . . there came onto the stage a Brother Timoteo of the Servi who sanctimoniously urged the wife of Messer Nicia to become pregnant] (93). What had been an instrument for Machiavelli becomes the problematic center for Grazzini when he fuses Callimaco and Timoteo. Before the stage, of course, the confessional had established a space for secrets, had become metaphor for speaking into the silent future.

The old man, Amerigo, lusts for his neighbor; the priest Fra Alberigo, arranges for Amerigo's wife, Caterina, to substitute for her neighbor in a proposed bed of adultery and to upbraid her husband, and for himself to become a licensed guest in Amerigo's household. As the latter says in a cloud of unknowing self-cuckoldry, inviting the errant priest into his (and Caterina's) bosom: "E da qui innanzi, poiché io ho visto in voi tanta dottrina e bontà, voglio che . . . siate nostro familiare" [And from this time forward, since I have seen in you so much doctrine and goodness, I want you to be part of the household] (118).

It is the husband's victimization by clerical venality that is the plot denouement, but the venality is interspersed in detail, the *fabliau* conclusion quite aside. Acknowledging tacitly the putative illicit behavior of keeping women in men's monasteries, Fra Alberigo places appearance above ecclesiastical rules, mentioned almost as an afterthought: "voi sapete che nel convento il tenervi le donne non par che si convegna, oltre che gli è vietato" [you know that keeping women in the monastery is not very convenient, in addition to being forbid-

Florence

den] (104). Near blasphemy is the friar's exchange with Caterina's maidservant-panderess about secrecy: "Io sono tanto lieta, Padre," says the girl, "di questa cosa, ch'io nol ve potrei mai dire" [I could never tell you, Father, how happy I am about this thing]. The friar returns a perverted benediction: "È per tua grazia" [It is through your grace] (114).

It is a small blasphemy that undermines piety's opportunity to convert chance and scheming and fortune, all those improbable structures supporting an exhausted Plautine formula, into providential agencies. The improbabilities are manifest enough that, did the priest's character not invalidate it, providence might be blamed rather than farcical dramaturgy. As he warns in the prologue, Grazzini foregrounds chance as characters arrive with perfect convenience: "Ma oh! eccolo appunto che ne vien di qua, e solo per ventura" [But, oh!, here he is coming this way right now, and only by chance] (102); "o diavolo! eccolo di qua appunto" [O devil! here he is right now] (103); "per sorte è la tua donna in casa" [luckily your wife is at home] (104); "la fortuna comincia a prospermi . . . ecco appunto la fante" [fortune begins to favor me . . . here comes the serving girl herself] (105); "Fortuna, siemi propizia questa volta" (106); [Fortune, be on my side this once] (106); and at the close Fortune provides the key to the space that encloses the friar in adultery: "Volle la fortuna ch'io m'abbattei fra questo mazzo di chiavi a una che aperse" [Fortune would have it that, out of this bunch of keys, I should hit upon the one that opened] (114). In fact, or plot, fortune generously provides.

The problem of social silence, though, is lightly enwrapped by a penumbra of infernal participation as well. Realizing that his own lust has been discovered by a scolding Caterina, Amerigo requests, then demands the only relief he can receive from his frustration and humiliation: "Io ti domando, e vorrei sapere, il modo che tu hai tenuto a côrmi a questo laccio. Non fustu strega o incanta diavoli?" [I ask you, and would like to know, how you have managed to catch me in this trap. You weren't a witch or a devil-conjuror]?

Caterina replies almost as would Iago: "Io sono stata per dirvi quel ch'io sono" [I was about to tell you that which I am] (116). Suggestions, but nothing more tangible, no disturbing overlay upon the Machiavellian plot. Just Fra Timoteo substituting for Callimaco, and none of Cecchi's later gyrations in *L'assiuolo*. Not now, though, the agreed-upon secrecy of the confessional box for the confessor; reminders, rather, that the role of the ecclesiastic has become dangerously vulnerable to public exposure: Fra Alberigo says, "Quel tanto ch'io voglio è che di questa cosa vi disponiate non favellar mai" [All I ask is that you resolve never to speak about this thing] (118); it is a wish that he had urged in bad faith upon Caterina just a few moments before: "per non dar di voi cattiva fama, di questo fatto mai più non parlerete" [in order not to give yourself a bad reputation, you must never speak again about this affair] (117).

These alarms at the possibility of publicity were dramatically disabled gestures revealing to some degree Grazzini's self-consciousness, his awareness that he had failed to realize the distinction between the historical form of the novella and the participatory form of drama. Elsewhere we have found drama cannibalizing the stuff of the novelle; here drama is drawn back into the historical web of the novelle. At the beginning of act 3, Caterina's maid makes a long narration of the central beffa, telling her version of the recent bed scene in which Amerigo is caught and reproved by Caterina while the smug priest anticipates the inevitable resultant triumph. Separated from participation, we hear the action desiccated into story, into history, at its penultimate and culminating moment. The secret the priest seeks to contain with his closing warning has already been revealed by report, obviating the formal conspiracy to extrapolate action through silence. Cecchi had observed his rival's novelistic myopia about Machiavelli's sense of form. *L'assiuolo* is not about such small matters as love or church. Nor was *La mandragola*.

Florence

Machiavelli's *Discorso o dialogo intorno alla nostra lingua* [Discourse or Dialogue about Our Language] is one of the more daring Cinquecento texts produced by the extended discussion of language versus dialect that preoccupied so many scholars, particularly in the early decades of the century. Not published until 1730, the *Discorso* was attributed to Machiavelli in a major manuscript written by his nephews in 1577. This long disappearance of a polemic work has brought forth several attempts to deprive Machiavelli of authorship, as has the internal demonstration that the work shows only superficial acquaintance with its primary target, Dante's *De vulgari eloquentia*. A scholarly majority, though, believes Machiavelli to be the author. Polemic circumstances explain the failure to publish the work in its own time (it was probably composed at the end of 1524, although there is legitimate argument for dating the composition a decade earlier). While the *Discorso* was in progress, the Venetian Bembo had targeted Dante in his codification of the pan-peninsular attack on Latin and literary Florentine in the *Prosa della volgar lingua*. No Florentine was likely to join at that juncture in the public derogation of Dante.[13]

Nonetheless, Machiavelli sets himself in debate with Dante, challenging the paragon of Tuscan pride with all the mock humility of Socrates. The question is set thus: "se la lingua nella quale hanno scritto i nostri poeti e oratori Fiorentini è Fiorentina, Toscana o Italiana" [whether the language in which our Florentine poets and orators have written is Florentine, Tuscan, or Italian] (5–6). It is a mild, disingenuous opening. Disingenuous, because Machiavelli condemns Dante's claim for "Italiana" from the poet's own words. If, as Dante says, he has borrowed from Lombardo, from Latin, and from Greek, he has simply enriched the suppleness of Florentine: "quella lingua si chiama d'una patria, la quale convertisce i vocaboli ch'ella ha accattati da altri nell'uso suo, ed è sí potente che i vocaboli accattati non la disordinano ma ella disordina loro: perché quello ch'ella reca da altri, lo tira a se in modo che par suo" [that language is called that of a country, which transmutes the words that it has borrowed from others to its own use, and is so potent that the borrowed words do not disorder it, but it rearranges them: because that which it takes from others, it draws to itself so that it appears to be its own] (53). The dialogue with Dante continues through some pages toward Dante's surrender. What interests us here, aside from the emphasis upon Florentine speech that will be reflected in *La mandragola,* is Machiavelli's abrupt parenthesis, toward the close of the *Discorso,* in which comedy becomes the test case for linguistic theory. There are modes that cannot flourish without incorporating "i motti et i termini proprii patrii" [idiomatic witticisms and terms of one's own country] (65):

Di questa sorte sono le comedie . . . perché le cose sono trattate ridicu-lamente, conviene usare termini et motti che faccino questi effetti; i quali termini, se non sono proprii et patrii, dove sieno soli intesi et noti, non muovono né possono muovere. Donde nasce che uno che non sia toscano non farà mai questa parte bene, perché se vorrà dire i motti della patria sua farà una veste rattoppata, facendo una compositione mezza toscana et mezza forestiera.

Of this sort are comedies . . . because things are treated with ridicule, it is appropriate to use terms and witticisms that make these effects; which terms, if they are not characteristic and native, where they are uniquely understood and known, they do not move, nor can they move one. Whence it comes that one who is not Tuscan will never do this part well, because if he wants to use the witty idioms of his native region, he will create a patched garment, making a composition half Tuscan and half foreign. (65–68)

Machiavelli concludes this warning with the example of a rival work, "una comedia fatta da uno delli Ariosti di Ferrara" [a comedy written by one of the Ariostos of Ferrara], which he praises for its classical form, only to deny it the stylistic wit necessary to comedy: "ma la vedrai priva di quei sali che ricerca una comedia; tale non per altro cagione che per la detta: perché i motti ferraresi non li piace-

Florence

95

vano, et i fiorentini non sapeva, talmente che gli lasciò stare" [but you will find it lacking in those witty turns that a comedy needs: and this for no other reason than that I have set forth: because he didn't like Ferrarese conceits, and, not knowing those of the Florentines, he left them alone] (69).[14] This allusion to the Florentine audience, of course, serves as the last turn of the vise upon Dante and the pan-Italian linguistic champions who followed him. Language and comedy both were viewed as having made their *translatio* from Rome to the Arno. It was a view fostered and developed in the literary gatherings of Florentine intellectuals at the Orti Oricellari during the first two decades of the Cinquecento, discussions in which Machiavelli participated and which echo in his *Discorso*. It has been persuasively argued that the catalysts for this long critical exchange were Angelo Poliziano's lectures at the Florentine Studio upon Terence's *Andria* and his commentary upon the prologue to Plautus's *Menaechmi*.[15] In brief, Poliziano argued from Roman practice upon Greek originals for an adaptation of comedy to the vernacular language and the mores it encompassed. But with this step one was halfway to Poliziano's determination that it was the morphology of comedy as a mirror of quotidian types and events that should be imitated, not—as was the case with Ariosto's experiments in Ferrara—particular ancient plays. Iacopo Nardi and Lorenzo Strozzi, both elite communicants in the Oricellari symposia, made early, primitive, and self-consciously defensive attempts at this new New Comedy,[16] and Machiavelli twice unsuccessfully rendered the *Andria* itself into the Tuscan vernacular, for *fiorentino* was the language of Florence. And Florence, being in Machiavelli's improbable optimism a world that harbored more comedy than tragedy, spoke in the language of *la vita privata*. The end of this comic vision was life in a family, like a family of languages gathered into choir, like the urban families that shared these languages of word and action. Communities, though, private or political, as we have noticed to be true of dialects also, do not have a natural tendency to openness. Carlo Dionisotti documented this centripetal force in Florence in the Quattrocento, which he characterized as a time during which

L'ambito della letteratura toscana si restringe e si municipalizza, e che allora si ha, per la prima volta forse in Italia, una letteratura dialettale nel senso vero e proprio della parola, fondata cioè sull'uso consapevole di un linguaggio di rango inferiore.

The compass of Tuscan literature becomes narrow and provincial, and then one has, perhaps for the first time in Italy, a dialect literature in the true and proper sense of the word, one founded, that is, on the conscious employment of a language of inferior status.[17]

Nonetheless, Tuscan was gradually supplying a recognizable baseline for a northern lingua franca. Such a situation makes for an ambivalent jealous pride; Dionisotti sums up the linguistic situation of the early Renaissance: "non i Toscani conquistano il resto dell'Italia, bensì il resto dell'Italia conquista esso la Toscana e ne rivede e spartisce a suo modo il patrimonio" [the Tuscans do not conquer the rest of Italy, but rather the rest of Italy conquers Tuscany and revises and divides up, in its own way, the Tuscan patrimony].[18] Dionisotti's summary presents the historical rebuttal to Machiavelli's optimism about Florence. When a dialect thus becomes a lingua franca it suffers these losses and invasions and falls into nostalgia for old purities and privacies. This is the linguistic aspect of a general cultural transition into which modern Florentine drama was born. It is not surprising, then, that we can recognize in Machiavelli a clear analogy between his linguistic polemic and his dramaturgical practice. Purity maintained through privacy is the crucial concern of the heroine of *La mandragola* in confronting her life-altering adventures.

Machiavelli's translation of *L'Andria*, written and rewritten shortly before the *Discorso* (current scholarship generally supports 1518–20) was, in spite of recent editorial claims,[19] not effectively transmuted into a Florentine text or context. There are small movements between an early, rather literal translation, written on the run, and a later and freer version: Tuscanisms such as "Io sono diventato pichino" [I am utterly done in] or "a fiaccacollo" [breakneck] (3.4), and ostentatious overuse of the (almost enclitic) Florentine pronoun

Florence

"e'." And there is the more socially circumstantial threat that Simo will send Davo off to cut and hoe in the fields rather than be assigned to grind in Terence's original mill (1.2). But these details do not represent that revolution promised by the nearly stillborn essay on the language. And *being* stillborn in the Renaissance, it was a text not likely available to Grazzini or Cecchi. Yet both must have sensed its tenor in Machiavelli's detailed descriptive and linguistic Florentinisms in *La mandragola*.

In the later *Cliǯia* one could observe an anomaly in the fact that the Florentine servant-parasite Pirro, that the farm supervisor Eustachio from Machiavelli's Greve, speak with fewer *fiorentinismi* than Nicomaco, the Florentine merchant who is Machiavelli's quasi-homonymic image; this reminds one that class is no restriction upon the public privacy inherent in dialect. A Plautine story partly taken from the *Casina* becomes a vehicle for Florentine intracommunal conversation. This is true not only of the language of the *Cliǯia* but of its content, the self-exposure of Machiavelli's affair with Barbara Raffacani Salutati, which reversed the usual borrowing to turn the play into a species of novella, a representation, but a representation of local tale-telling, gossip about a scandal. These dramatic experiments would scarcely have constituted a parenthesis in Machiavelli's development, had he not written *La mandragola*, had he not placed in the midst of his dramatic writing this piece of homage to the tradition we are exploring, which inspired the later Florentine imitations in homage to his own contribution.[20]

Il motivo del travestimento . . . ha una forte incidenza nella *Mandragola*. . . . Le sue radici più profonde vanno cercate nella linfa nascosta di un mondo carnevalesco, come direbbe Bachtin, dove la maschera elude l'ordine costituito e celebra la festa del mutamento, dell'anarchia vitale e della giovanezza che si sostituisce alla sterilità in un rito di rinascita. . . . La commedia, scrive il Frye, si fonda sul passaggio ciclico dalla morte alla vita, dall'inverno alla primavera, . . . e quasi a sostegno della sua tesi anche la *Mandragola* termina con l'idea di una rinascita.

Secret Sharers in Italian Comedy

The motif of disguise . . . is very evident in *La mandragola.* . . . Its most profound roots are to be sought in the hidden sap of a carnevalesque world, as Bakhtin would say, where the mask eludes the established order and celebrates the festival of change, of vital anarchy, and of youth that replaces sterility in a rite of rebirth. . . . Comedy, writes Frye, is founded on a cyclical passage from death to life, from winter to spring, . . . and almost as if to confirm his thesis, *La mandragola* also ends with the idea of a rebirth.[21]

Ezio Raimondi's notable studies on *La mandragola* culminate in this impeccable wedding of traditions: Frye incorporated into Bakhtin. It places Machiavelli at the apex of those comic orders that achieve their own fullest triumph in the Renaissance. But Raimondi's formulation is a seductively elegant error that reveals the necessity of separating precisely what he has joined, an error made apparent by his own enthusiasm for order when one sets it in contrast with *La mandragola*'s offspring by Grazzini and Cecchi. Raimondi's insight and error together gave impetus to the analysis by Giulio Ferroni, which continues to provide the most searching reading of Machiavelli's seminal drama.[22] In brief, setting *La mandragola* in the full context of Machiavelli's political anthropology, Ferroni can view the play as a sweeping demonstration of the notion that *"mutazione,"* change, adaptability, is the instrumental trait crucial to living wisely. The *savio,* wise prince or wise woman, adapts at need. This is more than pragmatism, though, and far removed from cynicism, because it comes through adaptation of that oldest of classical and Christian shibboleths: *nosce teipsum,* know thyself. And the paradox at the heart of wisdom is that it knows itself only in a *"riscontro,"* in a revelatory encounter with its opposite: "la sapienza ha scoperto che le è concesso affermarsi solo nel rapporto al proprio contrario, . . . nella polemica insistente ed ambigua contro l'irrazionalità e la follia" [wisdom has discovered that it can only affirm itself in relation to its own contrary, . . . in the insistent and ambiguous struggle against irrationality and madness] (57). Without attempting to do justice to Ferroni's probing of the stages of interaction among the characters, one can observe that he finds Callimaco undermined as a natural

Florence

99

protagonist by his dependency upon the parasite Ligurio, by his history as one who fled a troubled Florence for a life of Parisian leisure, and by his general indecisiveness. He less changes than is changed in circumstance by others. It is Lucrezia who emerges from Ferroni's reading as the *savia,* the protagonist and proponent of that wisdom which, recognizing the stupidity and narrow self-serving inherent in Nicia, Sostrata, Timoteo—even Callimaco—comes to honest self-knowledge through these *riscontri.* But she actually appears on stage in only two scenes before the final one:

Lucrezia è sempre lontana, spesso nominata ed esaltata con termini che ne mettono in rilievo l'isolamento . . . lo stesso momento definitivo della sua "mutazione" e del suo "riscontro" con la fortuna non si svolgerà sulla scena, ma sarà riferito da lontano dal soddisfatto Callimaco.

Lucrezia is always distant, often named and exalted with terms that emphasize her isolation . . . the very definitive moment of her "transformation" and of her "confrontation" with fortune does not unfold on the stage, but will only be recounted at a distance by the satisfied Callimaco. (81)

What makes Ferroni's reading of particular interest to our exploration of the anti-Plautine subgenre to which *La mandragola* makes such a major contribution is the critic's extension of this distancing to a consideration of Machiavelli's manipulation of his audience: "Lucrezia si trova, in parte, fuori della scena, a guardarla, come gli spettatori" [Lucrezia finds herself, to some extent, offstage, watching it like the spectators] (81). And with this, one recalls the prologue, which, as Ferroni observes (36–39), divides the audience into types parallel to those within the play, into *sciocchi* and *savii.* The former will denigrate the drama's action because they will be as inflexible as Nicia, so circumscribed in experience as not to know if they are dead or alive ("Che non sa forse s'e' si è vivo ancora"). On the other hand, this prologue appeals to the ladies in the audience who will recognize their own wisdom reflected in that of Lucrezia; such spectators will hear both the joking and the serious irony behind the prologue's wish

Secret Sharers in Italian Comedy

that they may share Lucrezia's fate: "Fu da lui molto amata, / E per questo ingannata / Fu come intenderete, ed io vorrei / Che voi fussi ingannate come lei"[23] [She was much loved by him, / And for this was tricked, / As you will hear, and I wish / that you could be tricked as she was]. This is the only instance I am aware of in which the audience is drawn into collusion before the beginning as well as after the end of the dramatic action. The effect is to immediately undermine all the metaphoric structure of ritual renewal in both language and action that *La mandragola* shares with its Plautine legators.

One should recognize little indices of difference, insistences that Machiavelli embedded within the Boccaccian-Plautine matrix of his comedy. The initial, most quietly stated and startling, is the elimination of the juventus-senex combat, the generational tug-of-war upon which New Comedy allegedly depends for its postritual structure. Callimaco is thirty years old, and Messer Nicia, if a fool, is not so through senility: "se non è giovane, non è al tutto vecchio" [if he is not young, he is not completely ancient] (1.1; 63). It is a judgment all the more convincing for being spoken by Callimaco himself. Thus, one source of comedic structure has balked expectation at the beginning. The Parisian exile and the Florentine husband are set at some approximate parity in age. And when Callimaco, carelessly forgetting the consequence that he will be unavailable to enter Lucrezia's bed, volunteers to join Messer Nicia in finding a victim for the deadly fertility potion, he parallels his own fecklessness with that of Nicia himself (4.2). Two mature men intermeshed in their absurd fears and desire, being maneuvered toward mutual satisfaction by the pimp Ligurio, all disguised literally ("noi abbiamo tutti a travestirci" [we all have to disguise ourselves]; "voglio che tu ti storca el viso, che tu apra, aguzzi o digrigni la bocca" [I want you to twist up your face, open your mouth, purse your lips or grind your teeth] [4.2; 147–48]) as well as in their purposes. And those purposes involve secrets to be kept in perpetuity. Nicia will forever seal the lips of his ragged victim in the silence of the love-induced death he presupposes; Callimaco will become the permanent guest of Nicia and Lucrezia. It is the deepest irony that *La*

Florence

mandragola laminates fecundity and death in a plot wholly alien to the New Comedy structure of marriages and banquetings, of regeneration and the rebirthing of society.[24] In a testing maneuver akin to the Ephesian widow motif, the Florentine matron Lucrezia is pregnant not only, presumably, with a child, but with the seeds of Venus she carries within. As Machiavelli so well knew, with all the Renaissance, the lesser gods carry their natural antipodes in themselves, potent even when only potential.[25]

There is no need to rehearse again how fortune threads the play as a theme from first to last; it is this element that is as important as any in inducing the allegorical interpretations associating *La mandragola* with *Il principe*.[26] But it offers a level of entry into the extremely mixed tonality of the play's action. On the one hand we have the sense of a tale told (this only apparently modifies rejection of the novella as ancestor). Fido has observed how thoroughly the dizzying theatrical events of *La mandragola* take place offstage, how often we overhear a narration of events unseen.[27] This characteristic signature of narrative imprints a surprising fairy-tale ambience as one matrix of Machiavelli's fable. "Once upon a time" in Paris a man was allegorically promised access to Sleeping Beauty, promising, in turn, to wake her from a sterile trance. His very name, Guadagni (profits), carries the promise of success in the archetypal quest, and more because he is "un giovane" (not inconsistently with the strictures above, if we remember the mature audience addressed in *Il principe*), and Fortuna, "come donna, è amica de' giovani, perché sono meno respettivi, più feroci, e con più audacia la comandano"[28] [as a woman, is the friend of young men, because they are less respectful, more fierce, and command her with more audacity]. A man born to win fortune's sweepstakes, as he does. His prize is sought on the basis of sheer hearsay but is absolute, too. A Florentine in Paris had informed him of the most beautiful lady in the world: "E nominò Madonna Lucrezia, moglie di Messer Nicia Calfucci, alla quale dette tante laude e di bellezze e di costumi, che fece restare stupidi qualunche di noi; e in me destò tanto desiderio di vederla" [And he named Madonna Lucretia, wife of Messer Nicia Calfucci, to whom he gave so much praise both for beauty and behavior, that he left every one of us stupefied; and he awoke in me as much desire to see her] (1.1; 61–62). Youth, beauty, and desire mediated through a narrative. The quest, too, is absolute: there are no intervening wagers or taunts of conquest, the usual motive factors in these searches, as in Shakespeare's *Cymbeline*. No line of action could be quieter, more distant from the busy circles in which Cecchi would embed it in *L'assiuolo.*

But Machiavelli anchors his action also in a matrix of social cynicism. The *giovane* Callimaco Guadagni is only a promise of the *Prologo;* in the play he is neither destined prince nor young. And it is his middle-aged rival who, as the parasite Ligurio says at the outset, has been favored by fortune: "Io non credo che sia nel mondo el più sciocco uomo di costui; e quanto la fortuna lo ha favorito! Lui ricco, lui bella donna, savia, costumata e atta a governare un regno" [I do not believe there can be a more foolish man in the world than this one; and how much fortune has favored him! He's rich; he has a beautiful, wise, refined woman, and fit to rule a kingdom] (1.3; 72). *La mandragola* opens upon this reversal raised on the back of Callimaco's mock fairy tale (1.1 and 2), and immediately fills it in with Nicia's thick local color as he boasts of his provincial travels from the cupola (one recalls the echoes in Grazzini and Cecchi) to the sea. The thickness of detail is reminiscent (or predictive) of nothing so much as Goldoni's social comedy in the villeggiatura trilogy, as Nicia remonstrates against the need to turn the domestic world upside down in transporting Lucrezia to the fertility-enhancing baths ("Perché io mi spicco mal volentieri da bomba. Dipoi, l'avere a travasare moglie, fante, masserizie, ella non mi quadra" [Because I drag myself away from my routines very unwillingly. Then, to have to transport wife, maidservants, household stuff, this doesn't square with me] (1.2; 69). Two plays in one, then, or more, the third being the classical sounding-board of the Lucretian legend with all its (here) ironic content. But it is a Florentine play, and it is perhaps in an older Florentine tradition that Machiavelli hones his ironies and echoes.

Florence

At the opening of act 4, Callimaco offers a short discourse that might be read as a wry response to the twenty-fifth chapter of *Il principe:* "Ed è vero che la fortuna e la natura tiene el conto per bilancio: la non ti fa mai un bene, che all'incontro non surga un male" [And it is true that fortune and nature balance accounts: they never do you a good turn, without some misfortune coming up on the other side] (4.1; 137). A love-induced impetuosity grasps opportunity in the guise of good fortune, even when experience teaches that it may lead only to future suffering. "Da ogni parte mi assalta tanto desìo d'essere una volta con costei, che io mi sento, dalle piante de' piè al capo, tutto alterare" [On every side such desire of being with this woman just one time assails me that I feel myself, from the soles of my feet to my head, all changed] (4.1; 139), laments Callimaco. *Patiens* alternating with *furor,* these poles of inspired love union and the suffering of separation were examined and reexamined by Machiavelli's older Florentine contemporary Marsilio Ficino. The latter may have inspired Machiavelli to embed a rich echo from the local ambience in the metaphoric structure of *La mandragola* with ironic and cynical intent. Callimaco yearns only for a single experience of love; and this is what Ficino had taught Cosimo and Lorenzo de'Medici to expect, at best, in his local platonic lessons on transcendence of the corporeal through the fury of love: "D'essere una volta con costei." [29] Machiavelli's is the profane echo of the ecstasy Ficino had promised the patient lover of God: a momentary resplendence illuminating the terrestrial night. And the action of *La mandragola* is enveloped in this darkness. Timoteo, tormented by his own venality, makes an easy peace that recalls the darkened bedrooms of *La venexiana,* of *L'assiuolo,* of Callimaco and Lucrezia: "la cosa conviene che stia secreta" [the business should be kept secret]. This conclusion, supported by Timoteo's generalization, is supported in turn by his dealings with earlier, perhaps even more deadly feminine innocents: "tutte le donne hanno alla fine poco cervello, e come n' è una che sappi dire due parole, e' se ne predica, perché in terra di ciechi chi v'ha un occhio è signore" [when you come down to it, all women are short of brains and, if one of them can string two words together, they all sing her praises, because in the land of the blind the one-eyed man is master] (3.9; 126).

Love has a double affect, then: it rushes blindly toward fortune as young men should do, grasping the moment; but in the oscillations of desire it learns to suffer (as well as triumph) in silence, *patire* in both senses. The almost oxymoronic quality of this favorite Florentine word, omnipresent from Ficino to folk advice (*"paẓienẓa!"*; Siro utilizes the popular version upon Nicia, "abbiate pazienzia" [2.5; 92]), is summed up in Callimaco's anguished cry of desire: "Se io potessi dormire la notte, se io potessi mangiare, se io potessi conversare, se io potessi pigliare piacere di cosa veruna, io sarei più paziente ad aspettare el tempo" [If I were able to sleep at night, if I could eat, if I could converse, if I could take pleasure in anything at all, I would be more patient in awaiting the time] (1.3; 74). And the pressure of time infuses *La mandragola* from the beginning, when Ligurio explains to Callimaco why Nicia will not discover that the newcomer is not really a physician: "la brevità del tempo . . . farà o che non ne ragionerà, o che non sarà tempo a guastarci el disegno" [the brevity of the time . . . will work so that either he will not think about it, or that it will be too late to spoil our design] (1.3; 77). This anxious imminence of time threads the play until it bursts out in Timoteo's audacious invitation of the audience into dramaturgical collusion with the lovers by fusing the interlocking spaces of time in the auditorium and in the plot: "voi spettatori, non ci appuntate: perché in questa notte non ci dormirà persona, sì che gli Atti non sono interrotti dal tempo" [you spectators, don't reproach us: because tonight no one will sleep, so the acts are not interrupted by time] (4.10; 170). Indeed, in Callimaco's opening exposition about how he was brought to abandon his Parisian comfort in a search for Lucrezia, he had intertwined time and fortune: "parendo alla Fortuna che io avessi troppo bel tempo" [it appearing to Fortune that I was having too good a time] (1.1; 60). Only a few lines later, though, long before the bed substitution has been plotted, Callimaco expresses a patient optimism in time's comprehensive turns: "Di cosa nasce cosa, e il tempo la governa" [One thing gives birth to another, and time governs this] (1.1; 67).

Florence

His faith in mutability is justified in the ripeness of time when Callimaco and Lucrezia together embrace their mutual good fortune.

"Secondando e' tempi" is a repeated phrase of both Machiavellian condemnation and advice, at least from the date of his cynical letter of 9 March 1498 talking of Savonarola and on throughout his counsel to Soderini and to the lesser Medici. It is unlikely, then, that the etymology was lost on Machiavelli when he has Fra Timoteo instruct Lucrezia to sleep with Callimaco in obedience to her husband: "ottemperare in questo caso al marito vostro" [to be obedient in this case to your husband] (3.11; 131–32).[30] One can, as Ligurio promises Callimaco in honor of his *cognome*, wait for a win when day turns to night; patience and time are the plague and the fulfillment of love: "tu te la guadagni in questa notte" [you gain her in this night] (4.2; 150). Servants, parasites, wives, husband, and lovers collude in the labyrinth represented by Callimaco's warning toward the climax: "ciò che tu vedi, senti o odi, hai a tenere secretissimo" [whatever you see, feel or hear, you must keep in the utmost secrecy] (4.5; 156).

It is Fra Timoteo, restlessly awaiting news of the outcome of the night's adventure (an adventure now stretching into an indefinite future, in spite of Callimaco's once limited hopes), who returns the metaphors in one phrase to the quotidian and ironically displaced symbol simultaneously. Returns them to the churching of classical Lucrezia and the unseen miracles of love: "andai in chiesa ed accesi una lampana che era spenta, mutai uno velo ad una Nostra Donna che fa miracoli" [I went into the church and lit a lamp that had gone out, (and) changed the veil on a Madonna who works miracles].[31]

Giovan Battista Fagiuoli: Degeneration as Revolution

I have chronologically reversed the history of dramatic invention in Cinquecento Florence in order to allow Cecchi's and Grazzini's original turns upon *La mandragola* to stand free as just that: originals that challenged a uniquely authoritative model. Let us now contemplate a later Florentine play that is generally asserted to belong in the mainstream of its author's pre-Goldonian corpus. But let us replace it into the larger "mainstream" of comedic structure that, with Florentine provincialism, one may call Machiavellian. Giambattista Fagiuoli's *Non bisogna in amor correre a furia* [In Love, One Should Not Run Furiously] is the play, written at the dawn of the eighteenth century. Before examining its heritage in the tradition from *La mandragola*, in the broader tradition of secrecy as form, let us pause to consider the problematic relations a text can exhibit between continuity and degeneration. Or, to put the matter in more problematic terms, whether degeneration of a cultural form is not as aptly observed as its regeneration. One is pointing the discussion here, of course, to the emergence of Goldoni from the tapestry of Italian Renaissance comedy whose weave we are tracing toward a recognition of his centrality.

Degeneration is a falling away from the generic norms, from one's kind, in the literary sense, with all its pejorative implications. It is a moldy history, often retold, that sees the late Seicento, the *barocco*, as a dramatic degeneracy from which Goldoni and Gozzi would rescue Italian comedy by their respective reactions. But should one play with the interplay of words that often lose their antinomy in time, we are faced with the proposition that regeneration implies some antigeneric status in a prior history of a corpus that was degenerate. We realize that for Goldoni's triumph a stage of dramatic degeneration was necessary. The pejorative implications, however, disappear at this point. If the late Seicento had not become centrifugal to the comedic history we have been sketching, the Settecento playwrights would have been left, like Grazzini and Cecchi, to do arabesques upon a form mastered by Machiavelli two centuries and a half earlier. Whatever intentionality there was or was not, the "pre-Goldoniani" — Maggi, Fagiuoli, Nelli — would not have been pre-Goldoniani unless they had been, to purloin a term, "contra-Machiavels." But it was in just this "degenerate" drama that the revolution within form would take its necessary origin.[32] From this perspective Fagiuoli appears as, if not a major dramatist, a major necessity, an indispensable parent of that regeneration of Italian theater in which Goldoni would not only inherit but transcend Machiavelli and *his* own forebears.

Fagiuoli was, like Grazzini, Cecchi, and Machiavelli, an encyclopedia of self-conscious Florentinisms. Like his predecessors, he was a provincial poet winking at his own extravagant regionalism.[33] Like Cecchi, he was an exponential expander of plot. *Non bisogna in amor correre a furia* in its skeletal structure is parodic of New Comedy formulae; Aretino (*L'ipocrito*) may have tried on five sets of reconciliations within a twenty-four-hour time scheme, but Fagiuoli mechanically raised the ante dramaturgically, doubling all of the cast staples of New Comedy: two senes, two innamorati, two innamorate, two servants, who would all interlace and yet overcome their misunderstandings. These misunderstandings would be expressed and controlled within that other relevant context of Tuscan proverbial wisdom that we have seen at work in Machiavelli's mid-century heirs. But the proverbial wisdom is revealed as a cracked vessel itself when it tries to house the action of *Non bisogna*.

Fra Timoteo dropped a veil over the eyes of the virgin; Fagiuoli continues the metaphor in a second Florentine proverb, "la cagna frettolosa fa i cani ciechi"[34] [the hasty bitch produces blind puppies]. Inured to the Dantesque and later Florentine world of metaphoric light, Cecchi, Machiavelli, and Fagiuolo inverted it. If one proverb announces that a thing given birth in haste produces blind results, the title proverb reminds one that Ficino may have been hasty in his vision, that love, too, has need of a little caution. Even as Ficino and he were about to die, Bernard Bellincioni, another artist kept by Lorenzo de'Medici, had written Fagiuoli's title into the language in his *sonetti:* "correre a furia," explains the Crusca, "vale operare sconsideratamente" [to run furiously is equivalent to acting without consideration], or, as Bellincioni puts it, "Chi corre a furia, tende rete al vento" [Who runs furiously, casts a net for the wind]. Fury,

Secret Sharers in Italian Comedy

then, from Ficino to Fagiuoli, is love in a hurry. After all, Ficino was unwilling even to await death's union of lovers with their God.

Fagiuoli's old proverbs were applied to new mores, to a society become complacent toward the institution of the *cicisbeo,* the married woman's extramarital social escort and confidant. This institution, indeed, was at the center of an early comedy by Fagiuoli whose Pirandellesque title encapsulates the institution itself, Fagiuoli's plotting tendency, and the tradition of secrecy as form: *Ciò che pare non è, ovvero il cicisbeo sconsolato* [That Which Seems Is Not, or The Disconsolate Cicisbeo] (1708).

The contemporaneous psychological setting, the clash between Amselmo, a father who is *soffistico,* a disgruntled and displaced champion of the old ways, pre-Goldonian *rustego,* and Orazio, the son, participating in *la moda,* life sophisticated in a quite opposite sense of the word[35]—this generational conflict and its inherent social ambiguities subscribe the play among the more popular precursors of Goldoni's comedy.[36] The title, when restricted to plot, is of little interest for the Florentine tradition we have been scanning: the father supposes his daughter-in-law to be a sexual conspirator with the fatuous cicisbeo until it is discovered that his own supposedly pious daughter has, instead, secretly played the part of deceiver all along. Here the secrets will out with the closure of plot, and one recognizes another play in the Plautine mode of *suppositi,* distant in its formal assumptions from the particular Florentine version of silence one conveniently labels Machiavellian. One can discern, though, Fagiuolo's attraction to the antirevelatory forms when the son expatiates on the modern husband's obligation to quiet collusion. It is the son, practitioner of the new punctilios of honor in the modern mode, who delineates the unspoken assumptions of husband, wife, and cicisbeo; silence is the sign of superiority: "Sarei notato di troppo pusillanimità se ritornassi dalla mia sposa, quando v'è altra persona: e mostrerei scioccamente, o d'esserne inamorato più del dovere, o che una pazza gelosia, senza ragione alcuna, mi

Florence

sovertisse la mente"[37] [I would be noted for too much pusillanimity if I should return to my wife, when there is another person there: and foolishly show myself either to be enamored of her more than I should, or that my mind was subverted by a mad jealousy without any basis] (1.3; 187).

This husband's stance reemerges as the plot node around which action and title are constructed in *Non bisogna in amor correre a furia*. But in the latter play it ties together the polarities of *furia* and *flemma,* the blindly precipitous and the blandly cautious, into a problematic plotting of contrasts, of psychological plottings and counterplots.

Dottore Bartolo, a macaronic lawyer recognizable from the commedia mask, makes an agreement with his friend Pancrazio to exchange their daughters in marriage to one another. Thus, not only will their aging lust be accommodated, but they will also save the annoyance of offering dowries with the young women. This opening scene, with its fulsome professions of friendship, is immediately succeeded by a mechanical repetition as Orazio and Lelio, two more appropriate young suitors to the same women, stress their own friendship and parallel desires. The women themselves, Florinda (daughter of the Dottore and beloved of Orazio) and Isabella (daughter of Pancrazio and beloved of Lelio), rebuff their fathers' plan and warn their lovers. The foursome agree that the young men will offer to take the daughters without dowry, in the hope that money rather than love guides the older men. But while all is apparent harmony and vows of faith among the young, Orazio admits privately to some doubts: "Bisogna dunque fondarsi sulla costanza di queste femmine, le quali, o minacciate o sgridate de'genitori, chi sa come potranno resistere. *'Femmina è cosa mobil per natura'* " [It is necessary therefore to rely upon the constancy of these women, who, should they be threatened or scolded by their parents, who knows how well they will be able to resist. "Woman is a thing fickle by nature"]. Lelio denies the proverbial premise in this particular instance, but undercuts his own confidence when he temporarily qualifies his assertion that their *amanti* will remain faithful: "non pensiamo *per adesso* più oltre" [*for now* let us not think ahead] (1.6; 317; italics mine).

The complications are drawn up from deliberately preposterous circumstances. Isabella injures her hand and so asks Florinda to write a love letter to Lelio by dictation. Florinda, in turn, asks Isabella to have her maid take for repair a box containing Orazio's miniature portrait. The doublings of plot are drawn into this prop: Isabella owns an exact duplicate of the box, hers containing Lelio's picture. The servants Brandello and Lisetta allow letter and box to fall into the hands of the wrong lovers, and Lelio and Orazio rush to accuse one another and the women of treachery. The men reject their *amanti;* the women in rash revenge agree to marry the old men. All four soon repent. Meanwhile, the oldsters eavesdrop upon the young foursome's complacent exchange of ideas of marriage (ideas much like those espoused by the husband in *Ciò che pare non è*) and feel relieved to have escaped such a domestic trial by permitting Lelio and Orazio to marry their daughters upon the dowry terms they had originally drawn up for one another.

This familiar-sounding plot takes on a psychological dimension, however, seldom found in intrigue drama. The beadroll of Florentine proverbs that is strung through the play embeds the principals' intuitions in the unexamined popular wisdom. Aging lust ("sotto la cenere più fredda, si cova il fuoco più vivo" [under the coldest ashes, smolders the hottest fire] [315]; "non tiro a merle, ch'abbian passato il Po" [I don't aim at blackbirds that have flown over the Po] [300]), luck ("nata vestita" [born fully dressed] [323]), testing will ("alla prova si scortica l'asino" [in testing one flays the ass] [310]), and testing gratitude (a servant "a'tempi d'oggi . . . lava il capo all'asino" [in these times . . . washes the head of the ass, i.e., does a good turn to one who cannot realize it] [358]) — such common experiences are capsulated in common figures. But there is one group of proverbialisms that carries the psychological weight of the plot.

Love blinds, of course, but so does spiteful revenge, the dark side of love. Determining to marry Pancrazio in order to punish the

Florence

rash jealousy of Orazio ("un marito geloso, è una furia d'Averno" [a jealous husband is a fury from hell (Avernus)] [367]), Florinda turns again to the eyes in ironic mockery of the Petrarchan metaphor: "Purché si cavino all'avversario due occhi, non disdice cavarne uno a se stesso" [Provided that two eyes can be gouged out of the adversary, there's nothing wrong with plucking out one of one's own] (366). The two strands intertwine causally. "La cagna frettolosa fa cani ciechi": the bitch botches her litter because she is "frettolosa," as is Florinda, who, in a rush to judgment, herself repeats the folly of which she accuses her lover: "Voglio gastigare la furia inconsiderata d'Orazio" [I want to punish the inconsiderate fury of Orazio] (2.15; 365). *Furia* and *fretta:* "l'abbiam corsa" [we have run] (3.12; 389), Lelio realizes; "siam tutt' a due corse in fretta" [we have both run headlong] (3.16; 395), Isabella admits to Florinda. *But,* claims Fagiuoli's title, love need not run blindly and at full tilt into disaster; and the title sentiment serves also to close the action as the principals gather together. Lelio and Isabella could be speaking for them all when he says, "Ecco rimesso in dolce calma quella fiera tempesta" [Now that fierce tempest has been restored into sweet calm], and she replies, "Che fu suscitata dalla vostra frettolosa passione" [Which was stirred up by your hasty passion]. Acknowledging this, Lelio closes by giving the title its full weight of authority as a statement of human control, of caution foreign to the traditions of crossed love: "Non *bisogna* in amor correre a furia."

What deterrent from disaster have these very modern lovers learned? *Flemma* is Lelio's word that comes closest to expressing a whole context of caution, of suspended judgment that counterbalances the varieties of *furia* (3.11; 385). Indeed, even as Lelio is entering his state of jealousy over Orazio's misplaced portrait, he concludes the first act with a counterpull toward rationality: "vo' sospender per ora ogni sinistra credenza" [I want to suspend for now every sinister suspicion] (1.16; 336). Later Orazio will reinforce this sentiment: "sospendiamo l'ire e i sospetti, finché non si sentano Florinda, e Isabella" [let's suspend anger and suspicion, until we hear from Florinda and Isabella] (2.10; 354–55). The hurried accusations, the spontaneous, immediate reactions of vindictive spite — these are not necessary (*non bisogna correre*) fires to temper love's shafts. But they have been perpetrated and (says Isabella) must be covered up to make the rashness of erring love itself appear a thing of value; citing yet another proverb, she says, "vendiamo loro il Sol di Luglio" [let's sell them the sun in July] (3.16; 398). Appearance, then, is all. But all appearance is not a faithful criterion for behavior; if the title phrase from another play is never explicit in this one, its inferential presence is ubiquitous: "ciò che pare non è." The mistaken judgments made in a fury serve happily to demonstrate the folly of believing what one sees when blinded by love. "Happily," because this lesson can be used to mask the secrets of marriage in a complacency as blinding as ardor.

This structuring theme of secret collusion branches out into the whole play from a beginning below stairs, in the love of the zanni Brandello for the maid Lisetta:

Lisetta: Ma quando sarò tua moglie, vuo'tu esser geloso?
Brandello: Di verno, come dire, sarò geloso, e anche gelato,
    se non avrò da scaldarmi.
Lisetta: Dico, se avrai sospetto di me.
Brandello: Di che cosa?
Lisetta: Che so io; se per disgrazia tu mi vedessi guardare
    un altro, parlargli, fargli cortesie?
Brandello: E così, che male è egli? Anzi questo è bene,
    che la moglie guardi, e parli, e faccia cortesie;
    se nò sarebbe cieca, mutola e malcreata.
Lisetta: O bravo: così ti voglio; far come fanno gli altri mariti . . .

Lisetta: But when I am your wife, will you be jealous?
Brandello: In winter, so to speak, I'll be jealous [*geloso*], and frozen [*gelato*] too, if I don't have some way to warm up.
Lisetta: I mean, will you be suspicious of me?

Florence

113

Brandello: Of what?

Lisetta: What can I say; if, by mischance, you should see me look at another man, speak with him, do him courtesies?

Brandello: And what harm is there in behaving like that? To the contrary, it's a good thing for a wife to look, speak, and do favors; if not, she would be blind, mute, and bad-mannered.

Lisetta: Oh, bravo! this is the way I want you; acting just as the other husbands do . . . (1.10; 328–29)

Sisters under the skin, Lisetta and Florinda agree that "un marito geloso, è una furia d'Averno," and an outdated one at that, "la moda" being punctilious only in ignoring what secret life may lie sinisterly beneath appearances:

Le maritate, io sento adesso, che tutte vivono con intera libertà, godendo insieme una somma pace co' lor consorti: e se vengon ossequiate e servite ad ogni ora in casa, e fuori in ogni luogo da giovanotti avvenenti e galanti, con cui non abbia attenenza di parentela, o necessità di negozio; non ostante son da'mariti accolti, come familiari ed amici; perlopiù come benefattori o compari, non mai, né men per ombra, avuti in sospetto d'amanti.

I hear now, that all married women live in entire liberty, enjoying together a complete peace with their consorts: and if they are waited upon and served at every hour, at home and in every place outside, by handsome and gallant young men with whom they have neither a family connection or the necessity of commerce; in spite of all this they are received by their husbands as familiars and friends; for the most part as benefactors or cronies, and never, not even distantly, suspected of being their lovers. (2.15; 367)

So Florinda explains modern life to Isabella, anticipating their gay "libertà" when they marry the hapless older men: "Non dubitate, viveremo lieti e felici co' nostri cari vecchietti: né ci mancheranno lusinghe per menargli pel naso a nostro piacere" [Never fear, we will live gaily and happily with our dear little old men: nor will we be short of schemes to lead them by the nose as we please] (368). The young women are mistaken in this vision, having forgotten that (like the *rustego* father in *Ciò che pare non è*) the Dottore and Pancrazio are of an older patriarchal generation of locked doors and marital surveillance. Secrets revealed and secrets accepted, the overheard and the overlooked: these become the thematics of Fagiuoli's play as well as its structural conclusion. The older men eavesdrop upon a reconciliation among the four young moderns in which the women dictate the rights of marriage. One need not append names to comprehend the general litany: "sarete più sospettoso / Mai più" [will you be suspicious anymore / Never more]; "vi verrebbe più voglia d'esser geloso. / Darò bando a questo pensiero in eterno" [should you ever feel like being jealous / I will exile this thought eternally]; "E se quando fuste mio marito, tornando a casa ci trovaste altri in mia conversazione? / Avvisato di questo, subito tacitamente mi partirei per non turbarla; né ardirei in quella di comparire, per non incorrer la taccia di malcreato" [And if, when you are my husband, you should return home and find others in my company? / Warned of this, I should depart immediately without saying a word, so as not to disturb you; nor would I dare to appear there, so as not to incur the reputation of boorishness] and so on (3.18; 401–3).

These promises of a secretive future draw the old men forward to reveal themselves and to cede their daughters to the young *amanti* with relief at their own narrow escape ("O guà, come si piglia moglie a'tempi d'oggi!" [O, pity, the way one takes a wife in these times!], cries Pancrazio).

The old generation gets the money, the young women get license for secret amours, and the young men get plucked as their haste into jealousy creates an equal haste into complacency; *furia* and *flemma* in the end seem equally disastrous to the comic harmony of the outcome, seem in the end indistinguishable.

Florentine drama and the secret refusal of structural closure it incorporated moved a long way in the two centuries separating Machiavelli and Fagiuoli. The latter's mechanical redoublings (*raddoppiamenti*), his substitution of metaphoric proverbs for individuated motivation, a falling-off of resonance—all of these elements

Florence

justify in some long historical view the consensus that Fagiuoli and his compeers at the beginning of the Settecento represent a degeneration in comic achievement. But, as argued at the beginning of this glance at Fagiuoli's grasp of the Machiavellian tradition in Florentine comedy, his work provided a necessary bridge, not the only one certainly, but one of the most consciously developed, by which our tradition could cross from one master to another, from Machiavelli to Goldoni.

Il manco male:
Maggi's Meneghino in Milan

" *M*eneghino": historical conjecture suggests the origin of the name in the patronizing use of the diminutive of Domenico in association with the Milanese vanity of hiring Sunday servants for parade even among the lower levels of society. The origin of the role is conjecturally traced to Nicolò Barbieri's commedia dell'arte masque of Beltrame. But sources aside, Meneghino became identified with the late-blooming zanni developed in Carlo Maria Maggi's corpus of plays focused upon Meneghino's dialect and presence as the most resonant voice of a dialogic cacophony.[1] I use the Bakhtinian term to emphasize the inconclusive structure of Maggi's dramas, a structural paradox inasmuch as Meneghino has emerged from his shadowy background to become a regional mask without infiltrating the commedia dell'arte troupes. He is a creature of words, a singular creation in the Seicento: a character theatrically successful without action. No Arlecchino this; just a spokesman of Maggi's sense of dialect vividness. Vividness: the cultural expression of life through talk.

Milan was outside the mainstream of the comedic continuities we can follow from early origins in Florence or the Veneto, Maggi, his city, and its dialect being under the pressure toward denaturalization from a long French dominance.[2] With Fagiuoli, Maggi is catalogued among the pre-Goldoniani but, not surprisingly, also among the rebellious importers of Molière and the *comédie italienne*. Justifiable, within the confines of such historical lines, is Maggi's relegation to a minor role in accounts of Italian drama. Placed within the comedic strand we have been following among his predecessors, though, Maggi emerges as a pivotal dramatist whose rank is not easily determined, whose work is not facilely comparable to that of any figure in the history of Italian drama after Ruzante, not exclusive of Goldoni himself. Maggi's corpus creates a culture: Meneghino as language, as character, as mask, henceforth would be the popular face of Milan. Without the precedents offered the Venetian and Florentine commediografi, without immediate successors to his dialect experiments, Maggi is sui generis—or would seem so did we not know that his work is illuminated by that of the other skeptics who refused to attend the optimistic Plautine feast. But nowhere has the structure of the secrecy been so explicitly announced as an antidote to classical commedia erudita as by Maggi.[3]

The plot of *Il manco male* is triple, a looser version of the testing in Goldoni's *La locandiera:* three suitors, Panurgo (with all the name implies) mediating for them with the young widow Pandora. Who could doubt that the secrets would be released from the dramatic box, would allow us to relax into the old all-revealing plot? Anyone would, of course, who took the title, *Il manco male,* seriously, or took seriously the first (Italian) prologue. Mario Apollonio made a plot summary as valuable for its conclusion as for its brevity:

I pretendenti di Pandora sono Trasone bravo, Fileride litigante, e Don Filotimo nobile ambizioso; la conclusione è che tutti falliscono le loro miré, ma pure evitano il peggiore; e Pandora si ritirerà nel "collegio delle vedove." . . . Tutto rifluisce dunque nelle posizioni iniziali. . . .[4]

The pretenders to Pandora's hand are Trasone the bully, Fileride the litigant, and Don Filotimo the ambitious noble; the conclusion is that all fail in their aims, but nonetheless avoid the worst; and Pandora will retire into the "college of widows." . . . Everything flows back, therefore, into the initial positions. . . .

Panurgo, the trickster tricked; the suitors resettled where they had begun; the widow returned to the *collegio* whence she had come seeking a liberator who never came.[5] This is the comic history emergent from Panurgo's frustrated result after he elicits from Pandora, whom he serves as financial adviser, a blank signed form, a carte blanche which he dangles before them to manipulate all the suitors. He shrugs as the adventure begins: "E se non mi riesce / Il mio fin principale, / Mi potrò consolar co 'l Manco male"[6] [And if I cannot gain / My principal end, / I will still console myself with the lesser evil] (1.30–32).

"Manco male," "manch maè"; the satisfaction that things are not worse, the settling for small gains against the spectacular possibility—the idiom stitches together the linguistic dissonances of the play as a structural rhythm so strong that it is even woven into the musical interludes (pp. 29, 61, 62, 75, 82, 119, 120, 124, 152, 154, 184, 200, 229–31). But set within this dull backing is the glittering promise—everyone evokes it from everyone else—of profitable secrecy. Through a myriad of ploys all parties seek their personal hidden treasure and settle for a standoff. The single exception that proves the rule is a subplot of servants' sexual tilting between a malaprop, Gelino, and Pandora's maid, Cricca, which eventuates in the only consummated marriage. It is as though the old happy plot paradigm discovered the last quarters for conclusiveness below stairs when modern comedy had withdrawn hope from a widow and her three suitors.

"Ve voi dir on secrett; / Ma, car vù, tegnì strett" [I'm going to tell you a secret; / But, my dear, keep it close] (1.534–35) might be placed as an epigraph to *Il manco male*. Panurgo is the master spokesman, promoting secrecy as well as the sublimation of desires; *his* cue phrase as busy manipulator might be the assurance that he is "sicuro del secreto in voi depongo / Il mio libero senso" [sure of secrecy, in you I deposit / my meaning openly] (2.26–27). Dicearco, mediator of difficulties and potential bridegroom, falls into Panurgo's web of secrets partially aware: "Qualche equivoco io temo" [I fear some trick] (3.294); this fuzziness reveals his simplicity when he ex-

Meneghino in Milan

plains to Pandora's aunt the late-arriving realization that his role is that of an intriguer instrumental within the plotting of *sciocchi*. With remorse he laments, "perché segreto sia fuori di sua casa" [it will remain a secret outside of the house] (3.692). One has in Dicearco a venial lay Fra Timoteo, caught up in a deceptive society quite by surprise. It is a society of *manco male* personified in Meneghino, joker and complainer but, at bottom, as Ireneo Sanesi calls him, "bonario sopportatore del male quando possa, tollerandone uno, evitarne uno peggiore"[7] [a good-natured sufferer of misfortune when, by tolerating one evil, he can avoid a worse one]. This draws one to the prologue, where the rationale of a new post-Plautine comedy is elaborated explicitly. Stage manager, maybe playwright, mostly just knowledgeable about comedy, the personification Manco Male, in pleading charity for his novel production, expresses Maggi's modest new sense of genre:

> Io sono un cuor sereno,
> Che fo del mal virtù,
> E, se non posso il più,
> Mi fo piacere, il meno,
> Se mal provvisto è il cuoco,
> Con dar sapore al poco
> Ancora nel digiun fo carnovale.
> Io sono per servirvi il Manco male.

> I am a serene heart,
> Who makes of the bad a virtue,
> And, if I can't get more,
> Content myself with less;
> If the cook is badly provisioned,
> By giving flavor to the little there is,
> Even in fasting I make carnival.
> I am Manco Male at your service.
> (Prologo primo, 11.25–32)

Secret Sharers in Italian Comedy

Manco Male has begun the critical discussion: "carnovale" is a comedic anachronism; but where there is no feast, one makes a festival with "make do." As one makes do with secret sexual arrangements, contrasted with comedy's quondam marriages celebratory of liminal renewal. The cook can always find a little seasoning for life. At the end, the unmasked Panurgo pleads with Dicearco to settle affairs quietly and allow him to depart without betraying his anticomic role as treacherous confidant: "Vi prego (e ben mi truovo assai con pena) / Risparmiarmi il rossor di questa Scena" [I pray you (and I find myself in great affliction) / to save me the embarrassment of this "scene"] (3.1390–91). They are his last words on stage, a reminder of the whole movement of this play away from the *lieto fine* toward, to borrow Mazzi's fine phrase for Sienese rusticali cited earlier, an ending "più o meno lieto." Meneghino will encapsulate the difference toward the close, when he foregrounds the contrasting rewards of comedic expectation and real life in this world of small winners and losers: "gnanch la Comedia me 'l conseia, / L'è manch maè quatter gnocch, che andà in galeia" [not even comedy advises it to me; / four knocks are lesser evils than going to prison] (3.831–32).

In *Il manco male* the buried but self-conscious antagonism between two conceptions of the comic frame becomes a litany of endorsement for the quieter new form identified with "manco male," as each suitor, like Meneghino, Panurgo, and Pandora herself, equates the phrase with the settling of ripples, dropped stones disappearing in the deep with diminishing trace. A secret hope (2.282, 928, 1045, 1163; 3.122, 299, 692, 1297) loses immediate force but extends in time. "Manco male": no great feast, no great loss.

"Guardemm a mi. Manch mael" [Look at me. Could be worse], responds the lusting Dottore in *Il Barone di Birbanʒa* [The Baron of Roguery] (2.363) as he is being drawn into a Boccaccian beffa that will leave him a soaked and wilted mock plumber in a nunnery garden. Meneghino himself in this play, emerging from a *laʒʒo* trick involving a false magician and spirits, cries out in the refusal of despair that the phrase embodies. He foresees criminal accusations and exile from his beloved city to the galleys but decides (for the moment), "L' è manco maè / El mett i gamb in spalla / . . . Pù prest che batt el Maer, batt el taccon" [It is the lesser evil / to beat a hasty retreat . . . / and, rather than taking to the seas, take to one's heels] (3.200–203). Better to take to one's heels than to the galleys — in spite of his immediate lyric nostalgia for Milano. Later, having lost his master's watch and his faith in a fellow servant, Meneghino settles with an interior dialogue summed up with "Manch maè" (3.427). The phrase, coming almost at the close of the last act, is an unexpected transplanting of the Meneghino from *Il manco male* into *Il Barone*. Here Meneghino, ambivalent satirist (as so many critics have observed) of the Milanese world he loves, is prepared to flee from it with surprising alacrity, as we have seen, settling for the lesser evil. Nothing in the structure of *Il Barone di Birbanza*, though, is made to support this complacent retreat of Meneghino from center stage — except its end. With the aid of a clever servant the false baron ("Il titolo ho comprato" [I have bought the title] [1.337]) hopes to make a fortune by way of conning competitors for the falsely supposed riches of his unattractive daughter, this little baronina being kept safely in a nunnery meantime. The flighty and wealthy widow Polissena covets the girl (and dowry) for her son Polidoro. But her trusted financial adviser, the (commedia dell'arte) Dottore Campana from Bologna, also lusts for the Baron's putative fortune — in diaphanous Mexican whale bones. Add an invented Genovese merchant suitor who is a mere phantom, a supposed Venetian Pantalone created from the clever zanni Tasca's manipulation of the "stupid" zanni Meneghino, and one has the essentials of this belated Cinquecento intrigue plot crossed with *commedia lazzi* and satiric set speeches both in and out of character. A Cinquecento comedy, but a little tilted, as Meneghino himself notices in the prologue:

Impunemanch el Mond va alla reversa,
E ognun sa, che co'l Mond
L'è inversae el Dizionaerij,
E che i paroll s'intenden al contraerij.

Secret Sharers in Italian Comedy

In any case, the world is topsy-turvy,
and everyone knows that along with the world
the dictionary is turned upside down too,
and that words are understood backwards.
(Prologo secondo, 156–59)

World and Word: we hear the dichotomy/equation throughout the Renaissance. It was usually associated with the two books of Revelation, and all knew that in the beginning was the Word. But now the world is upside down, and therefore not only the word but the relationship between word and world is reversed. Worldly actions now dictate the meaning of those words that once so definitively created the world. At the beginning of the seventeenth century, John Florio's Italian dictionary translated *rovesciare* (*riversare*) twice for Englishmen: "to turn the inside outward, to topsy-turvy." Remembering Florio, as well as Maggi's own allusion to dictionaries, to the false sense of finality in words, we may think of Maggi's second dramatic effort, *Il Barone,* as a product of generic rebellion explicitly taking the stance of turning something "topsy-turvy."

The young Polidoro is more able than the senex (*Il Dottore*) or the grasping mother to see through the dowry arrangements based upon greed. What is most remarkably "topsy-turvy," though, is the status of *la baronina*. The girl should be a merry seductress escaping exploitation, or a nubile girl waiting for all her lusciously ripe fruits to be plucked in lovers' paradise. But here *la giovane* is not only bony and ugly but speechless and hopeless of improvement. The presentation has inverted the youth-and-age syndrome where it was most sacrosanct in drama: the young woman is presented as unsought. The Dottore doesn't care—money of any sort, no matter how washed out its vessel, will serve his need. Polissena is equally coarse (and open) in closing her eyes in order to profit. Indeed, her description, which provides our first indirect encounter with *la baronina*, is a parodic Petrarchan female anatomy lesson (albeit mostly "translated" by Meneghino; 1.1–310). Polidoro recites against his mother and her minion the realistic vision of *la baronina*'s shortcomings in

Meneghino in Milan

the eyes of a putatively sacrificial suitor ("È una verghetta / Gialla, secca, sottile, e curva in cima" [She's a stick, / yellow, dry, thin and bent over on top] 1.167–68]). But in reply to Meneghino's expressed fear of familial discord, Polidoro reassuringly promises to retreat into peace obtained through inner reservations: "per acquetar mia Madre, / E perché più molesta a me non sia, / Fingerò d'inclinar" [in order to quiet my mother, / and so that she won't harass me anymore, / I will pretend to be attracted] (1.308). There is something missing in the comedic contract to verify Florio's other translation of *rovesciare* as "inside outward" as well. Maggi justifies this translation, however, in his intermezzo between the first and second acts. Apparenza and Povertà debate in traditional moral terms. Apparenza has counseled Povertà on the contemporary way of the world: "Chi fuori mostra il ver / Buon condottier non è. / Oggi è meglio saper / L'arte di far parer quel, che non è" [Anyone who displays his true nature is not a good guide. / Today it is better to know the art of false appearances]. But Povertà resignedly reminds her proud interlocutor that there is another turn upon his facile paradox:

> Ma poi questa è la disgrazia
> Della maschera mentita,
> Che l'inganno ha corta vita.
> Io la maschera guardando
> Ho perduta la persona.

> But then this is the misfortune
> of the false mask,
> That the trick itself is short-lived.
> I, in looking at the mask,
> Have lost sight of the person. (42–50)

"Ho perduta la persona": the mask devours the masker, and false appearance has become the universal norm.

There is also something missing in the center of *Il Barone di Birbanza* as comedy. The missing element is an attractive innamorata to counter Polissena's pressure, to create the threat the *baronina* scarcely offers to Polidoro's free choice; a daughter, a niece, or other foil to the Dottore; a confidante to whom she can open her own heart before the audience. Secrets thick upon one another seem to promise some such figure at the center of a comic explosion of unmaskings. But instead they dissipate into the spread of gossip: "Ma l'ho in secrett" [But I have it in secret] (2. 174), promises Tasca, but he knows how secrets are broadcast: "E perché delle donne / Già so l'usanza antiga, / Ghe l'ho ditt in secrett perché la 'l diga" [And because I already know / the ancient way of women, / I have told her in secret in order that she will spread it about] (2.402–4).

False dialects abound in the play, impersonations, false wealth— all the familiar counters of an old comedy. But in creating Meneghino, Maggi insisted upon becoming, like the Florentines, a dialect preservationist.[8] As we noted before, in dialect there is a natural centripetal tendency excluding the outsider. And this is precisely what Maggi did not exploit. The master of secrets at the heart of his play is Polidoro, who speaks only Italian. World and word are coming together as the confused effect of Babel is recreated in the guise of collusive silence.

Dottore Campana has signed a betrothal pact with the Baron; Polidoro has come to full awareness of the latter's con game and positions himself as adviser and go-between to help each victim of greed escape the other without exposing a *brutta figura*, that is, without embarrassment. He begins the denouement with what might be epigraph or close of *Il Barone*: "Un prudente, concorde, alto silenzio, / Come il fatto non fatto," he advises, "Per vostra pace, / E men vostro rossore io ve 'l tacea" [A prudent, unanimous, profound silence, / As if the thing done were not done, . . . For your peace of mind, / and to lessen your shame, I kept it from you] (3.636–41) He hides the compromised victims in adjoining rooms, moves between them like an innamorato usurping the role of a servant to two masters with dizzying agility: "lasciate ch'io / Sepelisca la cosa" [let me bury the thing] (3.659–60); tearing the incriminating documents to shreds, Polidoro justifies everyone, every action, insofar as "di quanto fra loro oggi è seguito, / Non sarà più parola, o ricordanza" [of what has happened between them today / there will be no other word or memory] (3.709–10). And the whole negotiation is carried on in whispers ("il Barone tira da parte Polidoro, e gli parla sotto voce"; "il Dottore tira da parte Polidoro, e gli parla sotto voce" [the Baron draws Polidoro aside, and whispers to him; the Doctor draws aside Polidoro and whispers to him] (3.69–99).

We may recall again that audience collusion that separates novella and drama: we hear in the theater the present, not a history. Maggi, by calling attention to the stage at the very moment of expected closure, rather than ignoring or evading this difference, opens it to conscious view. The baron has worked himself into old debts in a world offstage before he came on. Polidoro joins comedy, word, and world in the reversal Meneghino had suggested: when the Baron reminds Polidoro of "qualche creditor, che mi tormenta" [some creditor who torments me], the latter responds, "Questo è il difficil più. Cotesti nodi / La comedia non scoglie" [This is the most difficult. / Comedy cannot loosen these knots] (3.671–73). So what Polidoro says is not quite true: "Così tutta quiete / Finisce la Comedia" [Thus the comedy finishes, all passion spent] (3.716–17). There is our world beyond, beyond closure. The Baron has his threatening debts yet to deal with; *la baronina* returns to a bleak but undefined future wearing "la socca baretina" of a religious order (Isella points up a pun on another meaning, "abbandonata"). A quiet play, a disquieting future suggested, all in whispers, shadows, of Cinquecento formulae. No marriages, no feasts. Just a relief that in looking at the masks we have fared no worse: "la maschera guardando / Ho perduto la persona." As we noticed the Dottore saying at the beginning: "Guardemm a mi. Manch mael."

Casanova went to Rome as a potential young warrior of the church, escaped into the army, and made his way from that adventure into those others that became the autobiography of a life that no one had ever lived. It was an account that might have taken as epigraph a phrase from Maggi's *I consigli di Meneghino* [The Counsels of Meneghino]: "Vuij cuntavv on secrett de Ciarlatan" [I'm going to tell you a charlatan's secret] (Intermezzo secondo, 21). The charlatan Maggi invokes here is Democritus, and his "bell secrett" (43) is the trumpet with which he can hear the laughter of all mankind: "al tirè foeura on gran trombon de tolla / E 's comenzè a casciall per i oregg / De tutta quella folla, / Parlandegh in secrett par el trombon" [He took out a big tin trumpet, and commenced to stick it into the ears of all that crowd, speaking to them in secret through the trumpet] (34–37). These secret varieties of laughter are the entry into the varieties of worldly experience in the modern comedy that Baltraminna (personification, representative, little muse or "musetta" of Milanese mores) in the prologue presents as hunting out the vestiges of classical comedy. "Desmettì st'antigaja" [Cast off this antique] are the opening words of the First Prologue of *I consigli*. Laughter, then, is a symbolic key to character as it is revealed in comedy; the myth of Democritus is superbly placed at the center of the simple plot nodes of *I consigli di Meneghino*, Maggi's post–New Comedy. But the encyclopedia of satiric laughter is grafted with a balancing mode at the play's close when Meneghino, old, experienced, venal, wise, reacts to his young padrone's affection with restrained emotion, emotion restrained by that very rough metaphoric crudeness that simultaneously reveals its sentimental underside better than a softer overt rhetoric:

> Al me mett tanto s'cess,
> Che no poss gnanch respond.
> Ma con sti gran carezz cossa voeur dì?
> Vorraevel maei morì?
>
> . . .
>
> Son staè da on Spizié
> Che a foeugh de veritaè lambicca i coss,
> E ho toeugg on rizipé da voià 'l goss.

> His words move me so much
> I'm not even capable of answering.

Meneghino in Milan

But what's he getting at with all this affection?
Does he intend to die?

. . .

I have been to a pharmacist
Who distills things by the fire of truth,
And I filled a prescription for making one spill the beans.
(3.525–35)

Experience teaches one to appreciate the feelings it teaches us not to expect. Not too much later, Meneghino will offer an extraordinary *plaudite* in which he admits that "la Comedia feniss muffa" [the comedy finishes "muffa"]; but, indeed, "tutt i spass del Mond fenissen muff" [all the entertainments of the world finish "muffa"] (3.835, 838). *Muffa* is a word both unmistakable and impossible. One translator's "amaro" (bitter) attempts to cut the knot of clouds— "moscio" (limp, flabby), says Isella, but that is a nineteenth-century anachronism, itself nebulous. Bitter, tired, useless, outdated (in spite of the prologue boastful of modernity)—but all this cluster of sensations seems both accurate and wholly inappropriate to a comedy. Or so it would have been to a less daring experiment. To lay Maggi's structural cards open at the outset, one must say that, having mastered the plot paradigm of secrets sustained, he had the daring to graft it where that would seem impossible: upon the rising comedy of feeling. As in Meneghino's self-expression upon discovering Fabio's affection, though, it is a feeling tempered with the restraint of experience.

Disappointed in her marital scheming, an aristocratic mother, always affected and silly in her preciously overblown periods and metaphors, rants against fortune. Ridiculous in its immediately local context, her lament resonates within the form of the play: "De zimoij de fortunna no me fid, / La traditora, quand la vuol fà piang, / La fa bocca de rid" [I don't trust Fortune's favors, / because the traitoress, when she wants to make us weep, / she puts on a smile] (2.354–56). The mother is echoing Baltraminna's phrase in the intermezzo that separates the first two acts. More than echoing, though, she is integrating the commentary and the plot. Baltraminna had begun her intermezzo by invoking this same character, Donna Quinzia (Intermezzo primo, 1–7), as representative of the ludicrously conspicuous self-consumption of Milanese society, high and low. The intermezzo is a long catalogue of satire on clothes and manners that (no critic has failed to affirm) is superb in its observed local detail. And it concludes with a general warning that we have just seen Donna Quinzia repeat in act 2, without realizing herself to be a symbolic example. In closing her soliloquy Beltraminna observes, "L'ambizion d'i bass la ne fa rid, / L'ambizion d'i Grand la ne fa piansg" [The ambition of the lowly makes us laugh, / the ambition of the great makes us weep] (Intermezzo primo, 194–95). Laughter and tears, as the mixed extremes of life, reflect the generic extremes of drama. This particular play is a comedy, and so in the second prologue to *I consigli di Meneghino* Baltraminna "scaccia la tragedia" [drives out tragedy], rejects the Seicento vogue of tragicomedy, and places the genetics of Italian dramatic genres in the religious context where it developed, the *sacre rappresentazioni* with their calendrical history: "Chi fa della Quaresma Carnevae, / O al contraerij, no fa nagott de ben" [He who makes Carnival in Lent, / or vice versa, does nothing good] (Prologo secondo, 21–22). One cannot divert the decorum of Christian or psychic seasons.

This is Maggi's comedy of both secrecy and sentiment. The sentiments are mixed, as Baltraminna and even Donna Quinzia realize. Cues, though—the rejection of tragedy, of tragicomedy, the recollection of the cycles of the church year—invite us to examine *I consigli* as a unique attempt to forge a new genre that we might label with an old title: to create *la commedia divina*.

Before testing this hypothesis, one can briefly review the plot. It is a fiction that brought me to invoke Casanova's adventures because they are forecast in the arc of youth that Maggi traces.

Donna Quinzia, aristocratic and pretentious widow, must marry her daughter Alba into the money of a new time, money without titles; she is forced by circumstance and the urgings of her pragmatic son Don Lelio to "intorbidar con altra sfera" [mix with another sphere] the pure family blood (1.16).⁹ Alba is a clone of *la baronina* in *Il Barone di Birbanʒa;* and the peculiar situation of an undesirable female candidate for marriage offered without a counter-balancing rival is repeated. Better marriage than the nunnery, but especially marriage with Fabio, handsome son of the wealthy merchant Anselmo. Fabio, however, has a passion uncharacteristic of comedy's innamorati: "Voeur fass Regilios [sic]," explains Baltraminna in the second prologue (77). He wants to enter the church. Frustrated by his father's recalcitrance, Fabio swings to the other extreme (as would Casanova) and determines to become an officer in the wars swirling around Milan. The first *consiglio* of his old servant Meneghino is a two-hundred-line tour de force against risking one's hopes and life in this arena. It is another study in class, men versus officers, in the dashing of brains and guts and, at the very least, fortune and self-respect against the hard boneyards of war (1.169–341). There has, I think, been nothing closer to Ruzante's *Parlamento.*

But this is to retail the story from the prologue, not the play — a point of importance. Spectators are made aware in advance of an action in which Fabio's clerical vocation is not hinted at internally until a third of the play is past (1.645–46), and then only through a report of vague hearsay.

The early action of the play proper swings about upon Meneghino's second consiglio, secrecy, silence: "Ha gran vantagg chi scolta con chi ciaerla, / Chi scolta compra, e quel che ciaerla vend" [He who listens has a great advantage over one who chatters, / He who listens buys and he who chatters sells] [1.367–68]. The advice is given within the context of Fabio's interview about the marriage with Donna Quinzia. The lady talks, probes, and Fabio listens. He keeps his own — and Meneghino's — counsel. Picking up intrigues from the earlier plays, Maggi develops a pseudo-duel between Fabio and Lelio over the marriage "agreements," introduces as arbiter the *Cavaliere* Costanzo, and permits Fabio to escape both violence and marriage. The duel has been so arranged by Lelio as to assure that it will not occur, even while he enhances his *bella figura.* Meneghino, on the other hand, has been tested and found wanting in preparations to serve as a possible second to Fabio, becoming for the moment a descendant of the cowardly Spanish *graçiloso*. Then, recovering his balance, Meneghino returns to advise and aid his young master as Fabio develops his own intrigue to escape Milan for Rome and the church. It is a simple story, with an atypical comedic ending. The feast will be at the altar in an unexpected manner.

But from this summary, one would not realize that much of the action evolves at the *parlatorio*, the visiting room, of a nunnery where Fabio's sister, who is also Donna Quinzia's friend, is used to extract the secrets behind Fabio's conduct. In this semisacred place where the hidden and the public meet, the religious resonance of the plot is enhanced while its apparent simplicity unwinds into a labyrinth.

The second action is also set in motion in the first scene of *I consigli*, as Donna Quinzia manipulates the nuns to combat the consigli of Meneghino and the vocation of Fabio. Carnevale and Quaresima, vocations and venal votaries, will be set into a quietly quotidian but desperate combat. The worldly widow sees the *monastero* as her likeliest strategic outpost:

> Ho pregà Donna Ersilia,
> Monica amica mia,
> Perché la ciamma Fabij sò Fratell
> Al Monaster, che vuoi parlar con lui,
> Per descoprir paes com'al la sent
> In sto particolar d'i trattament.

> I have asked Donna Ersilia,
> My friend and a nun,
> to call her brother Fabio
> to the nunnery, saying she wants to speak to him,
> in order to sound him out on how he feels
> in this particular of the negotiations. (1.129–34)

Meneghino in Milan

Chiesa versus *cielo*, the inversion of high and low cultures within a Christian framework, as in some anachronistic painting with the garmented priests as the center of a sacrifice and the sanctity represented by elderly, bearded anonymous faces at the edge. This is the structure Maggi imagined into being as he settled the center of worldly secrecy in the *monastero* and the counsels of God in Meneghino. Yet both are to become—the one as warning, the other as warden—conduits for Fabio toward his vocation. One must, though, return in plot and psyche to the nunnery and Donna Quinzia's friend Donna Ersilia. It is through the nunnery's parlatorio bars that the simple plot spreads into a secondary New Comedy, a parodic story of secret intrigues beyond the imaginings of the protagonist of the primary plot who is its unwitting center.

Tarlesca, factor for the nuns' business outside the *monastero*, is given monologues almost as free from interruption as Meneghino's long consigli. But hers are woven into the convent life, into plot following its secondary branch. She carries a secret missive from Ersilia to Donna Quinzia; but Donna Eulalia, senior sister to Donna Ersilia, has allowed Donna Eufrasia to learn through a displaced letter (all this at the *ruota*, the wheel of freedom that allows the nuns access to or beyond the parlatorio) falling into the wrong hands, before improperly prying eyes, and so on interminably. Donna Daria needs creams, Donna Flavia needs to complete a little mercantile exchange—Tarlesca's pockets and mind are filled with the trivia that connect those before and behind the parlatorio screen. But all the confusions have resulted in Donna—but do we need names any longer for such a farrago coming to a point, the point, here as elsewhere, being money. Donna Eufrasia thrusts her rich nephew forward as a rival candidate to challenge Fabio's supposed courtship of Alba. Lost letters are intercepted, family intrigues are carried on, within the nunnery. All this is advanced by the alternating stupidity and slyness of Tarlesca, female counterpart to Meneghino; peasants among plotters, they are oxymoronic controlling pawns to the encompassing plot. Or, Maggi suggests with his form, should we renominate plot as the human interaction with providence? This returns us to the species of secrecy embodied in Fabio. Hearing Mene-ghino's counsel, Fabio acts out his role as a comic innamorato. But he retains his secret reservations. No true innamorata in the immediate offing, no endorsement forthcoming for a young man's commitment to the church, Fabio moves between both seniors, father and coun-selor, to gain the path to Rome, that holy city that Meneghino has visited in some distant, mythic-seeming past.

That is the play. But there is in it another counselor who speaks to Fabio before his commitment. He is the worldly cavalier Cos-tanzo. And his counsel, echoing the venalities of the nunnery, is to embrace the shibboleth of the earlier plays: "Il manco male è il sommo ben del Mondo" [making do with the lesser evil is the high-est good in the world] (3.338). However, this conclusion arrives after a number of pieces of antiworldly advice or, perhaps, advice sage for those determined to operate within the world; Costanzo reminds, for instance, that rancors "rodono in secreto / . . . E con taciti morsi i vermicelli, / Stimolando a far mal, non paion quelli" [gnaw us secretly / . . . and with silent bites the maggots, / not recognized for what they truly are, urge us on to do evil] (3.242–46). Every rose has its thorns; youth should not seek a liberty that will later redound upon its head as license. Finally, Costanzo agrees that Fabio is right in seeking to go to Rome, and that he himself will be the vehicle to arrange his visit by counseling Fabio's father; as he smoothly says, "Non amo il mio consiglio, amo ben vostro" [I'm not in love with my own counsel, but rather yours] (3.278). He has even admitted that "il manco mal del Mondo è pien di mali" [the best one can hope is a world full of evils] (3.340). Meneghino had warned Fabio that, on the outside, Rome is a chest of vanities; Costanzo endorses Fabio's trip as a tour in this vanity fair. When Costanzo departs, Fabio sifts through surface to substance in weighing these counter-consigli:

> Ancor questa miseria hanno i mortali
> Che il manco mal del Mondo è pien di mali?
> Donque perché servir con tante pene
> Il Mondo miserabile, ed ingrato?

Meneghino in Milan

... Che farai Fabio? Andare.
Ma vita? anima? Dio? Niente; andare.
Questa legge fa il Mondo a' pari tuoi.

We mortals still have this misery,
That the best the world has to offer is full of evils?
Then why serve with so much pain
the miserable and ungrateful world?
... What will you do, Fabio? Go.
But life? soul? God? Nothing; go.
This is the law the world makes, for the likes of you.
(3.404–14)

Meneghino's account of Rome immediately follows (the collusion of church and world is extended from the nunnery with his
reminder that Fabio's uncle, with whom he went to Rome, was a
priest), a catalogue of the temptations by superficial sights that Costanzo ("constant" to those worldly images from which Meneghino
has withdrawn his senses) assumes will be the vacation of Fabio the
tourist (3.433–516). Meneghino knows better. He will not accompany
Fabio to Rome; he has already been with that whore in all her glitter.
But he does not reject the vocation called up beneath the confusions
of plot. This is the reason Baltraminna explained Fabio's deepest
needs in the prologue. We watch the intrigues of class, family, parlatorio, and the stunted innamorata pass over Fabio, while he watches
a world of *ciarlatani* as a secret agent who listens and abides. Meneghino has told him the way the world juggles illusions:

> In su la prumma
> Zuquer canded masnaè, ma andand innanz
> Al gh'è 'l sò pizzighent,
> Che nun co'l nost latin
> Ghe disem polver de prilimpinpin.

At first pure white powdered sugar, but as you go further,
along comes its sting,
which we in our "Latin" call "pirlimpinpin powder"
[apparently Maggi's nonsense neologism]. (3.493–97)

Fabio has taken it all in, in silence: Costanzo's venality, that of
the nuns, of the father, of that Rome Meneghino describes from
some distant archetypal time. Keeping his own counsel (and Meneghino's), Fabio disappears to begin his journey to his Rome. He has
chosen without the worldly benediction of his father, who perhaps
sums up this holy version of comedic secrecy best when he realizes that Fabio has followed his vocation "senza farmi un motto"
[without saying a word to me] (3.781). The lover has gone through
Vanity Fair into the Holy City. And that with the encouragement—
one might now not inappropriately say the inspiration—of the rude
servant Meneghino. His servant is a zanni, but a zanni who seems to
have known the ways not only of cities but of courts, who sees the
universal ways of the heart. Fabio knows that Meneghino cannot
know: "Meneghin, queste cose / Non son da te" [Meneghino, these
things / are not for you to know] (2.138–39). An old man; crude,
outside his young master's culture and inside his heart. The character of Meneghino, like the plot of *I consigli di Meneghino*, turns
expectation inside out, as though Maggi had found the old formula
of a hidden god and turned it to the silencing of worldly plots.

Maggi discovered Meneghino's potential for expression of his
particular sense of comedy as a form that could transcend, even
while incorporating, the resignation implicit in *Il manco male*. He
was able to invert the daemonic origins of zanni into another super-
societal figure. With this experiment, Meneghino reenters a pre-
dramatic tradition, installed as a guide through the labyrinths of a
comedy more divine than Maggi's predecessors had dreamed when
undertaking the subversion of what they insistently labeled New
Comedy.

Meneghino in Milan

Dopo la *Veniexiana*, la commedia a Venezia ritornerà alle grandi vette dell'arte quando l'autore guarderà nuovamente alla città . . . e sarà la commedia di Carlo Goldoni.

After the *Venexiana*, comedy in Venice will return to the great summits of art when the author will look anew to the city . . . and it will be in the comedy of Carlo Goldoni.

Giorgio Padoan, *La Veniexiana*

Goldoni

"la tresca senza conclusione veruna"
the intrigue without true conclusion.
(*Le smanie per la villeggiatura*)

*T*he volumes of the Pasquali edition of Goldoni's collected works are prefaced by pieces of critical autobiography. They constitute his first extended commentary upon his achievement and the life adventures in and outside of the theater from which so much of it was derived. Issued in Venice in 1761, the year before Goldoni's move to Paris, not the least embarrassing of these immodest essays was that in the first volume which displayed Goldoni's pride in his precocity as a child playwright. More was perhaps said, though, in the engraved frontispiece than in the verbal boasting.

The child author sits writing at an elaborate desk behind which one sees a crowded bookcase, and upon a few of the spines we can read the names of the comedic predecessors whom Goldoni the man superimposed upon this literal image of the boy: the Florentines and the Milanese, Gigli and Lemene, Fagiuoli and Maggi. Neither Machiavelli nor Molière but those end-of-the-century legatees of the Italian open form nearest to him in time had their names enrolled in this imaginary library of Goldoni's heritage. He recognized himself as the child of a tradition localized by the alienations of dialect and form, the contours of which we have followed as they developed into the beginnings of the Settecento.

Goldoni was the heir who was able to play upon the early and late Renaissance legacy. He stretched the possibilities of the undisclosed ending to limits again and again: did so as his theatrical career began, and continued to probe the form until his final farewell to

Venice and San Luca. If we close by sampling his engagement with this particularly Italian form of comedy, it is to rethink a major corpus that offers confirmation and yet wrestles for disentanglement as it emerges from what we can now describe as a distinctively Italian comedic subgenre.

Il frappatore

Il frappatore[1] (earlier and later titled *Tonin Bella Grazia*) is better known than often read, through its pivotal place in Goldoni's memoirs upon his career (1.51). The popular Pantalone, Cesare D'Arbes, confronted the quondam playwright in Pisa just at the moment when Goldoni the lawyer had become disillusioned with a career in a foreign society that protected and promoted its own natives over the hopes of a Venetian. D'Arbes requested a play and received the scenario (built upon a commedia dell'arte skeleton) that became *Il frappatore*. Prepared for D'Arbes, the play is built around the Pantalone merchant type, here named Fabrizio. Its popular alternative title character is a wealthy and unworldly Venetian simpleton, Tonin Bella Grazia, brought to Rome to initiate a delayed education. But the society into which he is initiated is fiercer, colder than one might anticipate from analogous scenarii. It is a world rivaling that of Pisani's *Philogenia* or Fagiuoli's vengeful nubile schemers. That coldness Goldoni was exploring in adjacent plays: murder and exploitation of the main chance enter into *Il servitore di due padroni, I due gemelli veneziani,* and *La buona moglie*.[2] A deeper mood of cynicism, though, finds form when we position *Il frappatore* in the canon of comedic secrecy.

The play opens upon anxiety about an explicit and acknowledged secret and the promise that, teasingly withheld, it will be revealed at the climactic time. We are in Rome at an inn peopled by commedia dell'arte characters: Arlecchino, Brighella, Colombina, and, of course, D'Arbes as Fabrizio, a name substituted for Pantalone owing to D'Arbes' decision to play *senʒa maschea* and Goldoni's decision to transfer his cynical society from Venice to Rome.

Colombina, maid at the inn, has established a sympathy and intimacy of sorts with Eleonora, a guest accompanied by her servant Arlecchino—in this instance, unlike the ambiguous zanni in *Il servitore di due padroni*, a pure simpleton.

The opening line is Colombina's tentative inquiry: "Compatitemi, signora, se entro in un proposito in cui non ci dovrei entrare" [pardon me, Signora, if I bring up a matter that I shouldn't]. She has watched Eleonora's obvious suffering through the six days she has lodged at the inn and wants to share the lady's trouble. But Eleonora immediately truncates further questions: "So che voi vorreste conoscermi, e che vi svelassi l'esser mio e le mie contingenze, ma questa è l'unica cosa, da cui vi prego di dispensarmi" [I realize that you would like to know me, and for me to unveil my identity and my circumstances, but this is the one thing from which I pray you to excuse me]. However, she also holds out to Colombina (and to the audience) a promise of imminent revelation of her secret: "Aspetto ancora due giorni, per vedere se capita una persona qui in Roma . . . e poi dopo risolverò, e forse pria di partire vi farò quella confidenza che desiderate" [I'm going to wait for another two days, to see if a certain person arrives here in Rome . . . and after that I shall decide, and perhaps before leaving I'll make you that confidence you desire]. The play opens its action, then, around a secret positioned to seem the spring that will reveal the denouement. No Plautine intrigue plot could begin with clearer conditions of expectation between author and audience. Nor more defiantly and repeatedly abort them. This begins at once. For Colombina, secrecy is less practice than temptation, source of another natural hunger: "E ho da star fin domani con questa curiosità in corpo? Quanto più mi cresce la volontà di saperlo" [3] [And do I have to wait until tomorrow with this curiosity in me? How much more, then, the desire to know grows in me] (1.2). No sooner wished than fulfilled. She skillfully draws from Arlecchino the information that Eleonora has been brought from the Veneto to Naples by an errant husband and abandoned. Penniless, she has come to Rome on rumor of his imminent arrival at this very inn of the Aquila. The rumor is true; Colombina knows more than her informant about this husband, one Ottavio Aretusi (*il frappatore*), a frequent and suspect guest. Arlecchino and Colombina pledge one another to secrecy about their revelations of Eleonora's circumstances, and in the next scene (the first and apparently pivotal secret having been given into the confidence of the audience as the play has only begun) a second secret masquerader appears: a young woman dressed as a man. Nor is this new puzzle of identity long withheld: straightaway she presents Brighella with a letter introducing her as Beatrice, a *fiorentina*. Goldoni's play with the cross-dressing disguise motif is itself an implicit suggestion of the exhaustion of an old Plautine ploy, because there is no rationale, no explanation in plot, and thus no disguise, in effect. It is a mechanism left, as was the old comedic form, without a function.

The letter Beatrice carries, though, and the story she relates, open the way to new intrigues: her letter of introduction is from Ottavio Aretusi. She explains circumstantially that she is a widow from Venice sent ahead to meet her betrothed in Rome. On the basis of his scheming story, she has entrusted him with her inheritance. Brighella immediately recognizes a dangerous situation: not knowing that the wife is Eleonora his guest, he nevertheless does know that Ottavio is married to a woman in Naples. Compassionate for the obviously betrayed Beatrice, Brighella supplies the rooms Ottavio has requested. But the request in the latter's letter introduces a new complication causing curiosity: Ottavio is accompanied by another party, "un giovane veneziano, ricco e semplice, raccomandato alla mia custodia" [a young Venetian, rich and simple, recommended to my custody] (1.3). Nothing is known to all in this growing party altogether; something substantial is known to each member.

Immediately upon Beatrice's heels the Venetian simpleton Tonin Bella Grazia arrives under the raven's wing of Ottavio. Tonin, who, unlike the others, speaks in dialect, is a species of urban noble savage ("no son mai stà fora de Venezia" [I've never been outside of

Venice]) who serves to remind us of one of the exiled lawyer-author's earliest oblique gestures of skepticism about the virtue of Venetian insularity. All of the dupes, after all—Tonin, Eleanora, Beatrice (one will discover)—have roots in the Serenissima. But it is Tonin who will become the touchstone upon which the larger world will display its commitment to calculation, to that self-serving that remakes a cast of apparently familiar prototypes into predators.

Ottavio expresses confidence that he can extricate himself from the net of deceit he has woven ("L'inganno non può durar lungamente; sono imbrogliato, ma troverò la via d'uscirne" [The deception can't last long; I am entangled, but I will find a way out] [1.7]), and Brighella begins his own exploitation of Tonin's secret desire: "Per dirvela in confidenza, me voria maridar" [to confide a secret in you, I want to get married] (1.6). Ottavio and Brighella wink knowingly at their mutual hopes for using Tonin, but Brighella is less understanding, more skeptical about Ottavio's story of a wife buried in Naples, her alleged death an event that would free him for Beatrice. As Colombina puts the question, discussing strange appearances with her master: "Che imbroglio è questo? Quante mogli ha il signor Ottavio?" [What sort of mess is this? How many wives does signor Ottavio have?] (2.10).

Beatrice encounters Eleonora and raises doubts in the latter's mind about Ottavio. Beatrice encounters Tonin, who immediately wants to marry her and also puts doubts in his mind about his guardian bad angel. The city booby begs her not to tell Ottavio about their discussion out of fear: "No la ghe diga gnente, che avemo parlà. Faremo le cosse in scondon" [Don't tell him we've spoken. Let's do things secretly] (2.7). And here the suspicious Ottavio bursts in upon their whispered converse with the demand, "Che sono questi secreti?" [What are these secrets?].

In all of this initial shifting and crossing of foreground characters and their abortive interactions, we may wonder that we have not yet seen that Pantalone whose role was created for D'Arbes, that of Fabrizio, uncle and guardian of orphaned Rosaura. Rosaura? Her appearance, with that of Fabrizio, is withheld almost until the

Goldoni

conclusion of the first act, when it comes into intersection with the other prepared expectancies without itself being prepared. Rosaura and Florindo, innamorati, are discovered at the inn in medias res.

Rosaura: Ma signor Florindo, questo passare sì francamente nelle mie camere, mi pare un coraggio troppo avanzato.
Florindo: Fra gli amanti, cara signora Rosaura, non si osservano le cerimonie. . . .

Rosaura: But signor Florindo, this passing so openly into my chambers seems to me too presumptuous.
Florindo: Dear Signora Rosaura, lovers do not stand on ceremony. (1.8)

And at this point Fabrizio enters to announce the arrival of strangers recommended by a Venetian friend: Ottavio and Tonin. Tonin and Fabrizio mesh in a dramatic symbiosis. The former, attempting to amuse Rosaura, at one point offers to parody in dialect that Pantalone whose legacy has passed to D'Arbes/Fabrizio: "La senta se la burlo. 'Flaminia. Fia mia. Dove seu? Dove diavolo ve cazzeu? . . . Oimei, oimei, el mio catarro. Son vecchio. Son cotecchio.[4] No posso più; o che catarro becco cornù'" ["See if I'm joking. 'Flaminia. Daughter mine. Where are you? Where the devil have you gotten to? . . . Oh me, oh me, my cough. I'm old. An old loser. I can't bear it any more; oh what a damn cuckolding cough'"] (2.12). But Fabrizio is a Pantalone from a new and shrewder world than that of the commedia stereotype. When Ottavio introduces Tonin into his household, Fabrizio watches the young Venetian commit folly upon folly in an immediate infatuation with Rosaura, a pantomine courtship carried on in the face of her lover and her guardian. Ottavio is desperate with apologies ("Compatite, signore, le sue stravaganze; non ha avuto educazione finora. Spero col tempo di regolarlo" [Forgive his extravagances, Signor; until now he has had no education. I hope with time to discipline him] [1.10]), but when the Neapolitan has left Fabrizio alone, the identity of the title character is suddenly made problematic. It is Fabrizio himself who will explain later to

Secret Sharers in Italian Comedy

Tonin that Ottavio has been abusing his simplicity and denominates the Neapolitan as "quel frappatore," explaining the epithet expansively: "Vuol dire ravvolgitore, raggiratore, uomo di mal costume e di mal fede" [It means someone who is a cheater, a swindler, a man of bad habits and bad faith] (3.1). But we are early brought to ask whether the title better fits the calculating Fabrizio than the self-entangling Ottavio. Having watched Tonin's obvious vulnerability to Rosaura, and having heard Ottavio's apologies, Fabrizio begins to weigh possibilities: "Non ho veduto niente di più ridicolo. Ma è ricco, e questo basta per una giovane che ha poca dote. Chi sa? non lo voglio perder di vista" [I've never seen anything more ridiculous. But he's rich, and this is enough for a girl who doesn't have much of a dowry. Who knows? I don't want to lose sight of him] (1.10, concluding lines of the first act).

We have been familiarized with this situation as the heart of Plautine form in hundreds of comedies: the blocking senex with a commercial view of love imposing his will between innamorati, only to be overwhelmed by nature's affinities, upon which he ultimately places his paternal (and generational) blessing. And the fatuous tool in the person of a rival lover is exposed to ridicule at the happy close. The future seems all clear, in every sense.

The first scenes of *Il frappatore* offer us mysteries to be revealed, the mysteries of Ottavio's tangled relationships. In the dedicatory epistle, Goldoni promises poetic justice: "non isdegnate di leggere le male arti di un Frappatore, che immerso nei vizi, cerca il modo di coltivarli alle spese di un semplice Giovanotto, e siate certo che al fine della Commedia ritroverete il vizio punito"[5] [don't be above reading about the bad ways of a *frappatore* who, immersed in vices, seeks a way of cultivating them at the expense of a young simpleton, and be certain that at the end of the comedy you will find vice punished]. The promise is fulfilled. Eleonora counterposes as Ottavio's sister and denounces him to the authorities. He flees, but as Florindo says, "La galera, a quel ch'io sento, non la può fuggire" [From what I hear, he cannot escape prison] (3.14). Fabrizio closes this Neapolitan career of heartless crimes against trusting hearts with a line that loops back upon the dedicatory promise: "Ecco il fine meritato dal Frappatore"[6] [Here is the end which the *frappatore* deserves].

But this expectation fulfilled is an anomaly that underlines the anomalous, mocking nature of a play (after all, is not Fabrizio, the alternate frappatore, quite at large?) that disguises its parts as *disjecta membra* of an apparent New Comedy scenario which, *scritto*, becomes instead a new development of the other tradition of the unresolved.

The innamorati are not seriously enamored (now we remember the formal restrictions of good taste that Rosaura imposes upon Florindo's "coraggio troppo avanzato"); Fabrizio is not a blocking senex; Tonin is not to be frustrated. If she has been introduced without a prior history, introduced, like her affairs, in medias res of *Il frappatore,* Rosaura is of one cultural blood, societally at one in her views, with her uncle. Fabrizio closed the first act with his calculations upon Tonin's usefulness; Rosaura echoes his pragmatism toward the close of act 2:

Il signor Florindo ci patisce un poco, ma che serve? egli non è al mio caso. Penso a star bene, se posso, e non m'importa di lasciar Roma. Il signor Tonino è un po' scioccarello, ma questo suo difetto non mi darà grande incomodo.

Signor Florindo suffers a little, but what's the point? He is not the one for me. I want to be comfortably off, if I can, and I don't mind leaving Rome. Signor Tonin is a bit of a blockhead, but this defect will not cause me much inconvenience. (2.11)

But what of Florindo, frustrated lover? Again Goldoni rouses traditional expectations as Florindo quarrels with the preening, cowardly fool Tonin over attentions to Rosaura. She ends the conflict, though, by openly adopting the wisdom of taking the main chance by betrothel to Tonin (2.13), a wisdom reinforced by Fabrizio. When the two suitors reencounter, Florindo sets the fearful Tonino at ease: "Le ragioni addottemi dal signor Fabrizio mi hanno disposto ad una perfetta rassegnazione" [The reasons offered me by Signor Fabrizio have brought about my complete resignation] (3.5). The reasons for all the trio to accept Tonin's marriage proposal are clearly etched upon this little modern history in two lines between the tepid lovers.

Rosaura: Signor Florindo, il signor Tonin ha d'entrata all'anno quattromila scudi. (*parte*)
Florindo: Per questa parte la compatisco; io non ne ho quattrocento.

Rosaura: Signor Florindo, Signor Tonin has an income of four thousand scudi a year. (*she leaves*)
Florindo: On that score, I can understand her; I don't have four hundred. (3.5).

Fabrizio, frappatore in mercantile costume (Brighella had early given a clue to contemporary values when he inquired of Ottavio if Beatrice, "quella zovene vestia da omo," is "Negozio vostro" [that young woman dressed as a man (is) your business] [1.7]), covers his sale of Rosaura to Tonin not only with the self-righteousness that rejects the other frappatore Ottavio but with that which pretends to hope for the improvement in the *sciocco* that Ottavio first pleads ("spero col tempo regolarlo" [I hope with time to discipline him]). Drawing the youngster into Rosaura's web, Fabrizio calls into evidence of good intentions his own good heart: "Parmi che in voi vi possa essere un fondo buono, ed una docilità da poter sperare buon frutto" [It seems to me that you may have a good foundation in you and a docility that portends good fruit] (3.6).

The entire plotting of the Plautine façade is waved away in the final scene with a gesture from Fabrizio toward Beatrice and Eleonora. To Ottavio's wives he has only this chill parting advice: "Voi, donne, andate al vostro destino" [You, ladies, go to your destiny] (3.15). The departure of these ladies with that of their expectations of a happy denouement is gathered between Rosaura's submission to Fabrizio ("Io mi rimetto a tutto quello che fate voi" [I submit myself to all that you do]) and this last great frappatore's com-

Goldoni

mand advice to his man puppets: "Nel corso di quest'anno il signor Florindo favorirà di non frequentar la mia casa, così volendo ogni riguardo ed ogni onestà" [During the course of this year Signor Florindo will favor us by not frequenting my home, since every consideration and honorableness demand it], while Tonin is instructed "imparate a seguire l'onestà e la virtù, e a detestare perpetuamente il vizio, gl'inganni ed il mal costume" [to learn to follow honesty and virtue, and to forever detest vice, deceit, and bad habits] (3.15). But these are the defining terms of a frappatore, not a Tonino. And if Fabrizio has made the equitable public request that Florindo avoid his household during this year of testing for Tonin, Florindo himself in a previous scene has already opened an alternate door. Resigning his rights of marriage, he asks Tonin: "E voi vi dolerete di me, qualora essendo vostra sposa la signora Rosaura, mi procuri l'onore di onestamente servirla?" [and would you resent me, in the case of Signora Rosaura being your wife, should I obtain the honor of honestly serving her]? Tonino puts the seal of approval upon his own folly, undertext to the public party of betrothal, an open secret for the trio who have arranged a modern marriage: "Gnente affatto," replies Tonin, "anzi me farè finezza, ve sarò obbligà" [Not at all, rather you will be doing me a courtesy; I will be obliged to you] (3.5).

La bottega del caffè

The door through which Florindo may walk into Tonin's bed is opened by the future cuckold himself. Or, better, held open against another day when the situation is mature that we only project in this metaphor. In *La bottega del caffè* [The Coffeehouse], one of the sixteen comedies of the famous season of 1750, the door is actual—a stage convention become metaphor. Goldoni gave stage-setting instructions for *La bottega del caffè* with unprecedented fullness; they constitute perhaps the most important dialogue of the play. I take the somewhat exaggerated liberty of calling it "dialogue" because this set of directions is a discursion over the heads of the actors, an initial pact that seals the ethos of author and audience independently of action. Since much of what immediately follows insists upon the hyperactivity of *La bottega del caffè* in both plotting and language, this might seem a perverse judgment. But if we keep in mind Goldoni's fascination with place as the eye of the storm, a meeting ground, we might say, for those centrifugal and centripetal forces intuited by Folena and Baratto (brought into the discussion below), the extended stage direction may lead from the theatrical into the dramatic. I cite it in its entirety:

La Scena stabile rappresenta una piazzetta in Venezia, ovvero una strada alquanto spaziosa, con tre botteghe: quella di mezzo ad uso di caffè, quella alla diritta di parrucchiere e barbiere, quella alla sinistra ad uso di giuoco, o sia biscazza; e sopra le tre botteghe suddette si vedono alcuni stanzini praticabili, appartenenti alla bisca, colle finestre in veduta della strada medesima. Dalla parte del barbiere (con una strada in mezzo) evvi la casa della ballerina, e dalla parte della bisca vedesi la locanda, con porte e finestre practicabili.[7]

The permanent scene represents a little piazza in Venice, or a rather wide street, with three shops: the one in the middle a coffeehouse, the one on the right a wigmaker and barber, the one on the left devoted to play, or a gambling house; and above the three above-mentioned shops can be seen several accessible little rooms, belonging to the gaming parlor, with windows opening on the same street. On the barbershop side (with a street in the middle) is the house of the ballerina, and on the gambling-house side can be seen the inn, with functional doors and windows.

"Praticabili," because they will be used extensively, these upper windows, opening and closing with an incremental rhythm until they become symbol for the festival within and the frustration temporarily shut out: "EUGENIO, DON MARZIO, LEANDRO e LISAURA negli stanzini della biscaccia, aprono le tre finestre che sono sopra le tre botteghe" [Eugenio, Don Marzio, Leandro and Lisaura, in the little rooms of the gambling house, open the three windows above the three shops] (2.20).

Here are all these masqueraders of another carnival comedy exposing themselves. By this juncture Eugenio, the gentle-born but obsessed husband of Vittoria, has lost everything gambling with the false "count" Leandro, seducer of the ballerina Lisaura, in Pandolfo's shady gaminghouse adjacent to Ridolfo's *bottega del caffè;* Ridolfo, the *caffettiere,* has tried to save Eugenio from his folly; Leandro's deserted wife Placida has arrived *in maschera;* Don Marzio, the Neapolitan *maldiciatore,* has watched and jumbled all of their affairs. As the windows are flung open for a desperate feast shared by lambs and wolves, the inside action mirrors the comings and goings in the complicated piazzetta that Goldoni so carefully describes. Everything that extends itself as sheer activity mirrors the chaotic action that parades as plot. Masked wives search the *campiello* to expose their husbands; gamesters and victims alike hide their fixations; and all of this activity of inner and outward betrayal, distress, and anxiety is reflected in that original carefulness of staging that Goldoni made so explicit. It is reflected, too, dramatically, in mirror characters: the caffettiere Ridolfo and Don Marzio. The Neapolitan busybody gradually emerges as personification of the place, its secrets, its transparency. Always in or adjacent to the bottega, with its flow of customers, Don Marzio places himself as observer. His head and imagination turn toward each might-be protagonist as he gazes from the center *"guardando sempre con l'occhialetto"* [continually looking around with a lorgnette] (3.18), a window upon a window—but one whose imagination makes over place itself into a human stream of unending lechery, as he insists upon the existence of a back door to the quarters of Lisaura. A Venetian metaphor from the sea becomes a venereal scene: "Flusso e riflusso, per la porta di dietro" [Flux and reflux, through the door behind] (1.6).[8] He is, though, this cynic Don Marzio, mirror to the good caffettiere Ridolfo. And it is just here that the complications of this extravagant play and Goldoni's immediately successive versions of Venetian society become problematic. Mario Baratto makes observations that help one see how closely Don Marzio's role is woven into that of the mise-en-scène itself. "La *rue*," he remarks, "n'est plus, ici, un lieu 'conventionnel,' établi pour faire rencontrer et parler des personnages; la rue est elle-même . . . un 'personnage,' un personnage qui suscite et donne vie à tous les autres" [The street here is not a "conventional" place, established to make the characters meet and speak; the street itself is . . . a "character," a character which excites and gives life to all the others]. Citing the *Mémoires*, Baratto concludes that "La solitude y est pratiquement impossible; ou elle est seulement concevable au milieu de la foule. . . . Venise propose à Goldoni une réflexion constante sur l'art de vivre ensemble, en société"[9] [Solitude is practically impossible; or it is only conceivable in the midst of the crowd . . . Venice proposes to Goldoni a constant reflection on the art of living together, in society]. This paradox of privacy in a crowd is incarnate in Don Marzio: "Don Marzio est bien un bavard et un médisant. Mais il l'est aussi, parce que les autres sont prêts à faire ou à écouter des confidences: c'est une responsabilité largement partagée par presque tous les personnages" [Don Marzio is a proper gossip and scandalmonger. But he is so, because the others are ready to impart or to listen to confidences: it is a responsibility widely shared among nearly all the characters] (71).

The secret confidence is, of course, the epitomizing exercise of that public privacy oxymoron that Baratto here proposes as the essence of Venetian living. Don Marzio betrays the fragile nature of the compact early in the opening act of the play when he broadcasts that Eugenio has used him as agent to pawn his wife's earrings. Ridolfo's garçon of the bottega returns us to the radical meaning of a common word when he muses upon such betrayed transactions: "Fra il signor Marzio ed io, formiamo una bellissima *segretaria*" [Between Signor Marzio and me, we form a very fine secretariat] (1.5; italics mine). The suggestions of the word are separated and regathered in Don Marzio's assurance to Leandro in act 3 that he will be available "Se vi occorre protezione, assistenza, consiglio e sopra tutto secretezza" [If you need protection, assistance, advice and above all secrecy] (3.2). Private counsel, that improbability in Venice, is the lure that wins Leandro's misplaced trust: "aprirò a voi tutto il mio cuore," he promises, "ma . . . raccomando la segretezza" [I will open my whole heart to you, but . . . I recommend secrecy]. Leandro's married state is revealed to his mistress; his mistress is in turn revealed to his wife by this secretary recording the proceedings of the bottega and environs. So it has fared with Eugenio; so it will be with the cardsharper Pandolfo. When police agents are about to descend upon his parlor, he seeks advice from Don Marzio. The advice is to secrete the cards in a safe place. The place is revealed to Don Marzio and relayed by him to the police, and Pandolfo is led away to prison. Secrets retailed lead to wholesale trouble, and all who have confided in him, all who have watched, join to hunt Don Marzio from the city and from the comedy ("Qui non serve il giustificarmi. Ho perduto il credito e non lo reacquisto mai più. Anderò via di questa città" [Here it is no use justifying myself. I have lost credit and I will never get it back. I will leave this city] [3.26]). Don Marzio is, of course, presented as a spirit from another dangerous country, whose betrayal of Pandolfo makes almost literal irony of a familiar proverb: "Io sono napolitano. Vedi Napoli e poi muori" [I am a Neapolitan. See Naples and then die] (2.16). We are provided through this figure a confirmation in miniature that the world is "flusso e riflusso," a place of alternating tides of peril. But there is justifiable cause to reconsider Don Marzio's exorcising in Baratto's warning about collusion "par presque tous les personnages" in breaking confidences. And it leads one to reconsider the role of that figure with whom we began: *il caffettiere*.

Ridolfo is a man of uprightness and gratitude, who has been enabled to become a caffettiere through a loan from Eugenio's father: "Ho aperta questa bottega, e con questa voglio vivere onoratamente, e non voglio far torto alla mia professione" [I have opened this shop, and with this I wish to live honorably, and do not wish to do wrong to my profession] (1.2). His gratitude leads him to make constant efforts to reform young Eugenio from his disastrous gambling, from that generally prodigal life which has estranged him from his

good wife, Vittoria. More than the particular circumstance of gratitude, though, he is motivated by a natural benevolence: "Poche
parole, ma buone, dette da un uomo ordinario, ma di buon cuore; se
le ascolterà, sarà meglio per lei" [Few words, but good words, spoken by an ordinary man, but one with a good heart; if you will listen
to them, it will be the better for you] (1.11). Man and *mestiere* seem
one; Ridolfo projects his good nature onto the *bottega del caffè*:

Fo un mestiere onorato, un mestiere nell' ordine degli artigiani, pulito,
decoroso e civile. Un mestiere che, esercitato con buona maniera e con
riputazione, si rende grato a tutti gli ordini delle persone. Un mestiere reso
necessario al decoro delle città, alla salute degli uomini, e all'onesto diver-
timento di chi ha bisogno di respirare.

I follow an honorable trade, a trade in the order of the artisans, clean,
decorous, and civil. A trade that, pursued with a good manner and reputation, makes itself acceptable to all orders of persons. A trade become
necessary to the decorum of cities, to the health of mankind, and to the
honest diversion of whoever has need of relaxation. (2.2)

And later Ridolfo projects the benevolent aspect of his place of
trade back upon his own innate character: "Questo nostro mestiere
ha dell'ozio assai. Il tempo che avanza, molti lo impiegano o a giuo-
care o a dir male del prossimo. Io l'impiego a far bene, se posso"
[This trade of ours provides a great deal of leisure time. Many employ the time left over either in gambling or in speaking evil of their
neighbors. I employ it to do good, if I can] (2.8). With this paean
upon his mestiere, with his plotting toward a *lieto fine* for Eugenio's
affairs (he will engage also to untangle those of Leandro and *his*
abandoned wife), with his centrality in the bottega that is at the
center of the stage set and of the plot action, Ridolfo enters a metaphoric dimension as avatar for the playwright only second to that
of Anzoletto in *l'ultime sere di carnovale*. But this analogy overlaps
with another that brings it under question. A director of affairs, yes,
but one whose direction is unsought, a director who stands at the

edges of things. In this Ridolfo looks forward to Fulgenzio in the villeggiatura trilogy: not a controlling author of events, but a well-meaning meddler. Fulgenzio, too, has a good heart: "son uomo," he says, "sento l'umanità, ho compassione di tutti" [I am a man, I feel humanity, I have compassion for all] (*Il ritorno della villeggiatura* [2.2]). His efforts, though, lead to the most disastrous, near tragic, marriage in Goldoni's comedies.

Ridolfo himself, pressing on like Fulgenzio, exhibits a nervous awareness that his behavior may seem less than natural, perhaps less authoritative than meddling to others: "Mi dirà qualcuno: perchè vuoi tu romperti il capo per un giovane che non è tuo parente. . . . Io l'impiego a far del bene, se posso" [Someone will say to me: why do you want to knock your brains out for a young man who is not your relative. . . . I employ [my time] to do good, if I can] (2.8); "Mi burla, mi fa degli scherzi? Basta: quel che ho fatto, l'ho fatto per bene, e del bene non mi pentirò mai" [You tease me, you make jokes about me? Enough: that which I have done, I have done for good, and I will never repent of doing good] (2.20). And this brings us to observe yet another analogy that brings not only *il caffettiere* but the whole society interacting at his bottega into disturbing question. The analogy is that between Ridolfo and the other insatiable observer and advisor of the play, Don Marzio. In the first act, Don Marzio's fantasy about the ballerina Lisaura as whore ("Ha la porta di dietro; pazzo, pazzo! Sempre flusso e riflusso" [She has a door in the rear; mad, mad! Always flux and reflux] is countered by Ridolfo's express insistence upon minding his own business: "Io bado alla mia bottega; s'ella ha la porta di dietro, che importa a me? Io non vado a dar di naso a nessuno" [I pay attention to my shop; if she has a back door, what does it matter to me? I don't go sticking my nose in anyone's affairs] (1.6). All that we know of his behavior, of course, will eventually contradict this stance of noninvolvement, of disinterest in the private secrets whose possession is so obsessively dominant as a motive with Don Marzio. But the "porta di dietro" and its secrets move one to recollect the first conversation of *La bottega del caffè*, that between the two bottegai, Ridolfo of the caffè and Pandolfo of the gambling house. Explaining how "con questa [bottega] voglio vivere onoratamente" [with this shop I want to live honorably], Ridolfo exasperates Pandolfo with his judgmental righteousness, and the gambler remarks that there are cheating tricks to every trade. Yes, Ridolfo agrees, but "di quelli non vanno le persone riguardevoli, che vengono alla mia bottega" [these don't go over with the respectable persons who come to my shop]. Pandolfo's response brings the exchange into unexpected range of Don Marzio's lubricious fantasy:

Pandolfo: Avete anche voi gli stanzini segreti.
Ridolfo: È vero; ma non si chiude la porta.
Pandolfo: Il caffè non potete negarlo a nessuno.
Ridolfo: Le chicchere non si macchiano.
Pandolfo: Eh via! Si serra un occhio.
Ridolfo: Non si serra niente; in questa bottega non vien che gente onorata.

Pandolfo: You also have little secret rooms.
Ridolfo: That's true; but we don't close the door.
Pandolfo: You can't refuse anyone coffee.
Ridolfo: The little coffee cups don't stain.
Pandolfo: Get out! You close one eye.
Ridolfo: We don't close anything; only decent people come into this shop. (1.2)

But even as he speaks, Ridolfo is serving the cardsharper, as he will serve Don Marzio in *that* exchange about doors.[10]

At the close of *La bottega del caffè* the actions overlap in a frenzy of developments. Ridolfo tries desperately to reconcile the accusatory but loving wife with a Eugenio whose emotions are a mix of penitence, anger, and shame. The young man is persuaded to wait in the private room inside the bottega until Ridolfo can bring his wife to reconciliation. But when she comes to join him, Ridolfo finds Eugenio has fled: "Signora Vittoria, cattive nuove; non vi è più! È andato via per la porticina" [Signora Vittoria, bad news; he's not here anymore! He has gone away through the little door] (2.26). So

Goldoni

there is sudden confirmation of Pandolfo's and Don Marzio's suspicions of secret doors. It is only a little irony, though, Ridolfo's motives being still good in all of his *maneggi*, his meddling: "Che cosa guadagnate in questi vostri maneggi?" [What do you gain from these schemes of yours?], asks Don Marzio, and Ridolfo again replies: "Guadagno il merito di far del bene . . . guadagno qualche marca d'onore" [I earn the merit of doing good . . . I earn some marks of honor] (3.17). But discovery of this "porticina" of escape is only a foreshadowing of other imminent discoveries.

Don Marzio advises Leandro to flee, once the "count" has revealed that he is really Flaminio, caught between his deserted wife and the seduced ballerina. Leandro seizes upon the cynical advice to take the first gondola out of the lagoon where both women wait to pincer him, and says "Uscirò per la porta di dietro, per non essere veduto" [I will go out through the back door, in order not to be seen]. Don Marzio's seemingly preposterous fantasy suddenly is revealed as truth: "Lo dicevo io; si serve per la porta di dietro" [What did I say? he uses the back door] (3.2). The door that focuses the action has been hidden even in Goldoni's elaborate staging directions, the author extratextually colluding with the devious form taken by his action. And soon we learn that Ridolfo has known of it all along. In his effort to reunite Placida with the erring Leandro, he sends her to the barbershop over which Lisaura and Leandro have been quartered: "si ritiri in bottega qui dal barbiere; stando lí, si vede la porticina segreta [go into the barbershop here; from there, you can see the little secret door] (3.4). How does he know? Who has stood there before, to observe what scenes?

The innocent *bottega del caffè* set next to the gaminghouse, the apartments with those apparently innocent windows that seem so open to the piazza, the ordinariness of Ridolfo's honest quotidian environment now loom as obscene enormities, harboring secrets in what appears a labyrinth of betrayals.

The last betrayal will be that of Pandolfo by Don Marzio. When disguised police agents descend upon the gambling den, Pandolfo rushes to Don Marzio for advice. They share some euphemisms, then discard all pretense as Pandolfo is advised to hide his marked cards. "Dove le vuoi nascondere?" [Where do you want to hide them?], asks the Neapolitan, and Pandolfo excitedly explains: "Ho un luogo secreto sotto le travature, che nè anche il diavolo le ritrova" [I have a secret place under the beams, where not even the devil can find them] (3.10). It takes the head of the police squad only moments to draw this knowledge from Don Marzio, and Pandolfo immediately is brought forth on his way to prison. And now the alter-ego aspect of the relationship between the character of *il caffettiere* and that of the *maldicente* foreigner casts a final light across the play. Don Marzio is astonished at what his gossiping desire to seem to know all has brought on: "Che ho io fatto? Colui che io credeva un signore di conto, era un birro travestito. Mi ha tradito, mi ha ingannato. Io son di buon cuore; dico tutto con facilità. . . . Dico facilmente quello che so; ma lo faccio, perchè son di buon cuore" [What have I done? That person that I believed a gentleman of mark was a police agent in disguise. He betrayed me; he tricked me. I have a good heart; It's easy to get me to talk. . . . I blurt out easily what I know; but I do it because I am good-hearted]. As Don Marzio laments the meddling of his own "buon cuore," that other good-hearted meddler, Ridolfo, emerges from the apartment of the ballerina with an apparently re-pentant Leandro, now, like Eugenio, reunited with his abused wife. Ridolfo cannot refrain from accusing Don Marzio of having tried to separate wife and husband, while he, Ridolfo, has reunited them. Don Marzio is incredulous: "Unirsi con sua moglie? È impossibile, non la vuole con lui" [Get together with his wife? It's impossible, he doesn't want her with him]. Ridolfo is smug: "Per me è stato pos-sibile; io con quattro parole l'ho persuaso. Tornerà con la moglie" [For me it has been possible; with a few words, I have managed to persuade him. He'll go back to his wife]. Then Leandro with a quiet aside brings tumbling about our ears the house of cards upon which the "buon cuore" of *il caffettiere* has pitched the conclusion of his own "New Comedy"; he will return to his wife only in appearance: "per forza, per non essere precipitato" [of necessity, in order not to be ruined] (3.14–16).

Goldoni

Don Marzio's fantasy of the "flusso e riflusso, per la porta di dietro" has been the absurd projection of an obscene imagination, and yet has been true. For all of his own well-meaning meddling in others' affairs, at least as inept as Ridolfo's, Don Marzio may be the wiser man about the ways of this strange Venetian world passing under the inspection of his ubiquitous *occhialetto*. If he has been right about the door, about Leandro's marriage, surely he cannot be right in his final fantasy; and yet . . . and yet: "io so perchè Eugenio è tornato in pace con sua moglie. Egli è fallito, e non ha più da vivere. La moglie è giovane e bella. . . . Non l'ha pensata male, e Ridolfo gli farà il mezzano" [I know why Eugenio has made peace with his wife. He's bankrupt, and has nothing more to live on. The wife is young and beautiful. . . . It isn't a bad idea he's had, and Ridolfo will play the pimp for him] (3.19; the ellipsis is Goldoni's).

We have seen much display of sentiment and more betrayal—too much of the former to give credence to this prediction, too much of the latter to entirely disbelieve.

The Villeggiatura Trilogy

Il frappatore and *La bottega del caffè*, exquisite cynical vignettes, possibly for this very reason have not been prominent in the commentary of *goldonisti*, in contrast with the villeggiatura trilogy (plays privileged as *capolavori* by numerous editions and rich critical exploration).[11] While capitalizing on the ironic antipastoral theme of villeggiatura, the luxurious "rustication" on the veneto's *terrafirma*,[12] Goldoni was making a major structural experiment. It was constituted by his most persistent, many-faceted search of a society's psyche through its mania (what word can describe the phenomenon better than Goldoni's own?) for transporting all the extravagant pleasures of the city into country villas. The complexity of the subject led Goldoni to adapt to modern life that serial form he had essayed in the "Persian" trilogy of the 1750s.

In his introduction, Goldoni explains to "chi legge" [him who reads] *Le smanie* (in, of course, a retrospective view of the reception of the entirety upon the stage):

Ho concepita nel medesimo tempo l'idea di tre Commedie consecutive. La prima intitolata: *Le Smanie per la Villeggiatura;* la seconda: *Le Avventure della Villeggiatura;* la terza: *Il Ritorno dalla Villeggiatura*. Nella prima si vedono i pazzi preparativi: nella seconda la folle condotta: nella terza le conseguenze dolorose che ne provengono . . . ciascheduna può figurare da sè, e tutte e tre insieme si uniscono perfettamente.[13]

I conceived simultaneously the idea of three consecutive comedies. . . . In the first we see the frantic preparations: in the second the absurd conduct: in the third the painful consequences arising therefrom . . . each of them can stand on its own, while all three fit together perfectly.

Goldoni goes on to conclude his remarks with a boast about a new triumph in consistency of characterization: "se una delle difficoltà del Dramma consiste nel sostenere i caratteri in un'opera sola, piacerà ancor più vederli in tre sostenuti" [if one of the difficulties of drama lies in keeping the characters consistent in a single work, it will be that much more of a pleasure to see them consistent in three]. It is a bold boast, given the wildly divergent descriptions of the three plays. But it is earned as a result of the stacking of comedic genres one upon another: farce, next a little comedy of manners, and the last that of secrecy. This latter form, we have seen, was capable of such modal variety that it produced farce in Pisani's *Philogenia* and a sort of divine comedy in *I consigli di Meneghino*. Machiavelli's Lucrezia recognizes the folly of her struggle with society's hypocrisy and internalizes the lesson to her own profit in secret pleasure. In *Il ritorno dalla villeggiatura* Goldoni's heroine will internalize the society's principle of masking, too, but with "conseguenze dolorose."

I have no intention of reviewing the trilogy again in the wake of Mangini, Fido, and numerous incisive, if less thorough, interpreters. That would be hubristic. But I will make brief visits to *Le smanie* and *Le avventure* only as they reflect upon Goldoni's just-cited conception and upon the movement that sweeps toward placing *Il ritorno* among the most fully realized achievements in the comedy of secrecy.

Le smanie per la villeggiatura. What a gay, disturbing set of expectations and recognitions the title must have aroused in Goldoni's Venice; and yet the Livornese setting deflects (broadens) what must have been an ambivalent pride and shame about a dubious tradition.

Let us recall the opening stage direction and dialogue to realize how from its beginning *Le smanie* straddles the allied precipices of farce and social commentary by way (so often Goldoni's way) of a property: "Paolo *che sta riponendo degli abiti e della biancheria in un baule*" [who is packing clothes and linen in a trunk]. As the servant packs for the country escape, his young master Leonardo enters with all the swirling misplaced energy that will justify the title and that will often make one feel displaced again into *Il servitore di due padroni:* "Che fate qui in questa camera? Si han da far cento cose, e voi perdete il tempo. . . . Ho bisogno di voi per qualche cosa di più importante. Il baule fatelo riempir dalle donne" [What the devil are you doing in here? There are hundreds of things that need doing, and here you are wasting time. . . . I've got more important work for you. Have the women take care of the trunk]. The *baule*, of course, is less symbol than a staged reification of the disorder and the disordinate pressure of frenetic action that is not (as in *Il servitore* and in the commedia dell'arte tradition) counter to but, rather, compounded by the tardy pace of self-recognition on the part of the Venetian (Livornese) *ceto borghese.* Leonardo cannot afford the country vacation, but owing to his jealousies on one hand and to the endless pressure of his sister and ward Vittoria on the other (her name, allegorical in *Le smanie,* becomes ironic in *Il ritorno*), he literally pawns his future for a fling. After the staging of what seem to be countless reversals of position as the party of lovers, parents, and parasites prepares for departure, in the final scenes of the play, Leonardo and the trunk reappear, wrestling together. They do so under the hurried chatter of Vittoria. Leonardo, exhausted by confusions, says only, "vo' rimettere in ordine il mio baule" [Let me get

Secret Sharers in Italian Comedy

my trunk packed again]. Vittoria frets, and Leonardo replies with Goldoni's implicit stage direction capsulating the farcical proceedings and, with them, Leonardo's reduction to a comic symbol of a society enclosing him, enclosing itself, as Goldoni will expose its more consequential imprisonment of Giacinta later: Leonardo becomes the inhabitant of a straitened, self-made space, as he shouts, perhaps less to his sister than to the spectator: "Non vedete ch'io fo il baule?" [Can't you see I'm repacking the trunk?] (3.4).

The plot of Le smanie, in its skeletal scenario form, is simple. Vittoria and Giacinta are very young friends both da maritare, both prepared and unready for marriage. Their friendship, however, is superficial, while their invidious envies run deep (it was a happy stroke that Goldoni, mocking the rage for French things à la mode, should have invented the sartorial tag for their rival gowns: marriages). Juxtaposed physically and socially in the city, the girls' families plan to travel together in the country, young Leonardo attempting to cut as grand a bella figura as that of Giacinta's father Filippo. This is and is not associated with the financially sinking Leonardo's desire to marry Giacinta; that is a motive, but one psychologically overshadowed by the dominant desire for pleasure, for preening, for play, for a mad potlatch existence that marks these summer months in the country. And there is the rival innamorato Guglielmo. Largely used as a nearly superfluous, mechanical pawn by the willful Giacinta, he has become a frequent attendant in her household through his friendly acceptance by Filippo, the father. And this friendship results in his being invited to join the party in the villeggiatura. The invitation sets off the dizzy on-again, off-again arrangements for coaches and companions that constitute the farcical actions giving major tonality to the play. All is set right ultimately by the judicious voice of Filippo's old friend Fulgenzio, who points out Filippo's weakness in allowing himself to be dominated by Giacinta's clever headstrong ways (Filippo admits that "Si va quando vanno gli altri, ed io mi lascio regolar dagli altri" [You just have to go when everyone else goes, and I let myself be ruled by the others] [1.9]); it is the opposite stance from that of Vittoria, who speaks for herself and for Giacinta

Goldoni

when *she* admits, "Non veggo l'ora di maritarmi; niente per altro, che per poter fare a mio modo" [I can't wait to be married; if for no other reason than to be able to do as I please] [1.7]).[14] Fulgenzio displays the ethical and social dilemma involved in having on hand in the country Giacinta's two rival suitors, points out to Leonardo the error of privately wooing Giacinta, and arranges a betrothal before their departure. As Fulgenzio says of himself, "Credo di aver ben servito il signor Leonardo. Ma ho inteso di servire alla verità, alla ragione, all'interesse e al decoro dell'amico Filippo" [I believe I have served Signor Leonardo well. But my true intention was to serve truth, reason, and Signor Filippo's own reputation and interest] (2.9). He has done so, of course, as Filippo acknowledges in the outcome ("Sempre più mi confesso obbligato al vostro amore, alla vostra amicizia" [I am more and more obliged to your affection and friendship] [3.10]). Leonardo and Giacinta publicly betrothed, the entire party departs decorously for the country. And Vittoria, not to be overshadowed too much, invites the quiet Guglielmo to ride "in calesso con me" [in the calèche with me] (3.17). The situation is a nucleus, a promise of another coupling that will satisfy Plautine demands for happy symmetry. But it is Fulgenzio who remarks at the embarcation for the journey and the end of *Le smanie,* "Non va troppo bene per la signora Vittoria" [Things aren't going too well for Signora Vittoria; my translation]. The conclusion of the love farce has been brought about by this hero of reason, protector of friends, purveyor and protector of the social mores of a class. It is he who has quieted into general contentment "i pazzi preparativi" that constitute the action of *Le smanie per la villeggiatura.* But his last remark, negligible within the closing context, combines with another passing moment to prepare the "completed" action for inversion, prepare ironic counterpoint to all of Fulgenzio's efforts when we and Goldoni review them from the results of *Il ritorno.*

In the chorus of frantic shouting and staged shibboleths, a little comment by Giacinta and her maid-confidante's response come early enough to be forgotten by the close. But it is the preparative for the change worked in the later plays of the trilogy which negates the perennial criticism that finds character inconsistencies.

Brigida: Diciamola fra di noi: voi l'amate pochissimo il signor Leonardo.

Giacinta: Io non so quanto l'ami; ma so che l'amo più di quello ch'io abbia amato nessuno; e non avrei difficoltà a sposarlo, ma non a costo di essere tormentata.

Brigida: Compatitemi, questo non è vero amore.

Brigida: Just between you and me: you don't love Signor Leonardo very much, do you?

Giacinta: I don't know how much I love him, but I do know that I love him more than I ever loved anyone else, and I'd have no trouble marrying him; but not if it means a life of torment.

Brigida: Forgive me, but that's not real love. (1.11)

Even here, in this farce, we are entrusted with a submerged secret. But its effect is much more serpentine than the mistakes and tricks that misdirect communication in New Comedy, in commedia dell'arte plots. It is a secret that will emerge again much later to give definitive form to *Il ritorno* and to the trilogy.

Le avventure della villeggiatura is a comedy of manners. Thinly covering the malice and treachery that are less close to the surface when this nervous society is at home in Livorno, *in città,* manners are worn as masks. Unlike *Le smanie* (and paradoxically so, since *Le avventure* is the only member of the trilogy set in the country), this sequel is in much of its structure a display of contemporary social mores as the bourgeoisie goes about its busy leisure, as in Goldoni's earlier mode from, say, *La vedova scaltra* and *La putta onorata.* It is, in this respect, largely devoted to particulars of local color—in spite of the translation of Venice to Livorno. This significant aspect is foregrounded in the opening scene where one finds Brigida, Paol[in]o, and their fellow servants aping their employers' ritual of morning chocolate while the other class sleeps off the long night of gambling.[15] This scene is later "placed," as the vacationing group of rivals and intriguers arrange themselves for a *conversazione* at the bottega di caffè—a scene arranged as a superb metonymy for the simultaneously social and anti-social activity of this miniature society. Having strolled to the caffè in perfectly arranged order, having seated themselves in pattern, the group bursts into chaotic cacophony as the waiter arrives: "Un caffè." "Un bicchier d'acqua pura." "Un cedrato." "Una cioccolata." "Un caffè senza zucchero." "Una limonata" ['A coffee.' 'A glass of cold water.' 'An iced lime drink.' 'A cup of chocolate.' 'A coffee with no sugar.' 'A lemonade.'] (3.11). We watch them arrange for play, selecting groups for each gaming table (2.10 and 11), and we watch them psychologically strive for position at a gala dinner complete with veiled symbolic gestures—as when finding Giacinta too attentive to Guglielmo, Leonardo manages to spill a bit of sauce into her lap (3.1). All of this action, though, is drawn into a tonal web that counters the mild satire of its surface.

Goldoni's introduction "a chi legge" makes reference to Fulgenzio's carefully implanted remark at the end of *Le smanie* ("Non va troppo bene per la signora Vittoria"): "I pronostici di Fulgenzio [sono] verificati" [Fulgenzio's forecasts come true]. Fulgenzio, however, was not so wise as Brigida and Goldoni in foreseeing trouble for Giacinta also. And the tonal counterpoint in this sequel, as well as its plot potential, is also established in the introduction when the author points out that if Guglielmo seemed a mechanical foil, "Questo personaggio si disviluppa a questa seconda Commedia, e lo stesso carattere freddo e flemmatico produce la principale delle Avventure, cioè l'azione principale di questo secondo dramma" [This character is given an opportunity to develop in this second Comedy, and the same cold and phlegmatic disposition produces the most important of the Adventures, in other words, the principal action of this second drama]. Nonetheless, "il titolo collettivo abbraccia più persone," Goldoni explains, and "Tutti i personaggi agiscono per lo stesso fine, e tutte le loro diverse azioni si riducono a provar l'argomento" [the collective title encompasses a number of persons. . . . All of the characters act toward the same end, and all of their different actions serve to advance the plot]. Many dramatists have made the same vague boast, but Goldoni insists upon it in great detail: "se ne introducono quattro nuovi [attori], i quali tutti contribuiscono a moltiplicar *Le Avventure della Villeggiatura*, e tutti servono all'azion principale" [four new characters are introduced, all of whom contribute to multiplying the *Adventures in the Country*, and all of whom serve to advance the main action]. The multiplying effect of these characters is to increase the number of marital intrigues and seems distant from Guglielmo as focus of the principal action. One intrigue is the unsuccessful attempt of the happy gigolo Ferdinando to marry the money of Sabina, Giacinta's self-deceiving and sexually infatuated sixty-five-year-old aunt. Ferdinando wheedles and embarrasses himself throughout the play ("Ho rabbia di dovermi in pubblico far minchionare" [I'm annoyed at having to make a fool of myself in public] [2.10]), but, having overplayed his hand, he admits at the close: "La vecchia è in collera. La donazione è in fumo, e la commedia per me è finita" [The old woman is angry. My settlement has gone up in smoke, and for me the comedy is finished; my translation] (3.16). The other new intrigue is that of Costanza, her destitute niece Rosina, and the nonetheless sweet "baggiano" (booby) Tognino. Costanza, worldly but generous, has taken up sixteen-year-old Rosina ("povera, miserabile, che non ha niente al mondo. Tutto quello che ha in dosso, glielo ha prestato la . . . padrona" [Poor, miserable girl who has nothing in the world. The patroness has to lend her every stitch that she puts on] [1.2]) to marry her off. Tognino is also a sixteen-year-old *in villeggiatura*. Son of a physician, the simple boy is being pushed, with collusion from his father's friends, to become a *medico condotto*, that is, a country doctor to certain assigned villages. But now all that he or Rosina can think about is having discovered one another and love in this happy round of vacation parties. As they depart for Livorno at the end, Costanza whispers to Rosina: "Andiamo, giacché Tognino è disposto, non ce lo lasciamo scappare" [Let's go. While we have Tognino in the right

Goldoni

frame of mind, let's not let him off the hook] (3.16). But if calculation enters into this arrangement, it reinforces the elective affinities of the youngsters. Goldoni's new cast additions have shown an unnatural marriage frustrated, a natural one advanced. And thus he has justified his claim that "tutti i personaggi agiscono per lo stesso fine," because these two actions invert the marital choices of the "azion principale." They further to fulfillment the natural desire of youth and deny the nightmare potential in the union of age and greed. If they are not an ultimate commentary upon the choices made in the main action, they shadow it with doubts. Which brings us to Guglielmo. An ineffective psychological double agent used to protect Giacinta from the nebulous fear of Leonardo's possible dominance in *Le smanie,* a pawn between the father and the threatening betrothal, Guglielmo had been usable against both. Usable because of his "freddo e flemmatico" character that both removed him as a threat and set him in contrast to the variously malleable and mercurial temperaments of Filippo and Leonardo.

Le avventure is another play and, as Goldoni says, Guglielmo is the principal. He has partially unmasked the man, and Giacinta's own mask of manneredness has been penetrated. Brigida had informed her that she did not love Leonardo; now Giacinta informs Brigida that she has fallen in love with Guglielmo: "quella maniera sua insinuante, dolce, patetica, artifiziosa, mi ha, mio malgrado, incantata, oppressa, avvilita. Sì sono inamorata, quanto può essere donna al mondo" [that insinuating, sweet, pathetic, sophisticated manner of his, that has charmed me, subjugated me, made me his slave, in spite of myself. Yes, I'm in love, as much as a woman was ever in love] (2.1). Only the unnatural aunt Sabina has observed the covert signs ("Se non si sapessero i suoi segreti!" [As if no one knew her secrets] [2.3]), and the jealous Leonardo has developed quieter suspicions. Then they are no longer covert: in the midst of visits, the carousel of socializing *in villeggiatura,* Guglielmo isolates Giacinta for a stolen unmasked moment: "Dirovvi solamente ch'io vi amo" [I will tell you quite simply that I love you]. The dropping of the mask is momentary, though; the "freddo e flemmatico" in Guglielmo's character has been frozen there by this society: "vi amo; ma che se l'amor mio potesse recare il menomo pregiudizion o agli interessi vostri, o alla vostra pace, son pronto sagrificarmi in qualunque modo vi aggrada" [I love you; but if my love could bring the slightest harm to your interests or to your peace of mind, I'm ready to sacrifice myself in any way you choose] (2.7). Daring and timidity revolve so rapidly in one another's psychic embrace that the question of mask or man has become irrelevant. And given Guglielmo's lead, Giacinta has been predestined by social rhetoric; confession and regression are the internalized image of order. "Sagrificarmi" is the word set against desire. But the sacrifice cannot be the savage's vulgar display of virgins mutilated before the higher gods—just a nubile girl following a nice man into the secret of enduring *melanconia*. And such love secrets are proper for the preserve of nature's hiding places. Which brings us again to a stage metaphor unavailable in the flanking members of the trilogy set in Livorno. Brings us, that is, to Pan's traditional home, to that setting in which man and nature by myth share their fertile generative powers, brings us to the *boschetto*.

The servants had mockingly mirrored their masters' manner in the breakfast *conversazione* of the opening scene of the first act. In the opening scene of the last act, a pair of these same servants, Brigida and Paolo, demonstrate their prudent propriety in love matters. In the evening, Paolo proposes, "verremo qui in boschetto" [We will come out here in the woods]. Brigida is shocked—"Oh! di notte poi nel boschetto . . ." [Oh! I don't know about the woods at night]— and Paolo concludes as properly as any bourgeois lover: "Via, via, ho detto così per ischerzo. Son galantuomo, fo stima di voi" [Go on, go on, I was teasing. I'm a gentleman, I respect you] (3.1). The passing joke becomes commentary when the next scenes bring Guglielmo and Giacinta together . . . alone in the secrecy of the *boschetto*.

Alone at first, Giacinta laments but accepts her act: "pazza ch'io sono stata, perché lasciarmi indurre sì presto e sì facilmente a dar parola a Leonardo . . . [ma] Quegli ha da essere mio marito, e voglia o non voglia, s'ha da vincere la passione" [what a fool I was!—Why did I let myself be persuaded so quickly and easily to give my word to Leonardo . . . [but] he must be my husband, whether I like it or not. I've got to conquer my passion] (3.2). When joined by Guglielmo, she admits her secret and repeats her decision: "vel confesso, io vi amo, dicolo a mio rossore, a mio dispetto, io vi amo," she admits, but "Farò il mio dovere" [to my shame I confess it, I love you. But . . . I'll do my duty] (3.3); and then they are discovered by Leonardo, who demands, "Quali affari segreti vi obbligano a ritirarvi qui col signor Guglielmo?" [What secret business brings you out here to meet with Signor Guglielmo?].

"Si tratta della riputazione" [It's a question of reputation], Giacinta had told Brigida earlier when the servant-confidante could not comprehend why Leonardo could not be discarded for Guglielmo before any marriage vows had been incurred (2.1). Now, here in the boschetto, it is the lie that will preserve the secret by pushing it deeper into the shadows that obscure love and duty. The sense of duty is real enough, the passion is real enough. The lie is real, too, though, so real that it mocks either of the other realities. The love secret is ignored rather than preserved; Guglielmo is the secret sharer, and Leonardo remains the skeptic. But both accept Giacinta's lie that saves them all in their silence, sacrifices them all for *riputazione*. She has met Guglielmo, she disingenously explains, to demand that he preserve the honor of the family by betrothal to Vittoria, who "in pubblico ha dimostrata la sua passione" [has shown her affection in public]. Confronted by Leonardo, her lover Guglielmo recognizes that Giacinta sacrifices "la passione al dovere" [her passion to duty] and accepts his own role of self-abnegating liar in order to retain the socially scandalous secret, responding to Leonardo, "Sì, amico, se non isdegnate accordarmela, vi chiedo la sorella vostra in consorte" [Yes, my friend, if you will be so good as to grant it, I ask for your sister's hand in marriage] (3.4). Again we are aware that "Non va troppo bene per la signora Vittoria."

It is not finished, though, this struggle toward social surrender. Leonardo coalesces place as plot and symbol: "Vuol il dovere che così si dica. Tutti non sarebbero persuasi del motivo che li faceva essere nel boschetto; intieramente non ne son nemmen io persuaso"

[I have to explain it this way. Not everyone would be convinced by their explanation of why they were in the wood. I'm not entirely convinced myself] (3.6). With the forbidden love so badly hidden, *Le avventure* concludes as a comedy of bad manners enacted by the undeserving, by refugees from some earlier Venetian satire piling open lies and love secrets one upon another until *Le avventure* at the end merges with the farce that was *Le smanie*. The conclusion is huddled together in a flurry of action, as the couples pair off only to rush back to Livorno, all matings left in abeyance for future consummation. Leonardo recalls the doubling of Truffaldino in *Il servitore di due padroni*, writing himself a letter that declares a false emergency in Livorno. It is a testing on his part, of course, but it encourages almost ebullient optimism for an audience promised a third play. Guglielmo's gloom is relieved with a little penultimate line of hope shared only by this audience and himself: "Respiro un poco. Qualche cosa può nascere" [I breathe again. Who knows what may happen]. It is an invitation to anticipate a *lieto fine* for the final play. The mood is enhanced by Ferdinando's farewell to his hopes that was cited earlier, because all is play: "la commedia per me è finita." His metaphor becomes statement in Giacinta's closing *plaudite*, that seems to wipe clean all the rhetoric of love and honor, to invalidate the effective commitments made within the action:

Signori miei gentilissimi, qui il poeta con tutto lo sforzo della fantasia aveva preparata una lunga disperazione, un combattimento di affetti, un misto d'eroismo e di tenerezza. Ho creduto bene di ommetterla per non attediarvi di più. Figuratevi qual esser puote una donna che sente gli stimoli dell'onore, ed è afflitta dalla più crudele passione. . . . La commedia non par finita; ma pure è finita, poiché l'argomento delle Avventure è completo. Se qualche cosa rimane a dilucidare, sarà forse materia di una terza commedia.

Ladies and gentlemen, at this point the author, with all the power of his imagination, had prepared a long speech of despair, a regular conflict of emotions, a mixture of heroism and pathos. I thought it best to omit it, to avoid boring you further. Picture for yourselves what a woman prey to

Goldoni

the promptings of honor and cursed by the cruelest of passions might be going through. . . . The play doesn't appear to be over; yet it is over, since the plot of the Adventures is complete. If there are still some loose ends left to tie, they may well provide matter for a third comedy. (3.16)

It has been a pair of playful plays, this stepping out of role argues; our involvement has been a trick of prestidigitation built around the meaningless secret we shared only with players, the characters having dissipated, as Ferdinando said of his hopes, "in fumo . . . e la commedia . . . è finita" [in smoke . . . and the comedy . . . is finished]. This is Goldoni's audacious dare, an implicit promise that he can disillusion us and draw us back simultaneously into that marginless ground between Venice and his stage.

Il ritorno dalla villeggiatura

Ritorno. The title has a psychic as well as geographic dimension. Re-arrived in Livorno, Leonardo is snubbed by the unhappy Giacinta, his jealousies now roused to full pitch. The society of these plays has, indeed, been touched by an autumnal version of midsummer madness in the country, in the boschetto of stolen encounters with unforeseen passions. But one returns from the manic mood of holiday to oneself. After a grim carnovale (Giacinta calls it "la troppo libera villeggiatura" [the too permissive stay in the country] [3.13]), *quaresima.*

In Goldoni's complex move, Leonardo has become the focus of *Il ritorno,* as Giacinta and Guglielmo had played in the foreground of *Le avventure.* It is not, I hasten to say, that their torrid infatuation is not still the center of action, the strand that dictates the effective expectations of the audience. But in this play much of the action as it manipulates our reaction is boldly thematic. Goldoni had given an explicit account of his structural intent: "Tutti i personaggi agiscono per lo stesso fine, e tutte le loro diverse azioni si riducono a provar l'argomento" [All of the characters act toward the same end, and

Secret Sharers in Italian Comedy

all of their different actions serve to advance the plot]. We are encouraged in this unusual fashion to seek out the "argomento." But, as this brief review of the first two members of the trilogy has suggested, the argument is a weighing of values at those peak times when passion and *il dovere* bring humans to a *bivio*. It is this Herculean choice that Goldoni promotes to the focus of our attention. And it is Leonardo who now embodies it while more fully aware of consequences than even Giacinta.

Leonardo returns to Livorno to find himself financially ruined by the expense of social high life that has culminated in his disastrous attempt to emulate Filippo's style *in villeggiatura*. He also finds himself in love with a Giacinta who (he is certain now) loves Guglielmo: "ella non ha per me né amore, né stima, né gratitudine . . . guai a me se io arrivasi a sposarla. . . . Mi vendicherò ad ogni costo. A costo di perdermi, di precipitarmi" [she feels neither love, respect, nor gratitude for me . . . Heaven help me if I should ever end up married to her. . . . I'll get even whatever it costs. Even if it means my ruin, my downfall] (1.10). But there is the other side of Leonardo's mind that sees past fury to discern his own responsibility for having ruined himself: "Qual vendetta vo' io meditando. . . . Chi è il nemico maggiore ch'io abbia fuor di me stesso? Io sono il pazzo, lo stolido, il nemico di me medesimo" [And to think I was plotting revenge! Do I have a worse enemy than myself? Oh, what a madman, what a fool, I'm my own worst enemy!] (1.11). The rejected passion is real, the self-abasement is real—and so is the realism about his social position. Marriage for love fuses as motive with money: "Sono impazientissimo. In primo luogo per l'amore ch'io porto a quell'ingrata, a quella barbara di Giacinta; secondariamente, nello stato in cui sono, l'unico mio risorgimento potrebbe essere la sua dote" [I'm a nervous wreck. In the first place, because I'm in love with that cruel, ungrateful Giacinta, and secondly, because, in my present financial condition, my only hope for salvation is her dowry] (1.1). A lover almost openly betrayed, a young man who retains self-knowledge even on the verge of desperation, a cynic on the make: this multisided psyche has brought Leonardo a long way from the profligate man-boy who

Goldoni

was struggling with his *baule* in *Le smanie*. But the shifts are too wide in their arc to allow one to identify with the character or "provar l'argomento" through him. Leonardo as puzzle, then, but one whose partial objectivity and open cynicism bring us to remember the clues sewn into the tapestry of *Le avventure* that promise a *lieto fine* upon this return. And the chorus of hope grows more insistent in *Il ritorno*.

Early on, his house invaded by creditors, Leonardo remembers "la porta segreta" [the secret door] by which he may escape. His servant warns him against plunging into the darkness: "la scala è oscura, è precipitosa"; "Sarà piena di ragnatele, si sporcherà il vestito" [the stairway is dark and steep; there are cobwebs all over, you'll get your clothes dirty] (1.1–2). Here is allegory to remind us of the dark secrets of the boschetto (and at last we may discern a reason beyond the geographic for the villeggiatura having been set in "Montenero," the black mountain) where the threat of staining the garment of *riputazione* is so strong.[16] But there is, in this case, light at the end of Leonardo's tunnel: he escapes the house to seek help and so reinforces the anxiety of hope for a romantically anticipated harmony.

Guglielmo, building his notion that "Qualche cosa può nascere" into action, begins a covert assault upon the fortress of Giacinta's *dovere:* "Convien dissimulare," he admits, "non son contento s'io non le [Giacinta] parlo ancora una volta" [I must pretend. I won't be happy till I've talked to her again] (1.8). Vittoria, scarcely less aware than her brother of a cool reception into enforced betrothal, prods Guglielmo with an ironic refrain as he drags out the social farce — "Signor Guglielmo, dormite?" [Are you asleep, Signor Guglielmo?] — recognizing that "Egli è tutto flemma, io son tutta foco" [He is all phlegm, and I'm all fire] (3.11). She is right to the extent that Guglielmo reiterates his hope even to the penultimate moment of the action. Filippo is extracting Giacinta's agreement to marry Leonardo and depart from Livorno; and while the entire interwoven group of interested parties awaits a foregone decision, Guglielmo says to himself: "Mi par di essere al punto di dover sentire la mia sentenza. Chi sa ancora ch'ella non sia favorevole?" [It looks as if

I'm about to hear my final sentence. Who knows if it may not yet be favorable] (3.11).

With all of these preparative directives, there must be the anticipated *lieto fine,* and there is. But it is an ironic embrace of those entwined opposites of natural passion: *riputazione, dovere,* and money. Goldoni was not careless in knitting together his "argomento."

I earlier remarked upon how the failed Ferdinando-Sabina courtship and the successful one of Rosina and Tognino reflected doubt upon Giacinta's apparent choice at the close of *Le avventure.* In *Il ritorno* these paired triumphs and failures are reversed. Ferdinando receives a letter of capitulation from Sabina, begging his return to Montenero with the bait of that substantial "donazione," demand for which had finished his hopes in the earlier play. Asked "Cosa risolvete di fare?" [So, what will you do?] Ferdinando replies: "Un'eroica risoluzione. Prendo immediatamente la posta, e me ne vo' a consolare, a soccorrere la mia adorata Sabina" [A heroic decision! I shall take the next coach, and go to console and succor my adored Sabina] (3.11). "Povera vecchia pazza" [Poor crazy old woman], sighs Costanza sympathetically. But in the interim, Costanza herself has not only engineered the marriage of the children but tyrannizes them. Hoping still to keep a hold upon the doctor, Tognino's father, she silences and maltreats the boy: "Andate, vi dico, che se mi fate muover la bile, vi caccio via di casa come un birbante" [Get out of here, I tell you! If you keep getting on my nerves, I'll have you thrown out like a thief]. In a farcical parody of the expected pleasures of marriage, Tognino can only cry out, "Son maritato, e son maritato" [I'm married, and I'm really married; my translation] (3.6). Rosina begs, Tognino cries out, but as the play is ending, Giacinta endorses Costanza in the only terms she now knows, the terms upon which she has accepted Leonardo: "Compatisco la signora Costanza, s'ella desiderava di celare un maritaggio che può essere criticato; e voglia il cielo che non si lagnino un giorno questi due sposi" [I sympathize with Signora Costanza for wanting to conceal a marriage that some people might criticize. Let's hope that this couple will never have cause to complain] (3.13).

Goldoni

Giacinta's glimpse into a dubious future echoes at a distance Fulgenzio's doubts in *Le smanie*. And reminds us that that well-meaning meddler looms large in *Il ritorno*. If he was willing to stabilize his old friend Filippo's *riputazione* in the earlier play using Leonardo's courtship as his instrument, in keeping with the shifting focus of *Il ritorno*, Fulgenzio hides an obsession under sentimentality. Without illusions as to Leonardo's conduct, he persists in aiding him to a happy denouement *because* he is unworthy: "A me poco dovrebbe premere, perchè non ho verun interesse con voi. Ma son uomo, sento l'umanità, ho compassione di tutti; meritate di essere abbandonato, ma non ho cuore di abbandonarvi" [What should I care, you're no concern of mine. But I'm human, I recognize my humanity, I have a soft spot for everybody. You deserve to be left to stew in your own juice, but I don't have the heart to do it] (2.2). Fulgenzio gives good advice on pride as well as debt (1.3), beards Leonardo's disguised uncle Bernardo in his own den in hopes of gaining support for the profligate,[17] and with great effort arranges a new dowry plan that appeals to Filippo's avarice and seals Giacinta's fate.

And Giacinta places a final seal of approval upon Fulgenzio's efforts. While Guglielmo hopes, while Vittoria and Leonardo fear, while the audience prepares for the secret love to burst into a final symphony of blessing upon Guglielmo and Giacinta (even the alliteration assures us of the inevitable), Fulgenzio discovers that Filippo can turn over his Genovese landholdings to Leonardo and Giacinta in lieu of the promised dowry Filippo is unable to honor,[18] that Leonardo can recover his debts with the income, and that he, Fulgenzio, can act as accountant and manager of affairs to guide the reformed profligate Leonardo. There will be another geographical and psychic translation, then. Giacinta, having fallen in the natural garden provided by villeggiatura, will now go with Leonardo into the wilderness, a larger, distant, and foreign world. There is no way to demarcate irony from social slavery in the results of this interference by a well-meaning senex when Giacinta addresses him to say: "Ringrazio il signor Fulgenzio del bene che dall'opera sua riconosco; e vi assicuro, signore, che non me ne scorderò fin ch'io viva" [I thank

Signor Fulgenzio for the good that has come of his efforts, and, I assure you, sir, that I will never forget it as long as I live] (3.13). She has chosen to go to Genoa: "e parto con animo risoluto di non rammentarmi che il mio dovere" [And I'm leaving with my mind made up to think only of duty]. We know and do not know Giacinta's mind. We know Vittoria's, Leonardo's, losses and gains; we know that, hoping to the last for a change of Giacinta's heart, Guglielmo has lost all. It was, after all, only Guglielmo who went *in villeggiatura* with no motive but that of winning Giacinta. He had lost her at the very moment of self-revelation through his socialized timidity, his concern for her *riputazione*. If the conclusion of *Il ritorno dalla villeggiatura* is bleakly inconclusive, it is owing to Goldoni's grasp of the structural possibility of secrecy posed as direct address. His frustrated lovers deploy this technique with the fool Ferdinando as instrument.

In this tracing of Italian comedic form, comforting or unsettling, secrecy has been a mode of conclusion without ending. Goldoni's trilogy replicates this pattern in that Rosina, Vittoria, and Giacinta all marry into a future extraordinarily problematic and uninterpretable from the action of the play. In achieving variously inappropriate marital pacts, they face a *lieto fine* that cannot be confused with a happy ending. Only Ferdinando's choice of Sabina and her "donazione" is unambiguously embraced by both parties in full knowledge of what they are getting in trade. In accord with Goldonian irony, it is appropriate that the most unguarded member of this little society should begin his guardianship of its secrets by simply standing between Giacinta and Guglielmo as she chides the latter through the allegorical vehicle of Ferdinando's supposed mistreatment of Sabina. Guilty of abusing love's avowals, the gigolo is an admitted master of deception: "E che cosa ho fatto io alla signora Sabina?" [And what did I do to Signora Sabina]? "Tutto," responds Giacinta, "quel peggio che far le poteste" [Everything; the very worst thing you could do]. The bill of particulars is extended at great length, beginning with the pointed reminder that "un galantuomo non ha da cercar d'innamorare una persona vecchia, o giovane ch'ella sia, quando l'amore non può avere un onesto fine" [a gentleman shouldn't try to make an old lady — or a young one for that matter — fall in love, when that love can never have a decent outcome]. Goldoni's stage direction justifies the intuition of Ferdinando as "*si volta a guardare Guglielmo*" [he turns to look at Guglielmo]. The stage direction reads, "*durante questo discorso, Giacinta va guardando Guglielmo*" [Giacinta is looking at Guglielmo as she speaks] (2.8).

There is a further distancing yet as we close upon a putative ending. Guglielmo has written Giacinta a letter under the duress of city pressures, the microscopic social surveillance preventing the privacy once found in the boschetto. It is a confession of weakness buried beneath strength. He promises not to write the promise of rites with Vittoria "se non quando vi vedrò maritata" [until you are married]. It is an epistle from the boldest among the timid: "*E assicurarvi che dal canto mio non soffrirete inquietudini, promettendovi sull'onor mio che, a costo ancor di morire, sfuggirò ogn'incontro d' importunarvi*" [And to assure you that you will not have to suffer any further harassment on my part, as I promise you on my honor that, even if it kills me, I will avoid any unwanted meetings in future] (2.11). Ripped between the tides of duty and passion, Giacinta chooses. Her response to Guglielmo's letter is unwritten; she follows Ferdinando into a permanent marital deception, publicly seeming to address him while privately directing a rebuke to Guglielmo on his error in writing as he, in turn, pretends to excoriate Ferdinando on his refusal to reply to Sabina's pathetic letter, saying, "Vuole la convenienza, che quando si riceve una lettera, si risponde" [When someone gets a letter, it's good manners to answer]. But, observes Giacinta, "Bisogna vedere se la lettera merita una risposta" [First, you have to see if the letter deserves an answer] (3.8).

Giacinta's technique is to paraphrase sarcastically every passage of Sabina's letter by seeming in Guglielmo's presence to be deploring the conduct of her *own* counterpart, Ferdinando. It is a buried dialogue of lovers' farewell, a secret to that onstage audience oblivious of Guglielmo's letter, of the despair beneath every innocuous word. Fulgenzio and Filippo remain in Livorno, they too oblivious of the drama in which they are important role-players. Guglielmo awakens into that nightmare that will be his life with Vittoria—after the assault upon happiness has been repulsed by Giacinta's choice. Ferdinando and Sabina are flung off in one direction from this Venetian Livorno, Giacinta and Leonardo in another. It is the last contrast in this congeries of unfinished domestic business. Goldoni has drawn from his tradition a way to justify Giacinta's *plaudite* upon the trilogy without directing it: "consolatevi con voi stessi della vostra prudenza, della vostra moderazione" [be thankful for your own common sense and restraint] (3.13). The course of the trilogy's education in the cost of secrecy makes one wonder whether this audience remembered some version of the colloquialism "fa un freddo che consola": it's cold out there.

Una delle ultime sere di carnovale

The villeggiatura trilogy was, of course, early in a triumphant series of Goldoni's most mature work, succeeded quickly by *Sior Todoro brontolon, Le baruffe chiozzotte,* and *Una delle ultime sere di carnovale* [One of the Last Evenings of Carnival]. It was also at the beginning of the end. Carlo Gozzi had begun the theatrical counterreformation attacks of the *fiabe,* and in the allegory of exile that is *Il corvo,* he satirized Goldoni's imminent departure from Venice. This mocking attack came in October 1761, in tandem with the first presentation of Goldoni's trilogy; the invitation from the Parisian Comédie Italienne had reached Goldoni in August. On Mardi Gras, 16 February 1762, Goldoni made his *addio* to Venice. He made it with his own theatrical allegory.

I conclude this sampling of Goldoni's achievement and of the comedic tradition that was its heritage with *Una delle ultime sere di carnovale.* One motivation is that which has tempted so many into critical accounts: the coalescence of theatricality, Goldoni's farewell in the title to one of the great carnivalesque societies of the eighteenth century, and the circumstances of this last first night he would see in the Venetian theaters which his work had revived after a very long drought. The sentimental leave-taking of Anzoletto has roused the sentiment and sense of concinnity in sympathetic critics from the first audience onward. But the yet more urgent motivation is to watch a form coalesced with a particular action with such skill that the form itself is exploded into a dimension undreamed in its recurrences during the three hundred years we have probed to uncover these experiments.

When one first considers the action of *Carnovale*, it seems to be a play in the Plautine-Ariostan tradition: secrets are openly concealed everywhere, displayed, discussed, and culminate in a *scioglimento* that joins the generations, joins six couples in marriages celebrated by feast and dance, the old regeneration of harmony from chaos reenacted. Reenacted in the household of a bourgeois merchant in the laboring and merchandising corner of Venice seemingly least adaptable to romance and romanticism: Cannaregio. It is a setting for a Venetian Pratolini, a *piccola storia popolare*. One of Goldoni's perceptive commentators sums up: "la scena, disegnata dalla semplicissima didascalia 'Camera e lumi sul tavolino,' rimane immutata fino alle ultime scene, quando si passa direttamente nel vicino tinello per il pranzo e di lì, nell'ultima scena, nel contiguo salotto illuminato per il ballo" [the scene, indicated by the very simple stage direction '*a room and lights on a little table*,' remains unchanged until the last scenes, when one passes directly into the adjacent dining room for the dinner, and from there, in the last scene, into the adjacent salon lighted for the dance]. But in the same breath, the critic is struck with the insubstantiality projected by this scenic stolidity: "il bellissimo titolo . . . proiettando nell'indefinito quell'occasione così concreta e irripetibile (*una* delle ultime sere), sembra esprimere il distacco, il valore esemplare e la straordinaria forza evocativa che la commedia ha per noi"[19] [the marvellous title . . . projecting such a concrete and unrepeatable occasion (*one* of the last evenings) into the indefinite, seems to express the detachment, the exemplary value, and the extraordinary evocative force that the comedy has for us].

Luigi Squarzina, the director who has most extensively commented upon role playing of thing and place in Goldoni's drama,[20] was naturally attracted by *Carnovale*, with its simple realistic setting, just described. But he, too, found it strangely dissolved:

C'è insomma dappertutto già una qualità di memoria e di rimpianto che smaterializza le cose, tanto che in sede di spettacolo si sente l'esigenza di ridefinire continuamente i contorni dello spazio scenico. . . . Nasce in questa sospensione fra passato e futuro.[21]

There is, in short, everywhere a quality of memory and of regret that dematerializes things, so much so that in the theater one feels the necessity of continually redefining the contours of scenic space. . . . It is born in this suspension between past and future.

It is this suspension that redimensions the quotidian properties, the banal card game and nervous dinner party. The sterile — sterile because self-defeating — niceties of manner from the trilogy are nowhere in evidence. The guests circulate both at play and at dinner in an erotic *ronde* reminiscent of rowdy children at a party. One hypochondriac faints, hacks, and laughs for attention; another overaged belle stinks so badly of perfume that the others spurn her from the table with wrinkled noses and wicked commentary. Everyone is prying into everyone else's secrets, which are displayed as loosely as the cards held by the inattentive players. And upon this chaos of physical and psychic movement Goldoni displays his own cards in the first sentence of his address "a chi legge": "In fondo di questa Commedia è un'allegoria" [At the bottom of this comedy is an allegory]. The allegory is the unfinished history of his own "sospensione fra passato e futuro."

The plot of *Carnovale* is simple. Zamaria, owner of a weaving factory and widowed father of young Domenica, institutes a gala party to celebrate the concluding days of carnival. He invites two other prosperous clothmakers and their wives, a woman who is an expert at gold thread, the somewhat wild but able *manganaro* Momolo, who operates the professional pressing machines for all the clothmakers, and Anzoletto, the artistic designer whose work is always in demand—and who is the innamorato of Domenica. At the party the rumor is confirmed that Anzoletto is going to Moscovy by invitation to "provar se una man italiana, dessegnando sul fatto, sul gusto dei Moscoviti, possa formar un misto, capace de piaser alle do nazion"[22] [test whether an Italian hand, designing on the spot, and on the basis of Muscovite taste, can create a combination capable of pleasing both nations] (1.15). In the interstices of entertainment, all is worked out so that Domenica is married to Anzoletto; the widowed father marries a libidinous older woman, Madame Gatteau, a French embroidery expert who has mysteriously obtained for Anzoletto his Russian invitation; and the quartet prepare to set out together on this great foreign adventure, leaving Zamaria's factory and affairs in the hands of Momolo, who will settle down in marriage with Polonia, the gold-thread weaver. "Ho fatto," explains Goldoni, "de' Commedianti una società di Tessitori, o sia fabbricanti di stoffe, ed io mi sono coperto col titolo di Disegnatore. L'allegoria non è male adattata. I Comici eseguiscono le opere degli Autori, ed i Tessitori lavorano sul modello de'loro Disegnatori"[23] [I have made the players a society of weavers, or clothmakers, and I have disguised myself with the title of designer. The allegory is not badly adapted. The players execute the works of the author, and the weavers work on the model of their designers].

An apparent disproportion both in the introduction "a chi legge" and in the middle of the play (where it occupies nearly one-fifth of the text: 2.2–4) is a long, detailed encounter with the popular Venetian card game called *meneghella*. Goldoni explains its rules thoroughly enough to instruct one to play, and the playing through in *Carnovale* is so complicated in its accuracy, amidst continuous changes in the players' seating, that Squarzina suggests Goldoni must have been dependent upon observing his actors "play" to produce the text. Fido has demonstrated the frequency in other parts of the corpus with which Goldoni utilized his own and Venetians' infatuation with gambling as a metaphor and mirror of social and dramatic choices of chance-taking upon the improbable.[24] But in *Carnovale*, the gambling dominates a text that (unlike *Il giuocatore* or even *La bottega del caffè*) has no significant gaming theme, that reveals no gamblers' obsessions. What the play at *meneghella* does emphasize, of course, is risk taking. Anzoletto, Zamaria, Momolo, Domenica, and the others are all putting themselves at risk in the great domestic and travel adventure that will move them beyond the physical and psychic confines within which they have lived to this point; all are making a break with the past as drastic as Anzoletto's. There is another aspect, however.

What Goldoni emphasizes both in introduction and scenic action is the secrecy at the heart of a game that pits hidden possibilities against mere probabilities, bringing to the fore the element of bluff: "un Giuocatore non avrà carta buona . . . e non ostante rinforza, ed aumenta l'invito. Questa si chiama una *Cazzada*, una bravata per far ritirar gli altri" [a player may not have a single good card . . . and notwithstanding responds, and raises the bet. This is called a *cazzada*, a bluff to make the others withdraw]. It is what Goldoni's avatar, Anzoletto, and all the other lovers do in the play: they half-reveal, half-conceal their hands in the game of love.

In the trilogy, Leonardo half-knew the truth about Giacinta and Guglielmo until it burst upon him in *Il ritorno*, even there to be finally repressed. In this later play about *una delle ultime sere di carnovale*, everyone seems to know, too, that Anzoletto is going to leave Venice. Polonia knows it legitimately, as she explains to Domenica, who only fearfully suspects it; Polonia is acquainted with the French seamstress Madame Gatteau, who has shown her the letter "dove che i ghe scrive de sior Anzoletto, a la m'ha anca dito, che la va in Moscovia con elo" [where they write to her about Signor Anzoletto, and she has also told me, that she is going into Muscovy with him] (1.14). Madame Gatteau, in turn, is equally open with Domenica about a secretly nurtured infatuation with the young designer: "Come! sè inamorada de sior Anzoletto?" "Hélas! mademoiselle, je ne vous le cacherai pas." "Lo salo elo, che ghe sè innamorada?" "Mademoiselle, pas encore tout à fait" [*D:* What! Are you in love with Signor Anzoletto? *Mme. G:* Alas! Mademoiselle, I won't hide it from you. *D:* Does he know that you are in love with him? *Mme. G:* Mademoiselle, not completely as yet] (2.7). Polonia has been almost as open about her "secret" love for Momolo: "Xe vero, che tra lu e Polonia ghe sia qualcossa?" [Is it true, that there is something between him and Polonia?], asks the worldly wife of the silk merchant, and without wondering where this question may have had its origin or whether Polonia would want privacy in which to make her private confessions, Domenica responds: "El dise. Ma in quella testa crédela che ghe sia fondamento? Ela si piuttosto credo che la ghe tenderia, se 'l disesse dasseno" [He says so. But in that head do you believe there is any basis? Yet I believe she would be willing, if he were speaking sincerely] (1.9). And so the chain continues: confidences given, confidences broken, all in a closed circle of women. But how *did* the silk merchant and his wife know of Anzoletto and Domenica? (1.7). We never learn. Then there is Zamaria's secret, announced to the assembled card players: "Che i zoga, che i zoga, che co i averà fenio de zogar, parleremo. Gh'ho una cossa in mente. Chi sa? Co se vol che 'l torna, so mi quel che ghe vol per farlo [Anzoletto] tornar" [Let them play, let them play, and when they have finished playing, we will talk. I have something in mind. Who knows? If she wants him to return, I know what will bring him back] (2.4). It is a tantalizing declaration, one that seems pivotal to the denouement. The father has overheard the love dilemma Domenica imposes upon Anzoletto (stay or take me away), and he holds the cards: Domenica will not be freed from her father's will to join Anzoletto in Muscovy. And, in any case, Zamaria has already elicited Anzoletto's promise to forward future designs from Moscovia (now we may freely read: Zamaria-Vendramin, Anzoletto-Goldoni). He can wait out lovers' magnetism in silence. But he has not yet encountered Madame Gatteau, the future bride who will carry them all to Russia with *her* unrevealed connections in that distant culture. So this culminating secret plan comes to nothing, dissipates into that other plot that has been written to include Zamaria but not his own schemes. The couples pair off properly, and Momolo even gives this concinnity an explicit imprimatur: "Tutte xe arente alla so colonna, e anca mi me son rampegà" ("tutti sono vicini alla persona che amano," and "Rampicato, cioè acquistato", Goldoni adds in two glossary notes explaining the idiomatic Venetianisms) [Everyone is next to the person they love, and I too have been grabbed off] (3.11).

It is this omnipresence of secrecy, this oscillation between veiled origins we cannot penetrate and the most venal revelatory exchanges in the social *rondeur* of a little group in Cannaregio, that creates the effect we have had described for us by *goldonisti* as a projection "nell'indefinito [di] quell'occasione così concreta e irripetibile," and "una qualità di memoria e di rimpianto che smaterializza le cose, tanto che in sede di spettacolo si sente l'esigenza di ridefinire continuamente i contorni dello spazio scenico."

"Ridefinire continuamente i contorni dello spazio scenico" expresses in a single exquisite phrase Goldoni's adaptation of the secret as comedic form in his own *addio* to Venice, to the theatrical world in which he had lived and written until half a decade toward his sixtieth year. Squarzina was not the first to suggest that the witty but dependable Momolo and the optimistic master of design Anzoleto are split halves of Goldoni at the end of a tradition. Anzoletto is given the unforgettable farewell passage. But it is Momolo who is left behind to keep things together until the return. For there will be a return, all agree, except those of us in succeeding generations who have learned the historical outcome of the story with Goldoni's death in Paris.

Goldoni himself, of course, did not know, probably did not even guess it. So *Una delle ultime sere di carnovale* of his last year in Venice exploded the petty secrets of his creatures into a form that finally accepted the playwright-God analogy by embracing a future whose secrets were concealed in something larger than the little Veneto houses in which *La venexiana* or *La Betía* had closed off the ending from their audiences.

The author's address on allegory "a chi legge" was written for the sixteenth volume of the Pasquale edition, appearing in 1778. And it goes to the heart of the secret that had always been implicit in the form we have followed, the playwright's reconnaissance of something that "nasce in questa sospensione fra passato e futuro." Given

Goldoni

the self-allegory, Goldoni admits that some will think it only proper that he give an account of what he has done in sending the designs of Anzoletto-Goldoni back to Venice from Moscovia-Paris. But, he says, "Mi riserbo di farlo in altra occasione, allora quando col racconto della mia vita arriverò a parlare della mia andata e del mio soggiorno in Francia [I will put off doing it for another occasion, when in telling my life story I will come to speak of my departure and of my sojourn in France].[25] Goldoni is confident that the past has already incorporated the future as history. The conclusion of the "allegory" begun sixteen years before is still unknown. But the not yet begun *Mémoires* seem in his imagination already written, a story for those who recognize the poet's leaves as the sybil's leaves, secrets half told and fully displayed.

Afterword on Secrecy and
Literary Genres

I made clear at the outset that this study was not conceived or intended as a continuous literary history; it constitutes a morphology of one dramatic form recurrent at widely separated chronological and geographic points. The geographic points are Italian, though, and these plays have sometimes seemed to gravitate toward connections that felt historical in spite of my general disclaimer. When that sense has become too strong to ignore, I have sewn separate threads together into speculations, harmless enough if disregarded, and useful if I have sometimes intuited relations correctly. Such speculations have been accumulating elsewhere, usually with equal diffidence. But as they accumulate they begin to suggest a new view of unity in the history of Italian drama, a network of panpeninsular relations through theatrical and publishing entrepreneurs where we had become accustomed to seeing regional developments.

More surprising, perhaps, is the persistent reappearance of plays with all the characteristics of a common rebellious antigeneric stance across three centuries. And this survival seems almost perverse when the principal characteristic the plays share is a secrecy, an insistence upon a pact, however implicit, that commits the audience to accept a product that goes against the grain of every instinct of narrative, staged or written. Theoretically, that is, we come to fictive narrative as relaxed vessels ready to be filled, passive in our expectation of being entertained by the news of what fools some other mortals have been. The plays we have reviewed frustrate that set of mind as they insist upon our participation, a species of choosing sides in silent collusion with one stage participant as he deludes another. They frustrate it, too, in that, sharing the secret, we also share contingency, or better, project our contingency upon the stage action — the story has not been told. We necessarily make judgments, guesses based in the accumulation of gathered clues as to its future course. But we cannot pass the story on, because it is incomplete. In this we are, I have been saying, forced into the play's action, forced to become part of its formal whole, a shaping vector as indispensable as any dialogue exchange of information, of plotting in both the dramatic and scheming senses of the word. But it is also possible to say that the play action is thus forced into society, the enactors become another group with whom we have entered into the social contract of partially shared exchange. It is just this need for vicarious comprehension that motivates our other social compacts, which are made with varied acquaintances. And, as with the play's characters, these groups may often have no contiguous area except ourself; we move into and out of each cluster with participant but contingent and discontinuous judgments. At the close of *Le avventure della villeggiatura* Giacinta reports that nothing has concluded, but at another time more can be learned. In this we have the comedy claiming a mode of discontinuous but recurrent intercourse analogous to that marking all but the most intimate social connections. And in this one might recall the difference between gossip, which is always a contingent judgment upon past or present actions as they may form future ones, and history, which is a form of closed narrative.

The recurrent mention of Boccaccio in these pages may serve to remind one that narrative, too, even where fiction assumes the form of history, as in the novelle of the *Decameron,* has its secrets. Alatiel's amorous adventures offered a case in point, but perhaps the written narrative comes closest to secrecy in what one might label modern Gothic, that is, narratives leading to the unknowable: it is an effect eponymous with its most widely read exemplar, Conrad's *Heart of Darkness,* and utilized variously in James's *Turn of the Screw,* Nabokov's *Pale Fire,* and Calvino's *Se una notte d'inverno un viag-*

giatore [If on a Winter's Night a Traveler], to cite familiar texts. In these Gothic versions, however, the collusion is between the author and his unstable narrator or narrators, and the effect of open form is thus to exclude rather than involve the reader. There is another not uncommon aspect of narrative secrecy that does include the reader, however, demanding a strenuous effort to reach a satisfying state of private understanding with and of the author. This is textual coding, all the practiced species of puzzle from cryptogram, anagram, or numerological ordering to the formal allusiveness of allegory insisted upon by Tasso retrospectively for *La Gerusaleme liberata*. Having decoded the parallel levels of the narrative, however, the reader is left in quite a different psychological position from that of the auditor forced into collusion with the secrets embedded in our group of plays. The reader, in decoding, has performed a critical act[1] and so has recovered the dimension of the narrative events expanded through their interpretation(s) by the narrator. He has, to restate what was put in a more abstract way when Boccaccio was first invoked, heard a history and been placed in a position to relate it to others—that is, analogously to the literary critic, he is now in a position to make the esoteric generally available. However sophisticated the insider may be in the explicatory maneuvers by which he recovers and relates the full significance of what he has read, at bottom he is the historian of the past who repeats what was completed once upon a time. That act of explicating a rereading has been once more exemplified in my literary critique of the several plays discussed here. It has been a critique aimed, however paradoxically, at recovering the form of an uninitiated viewer's original involvement: literary criticism subordinated to the service of theater. This double reading is just what the form forbids for the secret sharer of our antigenre of open-ended dramatic intrigues; "Whatever the risks, which come with the very notion of secrecy," Matei Calinescu observes, "a secret is ultimately better kept by a person than by a text" (259).

The last remark provokes me to an obvious truism. "In the beginning was the Word," and it was with this Word that the scriptural deity made all things: "God said, Let there be light, and there was

Afterword

light." He spoke things into existence, concluding his creation with man. And it must be a large portion of the playwright's satisfaction that he alone among writers performs an analogous act: once staged, his words become men, walking and talking in his image. Free Will, however, caught Christianity in the paradox of contingency within form. God's shaping will acts to its ends through Providence, but the ways of Providence are (to use an eighteenth-century term for them) "strange" — indirect and unanticipated — because man himself is strange in his own willfulness. And like the theater of the world, the smaller stage theater of the dramatist involves form and contingency so intimately as to make the notion of dramatic form sometimes seem an oxymoron. The author incarnates his words in the actors, but they are then to a considerable degree detached from his original conception, free interpreters, vehicles always for contingency, liable at any turn to self-calculated business, improvisation — in short, to the interjection of their humanity. This is the actor's peculiar rapport and kinship with the audience rather than the author, who, having spoken his creatures into existence, nevertheless loses authority moment by moment.

In writing the dramas of secrecy, the authors we have heard in the pages above built this paradoxical theatrical principle into the dramatic form. The audience is energized by becoming an insider privy to the staged secret intrigues, a position given value by the presence of excluded outsiders within the action. And now we should notice that the narrator of such modern Gothic fictions as were mentioned above are self-indulgently garrulous and notoriously assertive of their inside historian's authority. This characteristic is inherent in their role, of course; as exemplified by Conrad's Marlowe, they are devious, deluded, misleading as they place the teller before the tale. In contrast, the stage characters of our Italian dramas who invoke the audience's collusion in their secret affairs are role models of discretion. They have every motive for, and evince every intention of, keeping their own secret counsel. If we have learned their private plans, it has not been through their boastful overreaching but through our own indiscretion in stumbling upon them. The auditor's collusion in protecting their still interesting future contingencies is a matter of nothing less than good manners, even if exhibited in a dubious cause. We have been given an unexpected trust. Thus falsely raised in self-esteem, we are coopted into honoring a stage character's often dishonorable confidence.

But by the same act, if we turn to the playwright's confidence in his art and his trust of our ability to transcend with him the prejudices of expectation, social and generic, the collusion may justify a sense that we are estimable auditors. The audience, like the playwright, permits these dramas, like themselves, to exist perpetually suspended between that past or future that would reduce them to mere history, shadow puppets reflecting the stuff of one upon another time. This suspension was, as we have seen, best sustained by the eighteenth-century heir to a remarkable tradition in Italian comedy. In this respect, my readings in earlier comedies can be understood as homage to Goldoni.

Afterword

189

Notes

Introduction

1. Northrop Frye, "The Argument of Comedy," in *English Institute Essays 1948*, ed. D. A. Robertson, Jr. (New York: Columbia University Press, 1949), 58–73.

2. George E. Duckworth, *The Nature of Roman Comedy: A Study in Popular Entertainment* (Princeton: Princeton University Press, 1952) 143–67.

3. E. K. Chambers, *The Medieval Stage* (Oxford, 1903), vol. 2; C. L. Barber, *Shakespeare's Festive Comedy* (Princeton: Princeton University Press, 1959); and Robert Weimann, *Shakespeare and the Popular Tradition in the Theater*, ed. Robert Schwartz (Baltimore: Johns Hopkins University Press, 1978).

4. Paolo Toschi, *Le origini del teatro italiano* (Turin: Einaudi, 1955).

5. Erich Segal, *Roman Laughter: The Comedy of Plautus* (Cambridge: Harvard University Press, 1968).

6. *The Masks of Menander: Sign and Meaning in Greek and Roman Performance* (Cambridge: Cambridge University Press, 1991), 131. Pages 59–62 expand usefully upon Segal's "festival" thesis. On the Atellan tradition and Plautus's participation in it as an actor before turning to his Greek models, see Duckworth, 49–51, and Niall W. Slater, *Plautus in Performance: The Theatre of the Mind* (Princeton: Princeton University Press, 1985), 7–9, 35, 145, 147.

7. Ferdinando Taviani and Mirella Schino, *Il segreto della Commedia dell'Arte: la memoria delle compagnie italiane del XVI, XVII e XVIII secolo* (Florence: La Casa Usher, 1982); plays written and published by members of the troupes are collected in two anthologies: *Commedie dei comici dell'Arte*, ed. Laura Falavolta (Turin: UTET, 1982), and *Commedia dell'arte*, ed. Siro Ferrone (Milan: Mursia, 1985–86), 2 vols.

8. Francesco Zeffi's account from his biography of Strozzi is reproduced

in Lorenzo di Filippo Strozzi, *Commedie,* ed. Andrea Gareffi (Ravenna: Longo, 1980), 37–38. In a later and fuller examination, Gareffi, starting from a notation added to the extant manuscript in a hand other than that of the original amanuensis that dates the play in 1506 (a year in which Strozzi was engaged in other entertainments in both Florence and Ferrara), examines the tangle of conflicting evidence on dating (*La scrittura e la festa: teatro, festa e letteratura nella Firenze del Rinascimento* [Bologna: Il Mulino, 1991], 119–28). But 1506 is made unlikely not only by Zeffi's statements but by the fact that it would, of course, make Strozzi's curiously aberrant play much earlier than either Machiavelli's *Mandragola* or the analogous experiments in neighboring Siena, discussed in chapter 3 below. Gareffi's later book contrasts Strozzi's (and Jacopo Nardi's) "public" and pro-Medicean conservative plays with Machiavelli's "private" and more subversive comedy (99–188). Strozzi's "commedia in versi" is cited in the text from Gareffi's edition.

9. Asked by his master to comment on his appearance, Catillo's servant observes: "Un po' più grossa è questa spalla manca / de l'altra; e questo non importa molto, / ché una vesta oggi ogni difetto cuopre" [this left shoulder is a little higher than the other; yet this doesn't matter much, because these days a garment covers up every defect] (1.4.188–90); references here and following are to act, scene, and line.

10. I am selecting almost randomly from the extensive summaries found in Bernard Weinberg, *A History of Literary Criticism in the Italian Renaissance* (Chicago: University of Chicago Press, 1961); I cite 1:239, 318, 397. The translations are Weinberg's. Although this history of critical theory is not organized to bring together the materials, it provides numerous critics' recapitulations of the function of *la meraviglia* in comedy.

11. Weinberg, *History,* 1:535–36. The translations are Weinberg's from a manuscript treatise titled *Che la favola de la comedia vuole esser honesta et non contenere mali costumi* [That the fable of comedy should be honest and not contain disreputable behavior].

12. Baxter Hathaway, *Marvels and Commonplaces: Renaissance Literary Criticism* (New York: Random House, 1968), vii. This "popular" little book focuses on the large body of Cinquecento materials analyzed in more detail in Hathaway's *The Age of Criticism: The Late Renaissance in Italy* (Ithaca: Cornell University Press, 1962).

13. I have found no credibly developed example of the open-ended comedic subgenre I delineate among plays with which I am familiar from Naples and the larger peninsular *meridione.* Among *commedie erudite* this

is perhaps not surprising. Bruno's complex arrangement of satiric Chinese boxes in *Il candelaio* was sui generis, and the prolific, influential Della Porta was a latecomer whose experiments were bounded by the proto-sentimentalism of *commedia grave*, hardly a focus likely to incorporate the final secrecy that this study addresses. (See Louise George Clubb, *Giambattista Della Porta, Dramatist* [Princeton: Princeton University Press, 1965]. Clubb analyzes this strand of comedy for its *gravità*, arising from "actions and characters fit for tragedy" and affecting the audience with "meraviglia, dolore e compassione," further, if still with particular focus upon Della Porta, in *Italian Drama in Shakespeare's Time* [New Haven: Yale University Press, 1989], 43–47, 53–57.) At the popular level, one speaks with caution owing to the paucity of surviving texts relative to the protodrama and its fuller offspring in the Veneto or Siena. There are occasional tantalizing suggestions, such as Caracciolo's lost farce "de quattro villani quali acconciano loro mogliere con altri" [about four peasants who settle their wives with others] (F. Torraca, *Studî di storia letteraria napoletana* [Livorno: Vigo, 1884], 65–81). But on the whole, this drama was so strongly dependent upon the topical satire of the *farse cavaiole*, and especially the self-presentation of Vincenzo Braca, that the love *contrasti* had little opportunity to develop, as they would in Siena and elsewhere (see the annotated anthologies of *Farse cavaiole*, ed. Achille Mango [Rome: Bulzoni, 1973], 2 vols; and Alfredo Barbina, *Giangurgolo e la commedia dell'arte* [Soveria Manelli: Rubbetino, 1989], 2 vols.).

14. While we possess numerous studies of the propagandistic court orientation of early Ferrarese drama and spectacle, including Lodovico Zorzi's notable study cited below, Paola Ventrone has impressively interwoven two relevant theses in great detail in *Gli araldi della commedia: teatro a Firenze nel Rinascimento* (Pisa: Pacini Editore, 1993). She sets the Ferrara model in the context of Medici Florence, where, owing to an ambiguous polity reflecting overlapping republican and absolutist tendencies, it could never flourish in pure form. Unlike the d'Este, the Medici had to adapt courtly spectacles to a long popular (sometimes populist) tradition emanating from the *cantori*, public performers of rhymed recitation, from the *canti carnascialeschi*, and from the mixed dramatic forms used in the *sacre rappresentazioni*. She also emphasizes the Florentine tradition of private performances from nunneries to private palazzi and academies, a tradition much more developed in Florence than elsewhere, unless it be in neighboring Siena (whose theatrics will be discussed in a later chapter). This

should remind one, of course, that Ruzante's experiments were also written for the indoor-outdoor theater at Alvise Cornaro's palatial villa in Padua; see Franco Mancini, Maria Teresa Muraro, and Elena Povoledo, *I teatri del Veneto: Padova, Rovigo, e il loro territorio* (Venice: Regione del Veneto & Corbo e Fiore, 1988), 3:36–56.

15. Ruzante, *Teatro*, ed. Ludovico Zorzi (Turin: Einaudi, 1967), 1596. Cf. Zorzi, *Il teatro e la città: saggi sulla scena italiana* (Turin: Einaudi, 1977), 30–32, and Emilio Lovarini, *Studî sul Ruzzante e la letteratura pavana*, ed. Gianfranco Folena (Padua: Antenore, 1965), 327–30.

16. Zorzi, in Ruzante, *Teatro*, 1431–33.

17. The letter is dated from Padua on 23 Jan. 1532; Ruzante, *Teatro*, 1253.

18. Cf. my reading of Ruzante's agon with Plautine pattern in *Dramaturgy of the Daemonic* (Baltimore: The Johns Hopkins University Press, 1984), 24–28.

19. Zorzi's essay "Ferrara: il sipario ducale," in *Il teatro e la città*, 5–59, is a contextual "reading" of the Schifanoia frescoes. Cf. the Albertian emphasis upon scenic space in the frescoes treated variously by Charles M. Rosenberg, "Courtly Decorations and the Decorum of Interior Space," and by Ranieri Varesi, "Proposte per Schifanoia," in *La corte e lo spazio: Ferrara estense*, ed. Giuseppe Papagno and Amadeo Quondam (Rome: Bulzoni, 1982), respectively 2:529–44 and 2:545–62. Proto-Vitruvian perspective and "le manie plautine dei ferraresi" (65) are conjoined in Marzia Pieri, *La nascita del teatro moderno in Italia tra XV e XVI secolo* (Turin: Bollati Boringhieri, 1989), 62–66.

20. See Felix Gilbert, "Machiavelli e Venezia," *Lettere italiane* 21 (1969): 389–402.

21. On the Venetian performances and editions see Niccolò Machiavelli, *La mandragola*, ed. Roberto Ridolfi (Florence: Olschki, 1965), 20; Antonio Enzo Quaglio, "Indicazioni sulla fortuna editoriale di Machiavelli nel Veneto," *LI* 21 (1969): 412–14. The description of the first performance is from Marin Sanuto, *Diarii*, 32, col. 458.

22. Gareffi, *La scrittura e la festa*, 110–11.

23. On Ariosto's attendance (as well as that of Strozzi) at the production of Nardi's play, see *I due felici rivali: commedia inedita di Jacopo Nardi*, ed. Alessandro Ferrajoli (Rome: Forzani, 1901), viii, xxv. On the pre-Machiavellian drama of Nardi in the Medici ambience, see Gareffi, *La scrittura e la festa*, 17–80.

24. The most comprehensive argument for a homogeneous theory of

"modern" comedy at the center of all the "contaminations" by means of which Cinquecento playwrights experimented with the genre is Clubb, *Italian Drama in Shakespeare's Time*. Clubb eschews seeking out traditional influences, instead indicating action and character clusters that she labels "theatergrams," core aspects of classical comedy open to countless recombinations. As the title implies, Clubb's study finds the Renaissance theatergrams available to Shakespeare independently of particular Italian sources.

Il Padano

1. Guido Ruggiero, *Violence in Early Renaissance Venice* (New Brunswick, N.J.: Rutgers University Press, 1980).

2. See Cesare Segre, *Le strutture e il tempo* (Turin: Einaudi, 1974), 151–53, on Alatiel's "mutismo."

3. See the collections edited by André Rochon, *Formes et significations de la "beffa" dans la littérature italienne de la Renaissance*, 2 vols. (Paris: Université de la Sorbonne Nouvelle, 1972, 1975). Especially useful is Anna Fontes-Baratto on the *Decameron*, 1:11–44.

4. *Le strutture e il tempo*, 155; cf. 136–41 on variations of the true-false "commutatore" in the *Decameron*.

5. Pisani, a Parmigiano, wrote the *Philogenia* while a student at the University of Pavia. If there was a "source," it may have been Leonardi Bruni Aretino's *Poliscena*, a play, however, that buries the travail of seduction under the medical sexual nostrums of the fifteenth century. See Ireneo Sanesi, *La commedia* (Milan: Vallardi, 1954), 1:131–44; *Teatro umanistico*, ed. and trans. Alessandro Perosa, which includes an Italian translation of *Philogenia* (Milan, 1965); Douglas Radcliff-Umstead, *The Birth of Modern Comedy in Renaissance Italy* (Chicago: Chicago University Press: 1969), 32–36; and Vito Pandolfi, "Le spurie origini del nostro teatro drammatico," in *Teatro goliardico dell' umanesimo*, ed. Vito Pandolfi and Erminia Artese (Milan: Lerici, 1965), ix–xx. The Latin text of *Philogenia* is cited from this volume, 171–285, by page number. This is the text of Codice Ashburn 188 in the Laurentian Library in Florence. Antonio Stäuble, *La commedia umanistica del quattrocento* (Florence, 1968), 39–48, 281–83, documents the extraordinary popularity of "una delle commedie più originali del secolo" (44). On the pavese goliardic aspects of Pisani's (probable) other come-

dies see also Paolo Viti, ed., *Due commedie umanistiche pavesi* (Padua: Antenore, 1982), 11–21, 90–106. Without ignoring the powerful influence of Milan, one should bear in mind the depth of intellectual imprint made across the Po Valley and throughout Lombardia by the Venetians. Quattrocento relations have been detailed in James S. Grubb, *Firstborn of Venice: Vicenza in the Early Renaissance State* (Baltimore: The Johns Hopkins University Press, 1988). This study of compromise in civic and juridical polities touches only briefly upon the arts (see esp. 168–72) but emphasizes interactions. In sum, says Grubb, "the peninsula-wide Peace of Lodi in 1454 ratified Venetian conquests in the Veneto and Lombardy. In the parlance of the day, the lion of St. Mark had come ashore" (6).

6. Stäuble, *La commedia umanistica*, 163–65. *Poliodorus*, a play derivative from *Philogenia*, exists in a unique manuscript version in the Biblioteca Colombina in Seville. See J. de Vallata, *Poliodorus: Comedia humanistica desconocida*, ed. Jose María Casa Homs (Madrid: Instituto Nicolas Antonio, 1953). This is a transcription with full historical discussions. The manuscript consists of a collection of early Italian Renaissance tracts and letters composed by Poggio Bracciolini and others, including a version of *Philogenia*. Nothing is known of Vallata, who tells us only that he composed the play at age eighteen. Owing to the Italian orientation of the manuscript and to the lack of a neo-Latin comedic tradition in Spain, Casa Homs tentatively attributes authorship to Giovanni Pontano writing under a youthful pseudonym. There is, however, no real evidence for this. *Poliodorus* follows the plot of *Philogenia* insofar as it masks an illicit liaison between a socially superior suitor and his *innamorata* through the device of marrying her to a dependent tenant on his farms. In this case, the continuation of the liaison seems limited to the eight days of liberty the girl demands before the rural wedding with which the play closes. *Poliodorus*, moreover, seems to be a reading text, not adapted to the restrictions of staging (Casa Homs, 127–34). In sum, *Poliodorus* appears most interesting as one more indication of the popularity of Pisani's *Philogenia*.

7. In this respect I disagree with the anticlerical analogies emphasized in Maristella de Panizza Lorch, "Confessore e chiesa in tre commedie del Rinascimento: 'Philogenia,' 'Mandragola,' e 'Cortigiana,'" in *Il teatro del rinascimento*, ed. Maristella de Panizza Lorch (Milan: Edizioni di Comunità, 1980), 301–48.

8. Galeotto del Carretto, *"Li sei contenti" e "La Sofonisba,"* ed. Mauda

Bregoli-Russo (Madrid, 1982). *Li sei contenti* is extant in only one slightly mutilated copy issued in 1542 and now in the Biblioteca dell' Archiginnasio di Bologna. Bregoli-Russo gives full biographical and bibliographical detail. Del Carretto's other two plays, *Comedia de Timon greco* and *Noʒe de Psiche e Cupidine*, are to be found in *Teatro del quattrocento: le corti padane*, ed. Antonia Tissoni Benvenuti and Maria Pia Mussini Sacchi (Turin: UTET, 1983), 557–725. All citations of *Li sei contenti* are from Bregoli-Russo's edition, with act indications and page number.

9. Vincenzio Martelli, *Rime e lettere* (Florence, 1563), 14.

10. *La venexiana* was uncovered and edited by Emilio Lovarini in 1928 from the Codice miscellaneo Marciano italiano cl. IX, n. 288. The colophon indicates that *Hieronymus Zarellus scripsi*. The name is elsewhere unknown, and Lovarini began the enterprise of conjectural identification by nominating Fracastoro. Giorgio Padoan reedited the manuscript (*La Veniexiana: commedia di anonimo veneʒiano del Cinquecento*, Medievo e Umanesimo, 20 [Padua: Antenore, 1974]), conjecturally dating it in the mid-1530s and placing it in San Barnaba and in the putative scandal of the Valier family. His thesis had been anticipated by Lovarini in a revised edition of 1947 (1535–37). Padoan's dependence upon Venetian arms laws for dating is inconclusive. But he notes that the novelty of thick local detail constitutes a reaction against Plautine formulae: "È con gli anni trenta che la situazione si modifica in modo decisivo. Dopo il grande successo delle recite plautine dei decenni precedenti vi era stanchezza per quella tematica troppo lontano dalla realtà contemporanea" [It is in the thirties that the situation is modified in a decisive mode. After the great success of the plautine performances of the preceding decades, there rose a weariness with that thematic too distant from contemporary reality] (14). I cite throughout the text in Padoan's transcription of the manuscript.

11. Padoan offers circumstantial evidence, in agreement with his dating, to identify Iulio as a Lombard. But the point in the play is, in this as in all else, indeterminacy (cf. Padoan, 2). See also Padoan's essay in *La commedia rinascimentale veneta* (Verona: Neri Pozza: 1982), 140–53, 251–64.

12. Padoan would complicate this offstage figure into yet another lover; 37, 153 n.79.

13. Cf. Padoan's conjecture (23) that this conclusion was a late textual addition, in connection with the claim common in novelle that the fabula is a "vera historia."

Notes to Padano to Veneto

14. Marzia Pieri, *La scena boschereccia nel rinascimento italiano* (Padua: Liviana, 1983), 85 n.1; Mango, introduction to *Farse cavaiole,* 1–7 and passim; and Toschi, *Le origini del teatro italiano.*

15. See pp. 61–74 below; Curzio Mazzi, *La Congrega dei Rozzi di Siena nel secolo XVI* (Florence: Le Monnier, 1882), 2 vols.; Giulio Ferrario, *Poesie rusticali* (Milan, 1808) and *Drammi rusticali,* in *Teatro antico italiano* (Milan, 1812), tom. 10; and Mango, *Farse cavaiole.* The principal analytic survey of interaction between classical pastoral forms and popular genres is Marzia Pieri, *La scena boschereccia nel rinascimento* (for Ruzante's—and Venetian—relations with the Rozzi and their predecessors see esp. 85–107). Pieri proposes the "ipotesi avventurosa" that the "rappresentazioni senesi e la loro capillare divulgazione ne facessero un serbatoio privilegiata di soggetti per i carnevali veneziani" [Sienese representations and their capillary distribution made of them a privileged reservoir of subjects for Venetian carnivals] (101). Cf. also Pieri, *La nascita del teatro moderno in Italia tra XV e XVI secolo,* 67ff., 100ff., 156–78.

16. Paolo Lagorio, "Per una struttura tematica del *mariazo,*" *Strumenti critici* 16 (1982): 64–106, offers an extended semiotic analysis of three groups within the *mariazo* corpus that variously interlink. He finds no single exemplar, however, that illustrates the ceremonial function of the genre as a marriage ritual together with its contestual, disputative aspect. Lagorio remarks that *La Betía* fits none of the subgroups of the genre, "e questa è una prima testimonianza delle difficoltà che un esame della commedia in questo contesto proporrebbe" [and this is a first witness to the difficulties that an examination of the comedy in this context would raise] (68); however, the primary difficulty is that Ruzante's play does incorporate both ritual and contest. Might *La Betía,* then, constitute just that ideal sought by Lagorio at the close of his essay on generic morphology: "non è forse così fantasiosa, alla fine, l'immagine di un grande *mariazo* ancora ignorato che ne percorra tutte . . . le tappe" [perhaps the image of a still unknown great *mariazo* that would extend across all of its stages is not so fantastic, in the end]?

17. My formulae summarize two books by Peter Burke that have been widely influential: *Popular Culture in Early Modern Europe* (New York, 1978) and *Culture and Society in Renaissance Italy, 1420–1540* (New York: Scribner's, 1972). Piero Camporesi's corrective critique of Burke is in *Rustici e buffoni: cultura popolare e cultura d'élite fra Medioevo ed età mo-*

derna (Turin: Einaudi, 1991). On the French *bibliothèque bleue* see Lucien Febvre's posthumous essay edited by Henry-Jean Martin, *L'apparition du livre* (Paris, 1958). Two important Italian applications of popular-elite interaction in the theater are Luciano Mariti, *Commedia ridicolosa: comici di professione, dilettanti* (Rome: Bulzoni, 1978), and Carmelo Alberti, *Il teatro dei pupi e lo spettacolo popolare siciliano* (Milan: Mursia, 1977).

18. Cf. *Dramaturgy of the Daemonic* 19ff. and n.32. Pieri, in *La scena boschereccia*, citing the pre-Bembo iconography of Cupid in fifteenth-century *contrasti*, arrives at *La Betía* (170–73) with a comment pertinent to the geographic distribution of our exemplars from the subgenre of secrecy: "Questo *sketch* [di Cupid] si ritrova identico in testi molti lontani e difformi . . . segno che la civiltà teatrale cinquecentesca è assai più unitaria di quanto normalmente si creda, a livelli di acculturamento in apparenza remoti" [This sketch of Cupid is repeated identically in texts very distant and diverse . . . a sign that sixteenth-century theatrical culture is much more unitary than is normally believed, at levels of acculturation apparently remote] (81). I cite act and line numbers from the text of *La Betía* in Ruzante, *Teatro*.

19. On the wide discussion of this intentional malapropism see Zorzi, in Ruzante, *Teatro*, 1454 n. 15 and 1466 n. 8.

20. Mikhail Bakhtin, *Rabelais and His World* (Cambridge: MIT Press, 1968).

21. Zorzi, in Ruzante, *Teatro*, 1345 n. 271.

22. Padoan, *La commedia rinascimentale veneta*, 41–62.

23. Cf. Zorzi, in Ruzante, *Teatro*, 1360 n. 356, on *novella* versions. He suggests the possibility that Beolco could have known Del Carretto's *Li sei contenti*.

Siena

1. "La 'Raffaella' di Alessandro Piccolomini," in Diego Valeri, *Conversazioni italiane* (Florence: Olschki, 1968), 97.

2. For the background and recent considerations of dramatic and societal relations in Siena see Roberto Alonge, *Il teatro dei Rozzi di Siena* (Florence: Olschki, 1967); Nino Borsellino, *Rozzi e Intronti: esperienze e forme di teatro dal "Decameron" al "Candelaio"* (Rome: Bulzoni, 1974); Daniele Seragnoli,

Il teatro a Siena nel Cinquecento (Rome: Bulzoni, 1980); Cristina Valenti, *Comici artigiani: mestiere e forme dello spettacolo a Siena nella prima metà del Cinquecento* (Modena: Franco Cosimo Panini, 1992); and Louise George Clubb and Robert Black, *Romance and Aretine Humanism in Sienese Comedy* (Florence: La Nuova Italia, 1993). On the historical and anthropological role of women for the *Intronati* cf. Gareffi, *La scrittura e la festa*, 337–85 passim, esp. 360–64.

3. The most extended study of *La Raffaella* is Marie-Françoise Piéjus, "Venus bifrons: Le double idéal féminin dans *La Raffaella* d'Alessandro Piccolomini," in *Images de la femme dans la littérature italienne de la Renaissance: préjugés misogynes et aspirations nouvelles*, ed. André Rochon (Paris: Université de la Sorbonne Nouvelle, 1980), 81–167. Piéjus is primarily interested in placing Piccolomini's dialogue in the context of fifteenth- and sixteenth-century female-conduct books, from which most of Piccolomini's details have been adapted into his unique structure.

4. A detailed analysis is "Il progetto drammaturgico di Alessandro Piccolomini: il personaggio e la 'fabula'," in Seragnoli, *Il teatro a Siena nel Cinquecento*, 93–134. Seragnoli posits an intellectual bond between Tuscany and the Veneto around "la maturazione di Piccolomini, a cavallo tra esperienze senesi e padovane" [the maturation of Piccolomini, straddling Sienese and Paduan experiences] (102). Piccolomini's stay in Padua placed him in contact with "una sorta di cultura 'internazionale' " [a species of "international" culture] roughly between 1536 and 1542: "Siena-Padova: asse portante di una rivelazione" [Siena-Padua: supporting axis of a revelation] (96). The revelation was Piccolomini's proto-formulation of a systematic philosophy of nature, but there was a theatrical dimension, as well, when Piccolomini participated in "un grandioso progetto—la messa in scena della tragedia *Canace* di Sperone Speroni recitata dal Ruzante . . . non realizzato per la immatura morte di Angelo Beolco" [a grandiose project—the staging of Sperone Speroni's tragedy *Canace* recited by Ruzante . . . never realized owing to the premature death of Angelo Beolco] (94–95). For details of the plan and the effect of Ruzante's death, see Nicola Savarese, "In morte di Angelo Beolco detto Ruzante: *La Canace* dello Speroni," *Biblioteca teatrale* 15–16 (1976): 170–90.

5. *La Raffaella ovvero della bella creanza delle donne*, ed. E. Camerini [Carlo Teoli, pseudo.] (Milan: Daelli, 1862), 1. All citations are to pages in this edition.

6. Characterization, to be dramatically revised later, has already begun

as Margarita protests: "E che peccati potete voi mai avere, chè vi veggio sempre co'paternostri in mano, e vi state tutto 'l giorno per queste chiese" [and what sins could you have, since I always see you with the holy beads in hand, and you are in and out of church all day long] (8).

7. There is more circumstantiality here, opening the frame of the dialogue into old relationships: Raffaella was so close to Margarita's mother "che si può dir me l'ho allevata io" [that I could say I raised her] because "la sorella sua era cognata del mio nipote" [her sister was sister-in-law to my nephew] (10) (presumably the aunt to Margarita who now seems debtor to Raffaella).

8. Piccolomini, as noted above, wrote retractions of the satire upon women's mores in *La Raffaella* and wrote two plays sentimentalizing extravagant constancy, *L'amor costante* (1536) and *L'Alessandro* (1544). The former, immensely popular, is posed as a counterlesson to the cynical love "constancy" of the *Dialogo* ("Imparate, donne, . . . a esser costanti," Piccolomini advises [Learn, women, . . . to be constant], from Lucrezia, *innamorata* of *L'amor costante*, because "non fu mai donna più casta . . . ne amor più costante" [there was never a woman more chaste . . . nor a love more constant] [5.9; 5.4]). However, chaste Lucrezia has been married secretly and demonstrates a lusty failure of *destrezza* when taken *in flagrante* with her man: "facevano un fracasso in su quel letto che pareva che lo volessero buttar a terra" [they were making such a racket on that bed, it was like they wanted to knock it to pieces] (3.7). *L'Alessandro,* as has been noticed, has its own Raffaella in the confidante Niccoletta, who urges her young charge to gather the rosebuds while she can: "cotesta età non è da perder indarno senza gustare i solazzi d'amore" [this age is not to be lost in vain without tasting the pleasures of love] in secret. Becoming more graphic than Raffaella herself, this Niccoletta cries, "Oimè, una giovane bella dormir sola? e stropicciarsi sola?" [O, a beautiful young woman sleep alone? and frig herself alone?] (1.3). Piccolomini did some retouching upon Girolamo Bargagli's *La pellegrina* (ca. 1567) ("a me non toccò di fare sennò di . . . accomodar qualche cosa" [all I had to do was make . . . some adjustments]), the most serious sentimental play to emerge from the Intronati, and it is tempting to hear an echo of Raffaella's voice even in this unlikely place when the servant Giglietta opines:

I mariti . . . non sono altro che fattori e guardiani degli inamorati. I mariti fanno loro le spese, i mariti lor fanno le vesti; gl'impacci, i rimbrotti, è fastidî che portan seco le donne son tutti de'mariti; i piaceri, i vezzi, le dolcezze tutte toccano agli amanti. Di questo quello che soleva dire sospirando un nostro cappellano: ch'a lui toccava l'uffiziare la chiesa, e un altro ne godeva l'entrata.

Husbands . . . are no more than the factors and guardians of the lovers. The husbands pay their expenses, the husbands buy their clothes; the embarrassments, the reproaches, and irritations that come with women are all the husbands'; the pleasures, the caresses, the tenderness are all the lot of the lovers. It reminds me of what our curate used to say with a sigh: it was his job to take care of the church, while other people had the pleasure of entering. (1.2)

I cite from *La pellegrina*, ed. Florindo Cerreta (Florence: Olschki, 1971). See 12–16 on Piccolomini's part in the composition.

9. Curzio Mazzi, *La Congrega dei Rozzi di Siena nel secolo XVI* (Florence: Le Monnier, 1882), 1:163–164. Mazzi presents a bibliography of the Rozzi literary productions, of which far the largest number consist of the *rusticali* both in print and in manuscript collections. This standard source has been expanded and partially superseded by Valenti's magisterial biobibliographical studies in *Comici artigiani*. Valenti distinguishes the popular *artigiani* who wrote, produced, and acted, even while exploiting their *mestieri* as blacksmiths, painters, tailors, and others from their Rozzi compatriots. She demonstrates that, adapting local folk forms to professional entertainments outside of Siena, these men created a new dramatic genre both in production and in print (12, 54–69). She traces the highly visible presence of the Sienese author-entrepreneurs in Rome and at the *corti padane* through direct ties to Agostino Chigi and the papal entourage of Leo X, as well as through the broad demographics of publication, which saw many editions of their works issuing from Venice and Rome, as well as Siena. The fullest exemplary detail is provided in Valenti's account of Niccolò Campani's [lo Strascino] entertainments in Rome, Mantua, and Milan (34–69, esp. 49–54). Similar to Seragnoli's emphasis upon Piccolomini's Siena-Padua "axis," Valenti's work offers a new piece of the accumulating evidence for a pan-peninsular dramatic network long hidden by regional literary histories. Sienese relations with another cultural center are the focus of Clubb and Black in a monograph with an edition of Giovanni Pollastra's *Parthenio*, staged at the University of Siena in 1516. They detail the presence and influence of Pollastra as a conduit of the erudite humanist tradition of Arezzo's prestigious grammarians interacting with the artigiani playwrights both in

Siena and in Medici Rome. See *Romance and Aretine Humanism in Sienese Comedy,* esp. 31–37, 67–89, 148–52.

10. I cite *Mezzucchio* from Valenti, 286.

11. All citations are to the edition in *Annali di storia del Teatro e dello Spettacolo,* 1 (1966), 141–75, by line number. On Pier Antonio Legacci dello Stricca's canon see Valenti, 265–344. Eight extant editions of *Tognin del Cresta* were all apparently issued in Siena at intervals throughout the Cinquecento. But Legacci's works received broad distribution even when issued in Siena; see Valenti, 74–75.

12. It is not surprising that these plays are a cornucopia of proverbialisms, as in this and the following citation, for example. However, one should observe that "segreto come al forno" illustrates a not infrequent artistic sophistication of the linguistic material from which the authors work. *Ficcarsi in un forno,* to hide oneself in the baker's oven, is a proverb with negative connotations of hiding for shame, as in the Crusca citation of the Cinquecento Florentine Grazzini. Legacci is, of course, aware of this, but Lenzo is not; yet both draw attention through misappropriation of the proverb to Lenzo's own shameful proposal.

13. Mazzi, 2:188.

14. *Commedie del Cinquecento,* ed. Aldo Borlenghi (Milan: Rizzoli, 1959), 2:906. Borlenghi's anthology includes *Capotondo* (2:951–90). All citations are from this edition by act and line numbers.

15. All citations are from the edition in *Annali di storia del Teatro e dello Spettacolo,* 1 (1966), 73–102, by line number. On Manescalco's canon see Valenti, 369–422. There were more than a dozen editions of *Il bichiere* (*sic*) in the Cinquecento issuing from presses in Siena, Florence, and Venice.

16. " 'Decameron' come teatro," in *Rozzi e Intronati,* 20. Pamela D. Stewart develops the interaction between Boccaccio's *novelle* and the drama in the several essays gathered in *Retorica e mimica nel "Decameron" e nella commedia del Cinquecento* (Florence: Olschki, 1986). Most immediately pertinent to the present discussion is "Il testo teatrale e la questione del doppio destinatario: l'esempio della *Calandria*" (103–23), which extends Borsellino's observations by systematizing the overlap between narrative and theatrical audiences in relation to the text.

Notes to Siena

1. Anton Francesco Doni, *I marmi* ([1553]; Bari: Laterza, 1928), 1:51. I owe this citation to the kindness of the late Professor Douglas Radcliff-Umstead, who supplied an expansion of his observation in *Carnival Comedy and Sacred Play: The Renaissance Drama of Giovan Maria Cecchi* (Columbia: University of Missouri Press, 1986), 95.

2. Giovan Maria Cecchi, "Prologo," *L'assiuolo*, in *Commedie del Cinquecento*, ed. Nino Borsellino (Milan: Feltrinelli, 1962), 1:128. All subsequent citations are from this edition, with page numbers preceding act and scene indications.

3. Prologue to *Le maschere*, in *Commedie* (Milan: Silvestri, 1850), 1:31.

4. There is an extended account in Luigi Squarzina's review of preparation for his own production: "questo ventaglio è l'unico oggetto che dia il nome a una commedia. Emblema di potere . . . indice di *segretezza* e di mascheramento" [this fan is the only object that gives its name to a comedy. Emblem of power . . . index of *secrecy* and of disguise] (italics mine); Luigi Squarzina, "L'addio a Venezia," in *L'interpretazione goldoniana critica e messinscena*, ed. Nino Borsellino (Rome: Officina, 1982), 246 and passim.

5. Cf. Alessandro D'Ancona, *Origini del teatro italiano* (Turin: Loescher, 1891), 2:157–62; introduction to Beatrice del Sera, *Amor di virtù: Commedia in cinque atti (1548)*, ed. Elissa Weaver (Ravenna: Longo, 1990), 20–34.

6. Radcliff-Umstead, *Carnival Comedy and Sacred Play*, 87–88. Cecchi's realization of having attained parity with his source is expressed through an internal acknowledgment: when Giulio recounts locking Ambrogio in a cold courtyard, Rinuccio replies, "I' ne disgrado messer Rinieri del Boccaccio" [I'm going Boccaccio's Messer Rinieri one better] (5.2; 183).

7. Niccolò Machiavelli, *Lettere*, ed. Franco Gaeta (Milan: Feltrinelli, 1961), 33, 230–31. The letter, its recipient, and the date (1506) have been definitively established by Mario Martelli, "*I ghiribizzi* di Giovan Battista Soderini," *Rinascimento*, 2d. ser., 9 (1969): 147–80, esp. 176–78.

8. "Corruzione popolare dello spagnolo *Quien es allá?* . . . frase forse pronunciata da soldati imperiali a Firenze durante il coprifuoco" [a popular corruption of the Spanish *Who goes there?* . . . a phrase perhaps used by the (occupying) imperial soldiers during curfew] (*Commedie*, ed. Borsellino, 1:165 n. 14).

9. This directed allusion is to the point in *La mandragola* at which Ligurio determines the signal of "San Cuccù" for the entrapment of Nicia's

sacrificial victim. The placing of Nicia "intra le dua corna" makes matters clear in *La mandragola*, but Girolamo Ruscelli's contemporary gloss goes more precisely to the focus of intersection with Cecchi's horned owl: "Cuccù in lingua Francese, significa il medesimo, che cornuto nella nostra, et però degnamente lo dà per nome in quella impresa" ["Cuccu" in the French language signifies the same as "cuckold" in our own, and it is therefore appropriate that he should use the name in that exploit] (*Delle comedie elette . . . con le correttioni, et annotationi di Girolamo Ruscelli* [1544], cited in Quaglio, "Indicazioni sulla fortuna . . . di Machiavelli nel Veneto," 413–14).

10. *Commedie del Cinquecento,* ed. Nino Borsellino (Milan: Feltrinelli, 1962), 1:93. All citations refer to this edition.

11. *Le rime burlesche,* ed. Carlo Verzone (Florence: Sansoni, 1882), 430. My attention was drawn to this allusion by Robert J. Rodini, *Antonfrancesco Grazzini: Poet, Dramatist, and Novelliere, 1503–1584* (Madison: University of Wisconsin Press, 1970), 92–93.

12. Grazzini archly underlines the traditional fabliau pattern by insisting that his farce is historical, "cosa seguita in effetto nel tempo dello Assedio [di Firenze]" [a thing that happened in actual fact in the time of the Siege of Florence] (94). This would, of course, make it very recent history, perhaps even a story à clef for many who had lived through the decade. Cecchi turns this upon Grazzini in his own prologue to *L'assiuolo* when he claims that he is recounting events "da un caso nuovamente accaduto in Pisa" [from an incident that recently happened in Pisa], rather than "dal sacco di Roma, o dall'assedio di Firenze" [from the sack of Rome, or from the siege of Florence] (128). The contrast, of course, serves to tie the two plays together in a rivalry and to suggest that, rather than recounting a modern scandal, Grazzini had written an ancient piece of fabulous history.

13. The examination of the context and authorship of the *Discorso* has been extensive, particularly in the past twenty-five years. Two important works appearing almost simultaneously made 1978 a watershed year. One was by a respected editor of Machiavelli, Mario Martelli, who represented the *Discorso* as a defense of the Florentine Academy against Benedetto Varchi, written around 1578–80, as argued in *Una giarda fiorentina* [A Florentine Fake] (Rome: Salerno, 1978). The other was Ornelia Castellani Pollidori, *Niccolò Machiavelli e il "Dialogo intorno alla nostra lingua"* (Florence: Olschki, 1978), with a critical edition of the text. Castellani Pollidori presented a full review of the previous debate on authorship and dating, confirming Machiavelli's claim and placing the *Discorso* in his de-

velopment. Martelli's approach was a summing of evidence in a courtroom atmosphere, and in a second work Pollidori rebutted it in like manner with a series of "tesi e antitesi" in *Nuove riflessioni sul "Discorso o dialogo intorno alla nostra lingua" di Niccolò Machiavelli* (Rome: Salerno, 1981). The most recent full treatment is the edition from the manuscripts by Paolo Trovato (*Discorso intorno alla nostra lingua* [Padua: Antenore, 1983]), who accepts Machiavelli's authorship and much of Castellani Pollidori's argument of detail and interpretation. Trovato places the text in the Florentine reactions to the whole language debate in useful detail, ix–xxxix. All citations are from this text, referenced to its paragraph numbering. Angelo Guidotti, *Il modello e la transgressione: commedie del primo '500* (Rome: Bulzoni, 1983), 131–64, esp. 134–35, discusses the *Discorso* in the double context of drama and *la questione della lingua*.

14. Castellani Pollidori shrewdly suggested that the vague denomination of the author of *Orlando furioso* as "uno degl' Ariosti di Ferrara" is a serio-comic by-blow, since "l'Ariosto dei *Suppositi* era in fin dei conti l'unico autore di commedie che potesse in qualche modo far ombra al Machiavelli della *Mandragola*" [the Ariosto of *I suppositi* was, in the last analysis, the only author of comedies who would be able in some way to overshadow the Machiavelli of *La mandragola*] (*Discorso,* 26). Unhappily, she seems to abandon this insight in favor of a textual emendation in *Nuove riflessioni,* 79.

15. Paola Ventrone, *Gli araldi della commedia: teatro a Firenze nel Rinascimento* (Pisa: Pacini Editore, 1993), 169–95. I owe my remarks on the Orti Oricellari theorists' development to Ventrone's study.

16. See the discussions in Luigina Stefani's edition of the texts of Nardi's *Amicitia* and *Due felici rivali* in *Tre commedie fiorentine del primo 5oo* (Ferrara: Gabriele Corbo Editore [for] Università degli studi di Firenze, 1986); Gareffi, *La scrittura e la festa,* 17–80, 99–142; and Ventrone, *Gli araldi della commedia,* 148–63, 180–84.

17. Carlo Dionisotti, *Geografia e storia della letteratura italiana* (Turin: Einaudi, 1967), 40; cf. 94ff. This appeared originally in *Italian Studies 6* (1951): from a University of London lecture delivered in 1949.

18. Dionisotti, *Geografia e storia della letteratura italiana,* 42.

19. Franco Gaetta, introduction to *Il teatro e tutti gli scritti letterari,* in Machiavelli, *Opere* (Milan: Feltrinelli: 1965), 8:xi; Mario Martelli, "La versione machiavelliana dell'*Andria*," *Rinascimento,* 2d. ser. 8 (1968): 203–10 and passim (this essay includes the earlier text of *L'Andria* with rele-

vant annotations); and Guido Davico Bonino, introduction to Machiavelli, *Teatro* (Turin: Einaudi, [1964], 1979), vii–x.

20. One historian has analyzed Machiavelli's mode of political "inquiry" in *Il principe* in a double relation. The anecdotal instances are "picaresque" disjunctive sequences; and the inquiry, as a whole, is the creation of theoretical worlds of possible, not historic, alternative. This "forces intimacy upon the reader": "we must read each exemplary narrative as enclosed in quotation marks: they are cited, not told. Each exchange implicates, making the reader complicitous in the handling of the tokens"; Nancy S. Streuver, *Theory as Practice: Ethical Inquiry in the Renaissance* (Chicago: University of Chicago Press, 1992), 175. The entire treatment of Machiavelli is found on 147–81, the "picaresque" analogy on 148–52. The complicity involved when narrative is withdrawn from historic "telling" into the bracketing of "inquiry" is patently analogous to the bracketing by transferral to dramatic presentation. And Streuver once again calls attention, as so many of the historical coincidences of our own inquiry have done, to Machiavelli's central place, implicit in our frequent return to *La mandragola*.

21. Ezio Raimondi, *Politica e commedia: dal Beroaldo al Machiavelli* (Bologna: Il Mulino, 1972), 214–15. Raimondi's notable essay first appeared as "Il teatro di Machiavelli," *Studi storici* 10 (1969): 749–98.

22. Giulio Ferroni, *"Mutazione" e "riscontro" nel teatro di Machiavelli e altri saggi sulla commedia del Cinquecento* (Rome: Bulzoni, 1972), 19–137. References to this study will be cited by page number in the text.

23. Niccolò Machiavelli, *La mandragola* per la prima volta restituita alla sua integrità a cura di Roberto Ridolfi (Florence: Olschki, 1965), ll. 14–17. All citations are from this edition. Ferroni cites their disguisings and their nervous reiterations of Ligurio's faithfulness as intentional emphases of "certi sottilissimi rapporti di comportamento tra Callimaco e Nicia" [certain very subtle relationships of similar behavior between Callimaco and Nicia] (54–55).

24. Luigi Vanossi observes the outcome of *La mandragola* to be antigeneric:

Se nel teatro classico i fraintendimenti e le ambiguità prodotte dall'intrigo venivano alla fine spianate, e la verità scendeva a illuminare tutti i personaggi, la chiusa della *Mandragola* istituisce invece una realtà bifronte, di cui Nicia continuerà a occupare il risvolto comico, la banda dell'illusione e della menzogna. Il gioco si salda in un ironico intreccio di battute, ognuna della quali presenta . . . una doppia superficie di esposizione.

If in classical theater the misunderstandings and ambiguities produced by the intrigue are in the end smoothed out and the truth descends to illuminate all the characters, the conclusion of the *Mandragola* instead institutes a double-faced reality of which Nicia will continue to occupy the comic side, the side of illusion and lies. The game is resolved in an ironic interweaving of witty exchanges, each of which presents . . . a double surface of exposition.

Vanossi analogizes this effect with Machiavelli's false preservation of tradition through maintaining appearances in *Discorsi*, 1:xxv, without pursuing it further (Vanossi, "Situazione e sviluppo del teatro machiavelliano," in Vanossi et al., *Lingua e strutture del teatro italiano del rinascimento* [Padua: Liviana, 1970], 56–57.) It is ironic and unfortunate that this insight should be cited by one of the recent historians of Cinquecento theater as the exception that proves the rule of New Comedy dominance: "più che di un contrappunto ironico si tratta di un vero e proprio ribaltamento, sia pur dissimulato, del lieto fine. . . . Sulla stessa linea si collocano pochi altri commediografi" [more than an ironic counterpoint, what we have here is a genuine overturning, even if disguised, of the happy ending. . . . Few other comic playwrights employed the same line] (Giovanni Attolini, *Teatro e spettacolo nel rinascimento* [Rome-Bari: Laterza, 1988], 246).

25. . . . as Machiavelli so well knew; see Franco Fido on the evolution of Chiron, "Appunti sulla memoria letteraria di Machiavelli," *MLN* 89 (1974): 1–12.

26. See Franco Fido, "Machiavelli, 1469–1969: politica e teatro nel badalucco di Messer Nicia," *Italica* 46 (1969): 359–75. The literature connecting Machiavelli's political philosophy with *La mandragola* is, of course, too large to be comprehended in this or any useful catalogue. Ferroni's version (*"Mutazione" e "riscontro,"* 99–103 and passim) is as judicious as any. It has been extended, focusing upon Fra Timoteo and the post-Savonarolan church politics of Florence under Leo X's papacy, in Gareffi, *La scrittura e la festa*, 189–217.

27. Fido, "Machiavelli," 364–65: "In questo senso . . . la più famosa commedia italiana del Cinquecento è anche una delle meno 'teatrali' che si possano imaginare" [In this sense . . . the most famous Italian comedy of the sixteenth century is also one of the least "theatrical" that can be imagined].

28. *"Il Principe" e "Discorsi,"* ed. Sergio Bertelli (Milan: Feltrinelli: 1960), 101.

29. Paul Oskar Kristeller, *The Philosophy of Marsilio Ficino* (New York, 1943), 299–300; Michael J. B. Allen, *The Platonism of Marsilio Ficino: A Study of his "Phaedrus" Commentary, Its Sources and Genesis* (Berkeley: University of California Press, 1984), 86–123, 206–7, and the texts and commentary in his *Marsilio Ficino and the Phaedran Charioteer* (Berkeley: University of California Press: 1981). Love is the highest in a hierarchy of *furores* in Ficino's system. *Furia* and *furore* are used in Italian along the full spectrum of connotations from being hasty to being transcendentally inspired. That the latter pole is implied in Callimaco's impatience is supported by Machiavelli's reference to "il furore d'uno innamorato" [the fury of a lover] in the prologue to *La Clizia*, and to "un giovane impazzato d'amore" [a young man maddened by love] when he catalogues comic characters in the *Discorso* passage on Ariosto discussed earlier. But these comments, along with some in the reading of Fagiuoli's play that follows, are made with the assumption that the notion of impetuosity conveyed by "furore" could not but have taken on fuller Platonic resonances in a Florence actively preserving Ficino's legacy. A theatrical employment of Ficino's concept nearly contemporary with *La mandragola* is found in the prologue of (Bietina's?) "farsa recitata agli eccelsi signori di Firenze," *Dell'uomo che si vuole quietare e vivere senza pensieri* [Farce of the Man who Wants to Be Tranquil and Live Without Worries], where the author admits that he is not especially gifted by nature with poetic inspiration: "manco da natura / dotato del poetico furore" (62–63). I cite the text in *Le farse morali fiorentine*, ed. Michele Cataudella (Salerno: Edisud, 1984). Cf. Ventrone, *Gli araldi della commedia*, 151–54, esp. 154 n. 49.

30. A major aspect of Ferroni's argument for placing the *"savia"* Lucrezia at the center of dramatic and political interaction in *La mandragola* is her "saper sempre adattare il proprio 'modo di procedere' alle 'variazioni' della fortuna" [always knowing how to adapt her own mode of proceeding to the variations of fortune] (*"Mutazione" e "riscontro,"* 80–88; I cite from p. 82).

31. Machiavelli's irony is enhanced by allusion to a particular Florentine icon. Gareffi, *La scrittura e la festa*, 207–8, notices that Grazzini's preface to *Il frate* speaks of Machiavelli's "Timoteo de' Servi." The seat of the Augustinian Servi was the church of the Santissima Annunziata. It was notable in the Cinquecento for the allegedly divine origin and powers of its icon of the Madonna, which was notorious for its popularity with the credulous

Notes to Florence

and hopeful who covered it with ex-voto offerings. It is this figure whose veil Timoteo changes (in echo of Lucrezia assuming a mask of matronliness to cover her changed role), remembering a time when one would find "cinquecento imagine" [five hundred items] before it.

32. An analogous symbiosis between degeneration and regeneration of a theatrical mode is elaborated by Siro Ferrone writing on the rise of the commedia dell'arte in "La vendita del teatro: tipologie europee tra cinque e seicento" in *The Commedia dell'Arte from the Renaissance to Dario Fo*, ed. Christopher Cairns (Lewiston, N.Y.: Edwin Mellen Press, 1989), 35–72, esp. 36–37.

33. Goldoni was put off by just this aspect: "Lessi il *Fagiuoli:* vi trovai la verità, la semplicità, la natura, ma . . . i suoi riboboli fiorentini m'incomodavano infinitamente" [I read Fagiuoli: I found there truth, simplicity, nature, but . . . his Florentine idioms disturbed me no end] (*Tutte le opere,* 1:644). Walter Binni, "Fagiuoli e Nelli," in *L'Arcadia e il Metastasio* (Florence: Nuova Italia, 1963), 207–43, gives a sympathetic overview of Fagiuoli as a linguistically self-conscious Florentine playwright. Roberta Turchi gives samples of Fagiuoli's self-censorship of satiric passages in preparing the plays for publication (*La commedia italiana del Settecento* [Florence: Sansoni, 1985], 7–18). Discussion of Fagiuoli as an anti-baroque reformist and creator of original Tuscan *maschere,* with some new material, is provided in Rossella Foggi, *Giovan Battista Fagiuoli* (Florence: Bruschi, 1993), issued in coordination with exhibits and a production celebrating the 250th anniversary of Fagiuoli's death.

34. *Commedie di Gio. Batista Fagiuoli Fiorentino* (in Lucca, Per Salvatore, and Giandomenico Marescandoli, *Con Licenza de'Superiori, 1734–37),* 6 vols. The passage cited is from 2:388, and all subsequent citations are from this edition. I give the title in full, as it is an edition not noted in the bibliography supplied in the Foggi volume.

35. Fagiuoli, *Commedie,* 6:188.

36. Turchi, *La commedia italiana del Settecento,* 8, provides an impressive roster of early-eighteenth-century performances across northern Italy and in Vienna, as well as a number of pirated editions of the play.

37. The social subjugation of husbands to the rites of *cicisbeismo* returns in a late play by Fagiuoli, *Il marito alla moda* [The husband a la Mode] (1734). In this work, Sempliciano Dolciati, a pleasant simpleton, wins a wife by default and happily promises to obey the rules of the new society,

with its secret *conversazioni* and *cicisbei*. However, *Il marito alla moda* displays none of the formal consequences found in *Non bisogna*.

Il manco male

1. Dante Isella, in Carlo Maria Maggi, *Il teatro milanese*, ed. Dante Isella. Nuova raccolta di classici italiani annotati, 6 (Turin: Einaudi, 1964), 1:xxvi–xxvii. All citations are from this edition.

2. Such a sweeping commonplace must be qualified, of course, especially in light of the linguistic studies of Dionisotti and Folena. A particularly valuable overview is found in Dante Isella, "La cultura letteraria lombarda," in *I Lombardi in rivolta* (Turin: Einaudi, 1984), 3–24.

3. Maggi's Milanese dramatic corpus is a product of his five very active last years, 1695–99; cf. Isella, *Teatro milanese*, 2:28–33. Maggi's plays did motivate and directly influence one classic dialect play written in emulation. This was *La sposa Francesca* (1703), by Francesco de Lemene, a patrician intellectual who lived out his life in his ancestral city of Lodi. The play, mixing classes and revealing their conflicts in a mixture of Tuscan and Lodinese, is a series of domestic mistakes and entanglements that are interspersed with satire on both ruling and serving classes, satire echoing that woven into Maggi's plays. There is nothing, though, of Maggi's formal secrecy (see Francesco de Lemene, *La sposa Francesca*, ed. Dante Isella [Turin: Einaudi, 1979], esp. pp. xvi–xxi of the preface dealing with Lemene's debts to Maggi). In the present context, one should note an extended negative critique of Plautine plotting and indecency made by Maggi in the jocoserious "parnassus" play, *Il concorso dei Meneghini*, esp. lines 128–215.

4. Mario Apollonio, *Storia del teatro italiano* (Florence: Sansoni, 1954–58), 2:328.

5. The *collegio delle vedove* was a Milanese institution established in 1631; cf. Isella, *Teatro milanese*, 1:11n.

6. In accordance with Isella's practice, all references to *Il manco male* will use act and line numbering, without scene divisions.

7. *La commedia* (Milan: Vallardi, 1954), 2:13.

8. Isella demonstrates throughout his annotations the cross-contamination of *Milanese italianizzato* and *Milanese pretto*, but the former

Notes to Meneghino in Milan

merged with commedia dell'arte techniques of adapting dialects through light suggestive cues (as with Pelegro, the supposed Genovese in *Il Barone di Birbanʒa*). Cf. 1:33ff and passim.

9. Maggi is tireless in underlining the overt consciousness of "class" divisions in a subtle exploration of crudity that is one of his just claims to being a *pre-Goldoniano*. Even as she is wooing the suitor from "l'altra sfera" on her daughter's behalf, Donna Quinzia assures him that "Intant sarà mia cura, che a Donn'Alba / Non manchi compagnia della sua sfera" [meanwhile it will be my care, that Donna Alba / may not lack companions from her own social circle] (1.553–54). One can note, too, how she falls into a Milanese idiom in the midst of her Italian from time to time. An example is in her statement of determination discussed below, when she decides to have Fabio pumped for information at the nunnery: "descoprir paes" ("scoprì paes," in proper Milanese) is literally "to reconnoiter the countryside" (1.1330).

Goldoni

1. "Frappatore" runs a gamut of meanings from busybody, meddler, to cheat. Cf. Fabrizio's list of synonyms cited below on p. 145.

2. Cf. my comments on *Il servitore* in *Dramaturgy of the Daemonic*, 118–21.

3. All Goldoni citations are from *Tutte le opere di Carlo Goldoni*, ed. Giuseppe Ortolani (Verona: Mondadori, 1935–56), 14 vols. Act and scene location will conform to this edition.

4. In the popular card game of *cotechio*, Pantalone's metaphor for age, the loser is the player with the most points.

5. *Tutte le opere*, vol. 2, p. 94.

6. The line is omitted from the Zatta edition because that edition does not reprint the dedication.

7. This description is from the Pasquali edition, to which Goldoni added extensive detail over that found in the editions issued by Bettinelli and Paperini. Cf. *Opere complete di Carlo Goldoni*, ed. Giuseppe Ortolani et al. (Municipio di Venezia, 1907–60), 4:209, 298; *Tutte le opere*, 3:1133.

8. I owe the resonances of the metaphor to Gianfranco Folena, *L'italiano in Europa: esperienʒe linguistiche del settecento* (Turin: Einaudi, 1983), 207.

9. Mario Baratto, *La letteratura teatrale del settecento in Italia (studi e letture su Carlo Goldoni)* (Verona: Neri Pozzo, 1985), 68–69.

10. The irony reflects upon Ridolfo, not the institution of the coffeehouse. When the foreigner Ferdinando demands a locked room in the *bottega* of the Venetian *caffetiere* Nicolò in *Le morbinose* [The Spirited Girls], Nicolò responds with a reprimand:

> In sto nostro paese ste cosse no se usa.
> In pubblico se vien a bever el caffè.
> E col se beve in pubblico, da sospettar no gh'è.
> Femene d'ogni rango da nu la vederà,
> In tempo delle maschere vegnir con libertà.
> Ma co la libertà xe resa universal,
> In fazza del gran mondo se schiva el mazor mal.

> In this our country one doesn't practice these things.
> One comes to drink coffee in public.
> As one drinks in public, there is no cause for suspicion.
> You will see, among us, women of every rank come here
> with liberty during Carnival [the time of the masks].
> But since freedom has been made universal,
> In the face of the great world one avoids the greater evil. (2.1).

Indeed, Goldoni reflects his admiration for English frankness and social honesty by projecting the Venetian custom of female patrons in the coffeehouses upon London in *Il filosofo inglese* [The English Philosopher].

11. Among these commentaries one can single out Nicola Mangini, "Il tema della villeggiatura nel teatro goldoniano," in *La fortuna di Carlo Goldoni e altri saggi goldoniani* (Florence: Le Monnier, 1965), 87–135, and Franco Fido, "Giacinta nel paese degli uomini," in *Da Venezia all'Europa: prospettive sull'ultimo Goldoni* (Rome: Bulzoni, 1984), 11–58, as well as Fido's introduction to Carlo Goldoni, *The Holiday Trilogy*, trans. Anthony Oldcorn (New York: Marsilio, 1992), a magisterial English translation of the villeggiatura trilogy. Except where noted, I have utilized Oldcorn's translations throughout the discussion of these plays.

12. See the essay and bibliography by Piergiovanni Mometto, "La vita in

Notes to Goldoni

villa," in *Storia della cultura veneta: il Settecento*, ed. G. Arnaldi and M. P. Stocchi (Verona: Neri Pozza, 1985), 5:1, 607–29.

13. *Tutte le opere*, 8:1007–8 (cf. Ortolani's annotations, 1409–10).

14. Cf. Giacinta: "Son donna, son giovane. Mi hanno sempre lasciato fare a mio modo, ed è difficile tutt'ad un tratto farmi cambiare temperamento" [I'm a woman, I'm young. They've always let me do as I liked. It's hard for me to change my ways and my character at one fell swoop] (2.6).

15. Goldoni here foregrounds the close functional relationship between *villeggiatura* and the Venetian *ridotti:* cf. Emanuela Zucchetta, *Antichi ridotti veneziani* (Rome: Fratelli Palombi, 1988), 8–10. The patrician *ridotti* were aped by *ridotti popolani* such as that behind "l'Osteria Selvadego a San Marco." It was "un casino istituto con regole, ordini, cariche, in tutto simili a quelli dei nobili, composto di camerieri, delle loro mogli ed altre donne di uguale condizione" [a casino set up with rules, orders, responsibilities, in all things similar to those of the nobles, composed of waiters, of their wives and other women of equal condition] (Zucchetta, 15).

16. The conception of *riputazione* as public appearance recurs throughout *Il ritorno* as the outer side of *dovere;* cf. "monete mettono a repentaglio la nostra riputazione" [money places at risk our reputation] (Vittoria; 1.3); "Questa è l'ultima mia rovina, la riputazione è perduta" [This is my ultimate ruin, my reputation is lost] (Leonardo; 1.11); "Che cosa mi ha trattenuto finora . . . non altro che il mio decoro, il giusto timore di essere criticata [What has restrained me to this point . . . (is) none other than my decorum, the just fear of being criticized] (Giacinta; 2.11).

17. Bernardo is the only new entrant in the cast of the trilogy, appearing in adjacent scenes of *Il ritorno* (2.5–6). Goldoni is at pains to justify this fresh incursion: "Vedrà il Lettore che non è inutile, e comprenderà facilmente che un carattere odioso, come quello di Bernardino, può essere sofferto e anche goduto in una Scena; ma diverrebbe noioso ed insopportabile, se una seconda volta si rivedesse" [The Reader will see for himself that Bernardino is not superfluous, and he will also realize that such an odious character may be tolerated, even enjoyed in a single scene; but would become obnoxious and unbearable were he to appear a second time] (["L'Autore a chi legge"], *Tutte le opere*, 7:1148). There is something disingenuous here. Bernardino is a laughing skeptic who is properly cynical about his nephew, whom he persistently calls "il Marchesino." He makes a mock encomium in praise of Leonardo's judicious ability to live a life of profligacy, and it is an attitude from which he refuses to be drawn out into

any serious consideration of the young man's dilemma. Far from odious, this clear Democritan eye on the ways of the world, and of Leonardo in particular, presents Bernardino the outsider as a welcome relief from the anger and self-absorption of the others. His function, though, is principally to set into perspective Fulgenzio's pompous reaction when his humanitarian proposals meet the impervious shield of irony: "Per me mi è venuto a noia la parte mia" [I'm getting fed up with my role in all this] (2.5).

18. An escalation of folly observed: *la villeggiatura* has bankrupted Leonardo through his emulation of the debt-pressed Filippo's extravagance.

19. Gianfranco Folena, *L'italiano in Europa*, 182, 185.

20. "L'addio a Venezia," in *L'interpretazione goldoniana critica e messinscena*, ed. Nino Borsellino (Rome: Officina Edizioni, 1982), 174–263; 206–18 comprise Squarzina's account of his 1968 production of *Una delle ultime sere di carnovale*.

21. "Note di regìa ('Una delle ultime sere di Carnovale' e 'I Rusteghi')," in *Studi goldoniani 2* (Venice: Casa di Goldoni, 1970), 193–214. I cite 196; the ellipses are Squarzina's.

22. The allegory surfaces into literalness when Momolo comments on "un dessegno di sior Anzoletto . . . che no gh'ha invidia a uno dei più belli di Franza" [a design of signor Anzoletto . . . that has no reason to envy one of France's finest].

23. *Tutte le opere*, 8:207.

24. *Studi goldoniani 2*, 179–88, reprinted in Fido, *Guida a Goldoni: teatro e società* (Turin: Einaudi, 1977), 89–101.

25. *Tutte le opere*, 8:211.

Afterword

1. Discussed in Matei Calinescu, *Rereading* (New Haven: Yale University Press, 1993). Calinescu's chapters on "Rereading for the Secret" (225–72) offer a stimulating analysis of the effects and motives of narrative secrecy.

Notes to Afterword

Index

Names from the notes have been cited only in those cases including discussion of subjects treated in the main text.

Index

Index

Index

Index

Jackson I. Cope is Leo S. Bing Professor Emeritus, University of Southern California. He is the author of *Robert Coover's Fictions, Dramaturgy of the Daemonic: Studies in Anti-Generic Theater from Ruzante to Grimaldi, Joyce's Cities: Archaeologies of the Soul, The Theater and the Dream: From Metaphor to Form in Renaissance Drama, The Metaphoric Structure of Paradise Lost*, and *Joseph Glanvill, Anglican Apologist*.

Library of Congress Cataloging-in-Publication Data

Cope, Jackson I.
Secret sharers in Italian comedy : from Machiavelli to
Goldoni / by Jackson I. Cope.
p.   cm.   Includes index.
ISBN 0-8223-1760-5 (cloth)
1. Italian drama (Comedy)—History and criticism.
2. Secrecy in literature.   I. Title.
PQ4149.C67   1996
852'.052309353—dc20   95-49319   CIP